The Guinness Guide to
Motorcycling

The Guinness Guide to
Motorcycling

Peter Carrick

GUINNESS SUPERLATIVES LIMITED
2 CECIL COURT, LONDON ROAD, ENFIELD, MIDDLESEX

Editor: Anne Marshall

Layout: David Roberts
© Peter Carrick and Guinness Superlatives Limited 1980

Carrick, Peter
   The Guinness guide to motorcycling
   1. Motorcycling
   I. Title
   796.7   GV1059.2

ISBN 0 85112 210 8

Published by
Guinness Superlatives Limited
2 Cecil Court, London Road,
Enfield, Middlesex

Guinness is a registered trademark of Guinness Superlatives Limited

Typeset by Brown, Knight & Truscott Ltd, Tonbridge, Kent and printed and bound by W S Cowell Ltd, Ipswich, Suffolk
Colour origination: Newsele Litho Ltd.

Frontispiece: Kenny Roberts, America's first motorcycling road race world champion *(All Sport/Don Morley)*.

Title page: It's 1911 and the Royal Mail gets through, by courtesy of the motorcycle

Acknowledgements

I have been helped in the preparation of the *Guinness Guide to Motorcycling* by numerous friends and colleagues who have offered expert advice and guidance and verified facts, dates and incidents. Particularly do I wish to thank Vic Willoughby and Charlie Rous for their work in connection with chapter 4 and chapters 11 and 12 respectively, and employees and officials of the Auto-Cycle Union, who were always patient and helpful, despite the frequency of my calls to check with their records.

I am also grateful for the cooperation of Mick Woollett, Bob Currie, Mike Winfield, Cyril Posthumous, the Motor Cycle Association of Great Britain Ltd., the Speedway Control Board, and the editorial staffs of *Motor Cycle News* and *Motor Cycle Weekly*.

My special thanks are extended to Rosemary Wetherall, who gave considerable help at all stages of the project and I am also indebted to her, and to Diana Davis and Pat Birchall, for typing the manuscript. I am also grateful to editor Anne Marshall of Guinness Superlatives Ltd. for her constructive guidance and help and for her considerable contribution in tracking down and selecting illustrations.

The extract from C. F. Caunter's book *Motor Cycles, a Technical History,* is reproduced by permission of Her Majesty's Stationery Office, the extract from *The Story of Honda Motorcycles* by permission of the publishers Patrick Stephens Ltd., and all photographs, as individually acknowledged.

Contents

Preface

Motorcycling has existed for close on one hundred years and in that time has developed almost beyond recognition. Technical advances have been staggering. The entire concept of riding a motorcycle has been revolutionised. The industry has in turn progressed, faltered to become at times almost extinct, only to rekindle and flourish until today, in the 1980s, it is perhaps more buoyant and stimulating than at any time in the past.

Motorcycle sport also has advanced considerably over the years and the world's best and most successful racers are now international celebrities enjoying enormous popularity and prestige. The entire motorcycle scene is diverse and dynamic and it is something of this colourful, fast-moving kaleidoscope which I have attempted to capture for the readers of the *Guinness Guide to Motorcycling*.

The book is comprehensive and absorbs virtually every aspect of motorcycling from the early formative years to the present day. I have tried to avoid a tedious repetition of facts and figures (though the book contains plenty of statistics), but with a readable style, I hope to have conveyed something of the excitement, satisfaction, glamour, romance, skills and thrills of motorcycling, yesterday and today.

Chapter 1

Make Way for the Motorbike

For all practical purposes the motorcycle, in any form remotely significant today, came into being in 1885. That year, in Mannheim, Germany, Karl Benz developed a three-wheel vehicle driven by a single cylinder, internal combustion engine, and Gottlieb Daimler, a former gunsmith who had moved into engineering, more significantly to our story, produced his historic, two-wheel boneshaker. The world's first petrol-engined motorcycle had arrived.

Hurriedly, and in some ways, crudely put together with hard-wood frame and timber-spoked, iron-tyred wheels, the *Einspur* (one-track) as it was named, nonetheless incorporated a number of surprisingly inventive features for that time: a handlebar 'twist' control, float-type carburettor and fan cooling; same-size wheels, and a centrally-located petrol engine with flexible mountings. Daimler used a light 264 cc four-stroke engine capable of running on either petrol or coal gas.

Earlier, Daimler and his colleague Wilhelm Maybach – later to design the classic Mercedes cars – had worked for the Deutz Engine Company, just outside Cologne, run by Dr. Nicolaus Otto and Eugen Langen. Otto and Langen, almost a decade before in 1876, had patented the four-stroke principle, while at the Deutz works Daimler and Maybach had produced a four-stroke gas engine. But while the Company prospered by producing and marketing the engine for stationary use, and saw little cause to change, Daimler's visionary approach already foresaw the enormous potential of mounting such an engine on a *moving* vehicle which carried its own fuel. Daimler left the Deutz Company in 1882 to concentrate on research into liquid fuels, being joined shortly after by Maybach. In three years the vision had become reality with the unveiling of the boneshaker.

Engines themselves, by this time, were not the novelty. Nor was transport. Railways and ocean-going ships were already firmly established, but steam was the motive power. So what more natural than that early pioneers should look to steam in their attempts to hoist the ancient 'hobby horse' type of personal transport popularised around the mid-1880s by the Frenchman Pierre Michaux, who fitted cranks and pedals, into a self-propelled

German engineer Gottlieb Daimler (1834-1900). His 'boneshaker' of 1885 made a significant contribution to the development of the motorcycle (*National Motor Museum*)

age. In fact the first steam-powered cycles were in existence before 1870. In France, Michaux and L.G. Perreaux patented their version in 1888 while, at about the same time, Sylvester Howard

Karl Benz developed in 1885 a three-wheel vehicle driven by a single-cylinder internal combustion engine (*National Motor Museum*)

MAKE WAY FOR THE MOTORBIKE

Daimler's historic machine, the *Einspur*, shown with its stabilising small wheels (*National Motor Museum*)

Roper was popularising the Roper steam motorcycle in America.

The revolutionary aspect of Daimler's machine was the abounding implications it was to hold for the development of *personal* transport. Steam engines worked more efficiently with size and thus found an ideal application in ships and trains; and even the early airships of the 1880s. Daimler changed direction towards the development of small engines with a high power-to-weight ratio, thereby signposting the way, more than 60 years later, to the 'wheels' revolution of the post Second World War years.

Daimler himself quickly moved over to become more significant to the progress of four-wheel travel than in the further development of the motorcycle, but not before his curious-looking creation had written itself into motorcycle history. In developing the machine, Daimler had set up a workshop at a place called Cannstatt, near Stuttgart, and it was from there to the nearby village of Unter Türkheim, a round trip approaching 12 km (7½ miles) that the revolutionary machine was given its maiden outing, ridden, it is now generally accepted, by Paul Daimler, the inventor's 17-year-old son. The date was 10 November 1885, and the world was never quite the same again. Remarkably, perhaps, the unveiling of Daimler's trendsetter was still some 20 years before the first motorcycle race of any significance, which was held near Paris in 1904.

Improvements to Daimler's machine added a primitive two-speed transmission, but by the time the original *Einspur* had been destroyed in a fire at the Daimler factory in 1903, its inventor had long since turned his attention to four-wheel development, the challenge of two-wheel progress

being taken up by a host of enthusiasts fired by Daimler's inspiration.

Curiously, further development was based largely on the search for a viable steam-powered bike and not for another nine years was attention once more turned seriously to the internal combustion engine. A notable exception was the work of the brilliant British inventor Edward Butler who, but for lack of funds and good fortune, might have brought forward the development of the motorcycle by half-a-dozen years. His three-wheel Velocycle, closer in concept to a motorcycle than a car, had its single seat position between the two front wheels and used the two-stroke principle. But Butler was unsuccessful in his search for backers for the project and the machine, well ahead of its time when plans were shown for the first time in 1884 (that's a year before Daimler's creation!), didn't get beyond the design stage.

In 1887, two years after Daimler's machine had been unveiled, Butler got the backing he needed and tested a revised prototype in 1888. This was further improved by the use of rotary valves and the first ever float-feed carburettor, but Butler's exciting project, now called a Petrol-Cycle, was hampered, first because of the speed limitations on British roads—4 mph (6 km/h) in the country and 2 mph (3 km/h) in towns!—and, then, in consequence, by the decision of the financial syndicate behind the project to develop the engine for use in boats and for stationary means.

Although the Petrol-Cycle was advanced to a stage when it could be driven at a speed of 12 mph (19 km/h), further development was halted as the syndicate ran out of capital and Butler's enterprise was finally buried in 1897 after a 'rescue and exploitation' exercise by the British Motor Traction Company failed.

By this time other pioneers had their heads well down developing the idea of petrol-driven bikes. In 1887 Felix Millet produced the first multi-cylinder motorcycle, and America was also active during these experimental years. Comte Albert de Dion and his partner, Georges Bouton, in France; Colonel Henry Holden in England; and in Germany, Heinrich Hildebrand and Alois Wolfmüller, were all names destined to make an indelible mark on motorcycle history. Ten years after Daimler's boneshaker had first seen the light of day, de Dion and Bouton had produced a three-wheeler powered by a petrol engine, which ran at an exciting 1500 rpm, almost double the shaft speed of Daimler's engine. Within three more years, by 1898, the firm set up by de Dion and Bouton was producing what amounted to over-the-counter engines for use in Britain and certain Continental countries, and even the United States.

This Holden motorcycle of 1902 was the brainchild of Henry Capel Lofft Holden, who built the first four-cylinder motorcycle. The engine is exceptionally low in the frame (*National Motor Museum*)

It was that same year 1898, that a Major from the Royal Engineers, later Colonel Henry Holden, put Britain into the record books by planning, through a London company, the limited production of what was the world's first four-cylinder motorcycle. With two sets of twin cylinders, the engine was mounted low in the frame, but overheating problems dictated a reluctant switch to water cooling and the added cost made the machine uncompetitive against the contemporary light car, with its added comfort and reliability, and reasonable price. Holden patented his design in 1896 and it is described in C. F. Caunter's *Motor Cycles, a technical history* (HMSO, 1956), as follows: 'The first model had an air-cooled engine with a cylinder bore of 2·125 in and a stroke of 4·5 in. The pistons moved together, but the impulses were arranged to occur alternately in one cylinder at each end so that there was a power impulse at each piston stroke. The surface vaporiser consisted of a tank containing the petrol, with a vertical longitudinal diaphragm of copper wire gauze, through which the air passed on its way to the mixing valve, and part of the exhaust heat was

used to warm the fuel to assist vaporisation. Ignition was effected by means of a coil-and-battery system, working in conjunction with a high-tension commutator type distributor, which was driven from the exhaust-valve camshaft. Since there was no rotary motion in the engine itself, a chain-drive had to be arranged from the rear wheel to drive the camshaft. The machine weighed 123 lb and was capable of a maximum speed of about 24 mph.'

It was at about the time that Colonel Holden was patenting his design in 1896 that the production of motorcycles as a business was first seriously contemplated. The now legendary Hildebrand and Wolfmüller of Munich showed the way. The Hildebrand brothers, Heinrich and Wilhelm, had earlier teamed with fellow Bavarian, Alois Wolfmüller and another clever engineer, Hans Geisenhof, but the parallel twin four-stroke unit which was first produced didn't sit well in the frame for which it was originally intended. In a new frame, based on the former Hildebrand 'steamer' of 1889, the horizontal engine fitted perfectly, however, and as the partners formed a company to market their new product, it seemed they had achieved success.

The Hildebrand and Wolfmüller of 1894 was a truly remarkable machine. The bore and stroke of the two horizontal cylinders were 90 × 117 mm to give 1489 cc and the machine was said to be capable of 28 mph, (45 km/h), frighteningly fast for a two-wheeler in 1894. It was the biggest engine fitted into a production two-wheeler up to that time and the first to be generally known as a motorcycle. It was really the first production motorcycle, the first model to be produced on a commercial scale, for in the pioneer years inventors hand built their creations and had no thought of offering them for public sale.

Orders poured in. The company planned a new factory to cope with production. The machine, through licence, became available in France as the *Petrolette*, but tests and demonstrations which were designed to consolidate the machine's reputation only served to show up its shortcomings. The situation worsened as many owners, complaining about poor starting and numerous other difficulties, demanded their money back and the project was doomed when the company discovered they were selling the machines at a price below the cost of production. The business finally collapsed in 1897 in both Germany and France, but Hildebrand and Wolfmüller had demonstrated beyond all question that the motorcycle had a future far beyond the limitations of an engineering exercise.

Continental Europe, the Hildebrand and Wolfmüller failure notwithstanding, forged ahead while Britain limped well behind, hampered and frustrated. It wasn't that inventive flair was lacking. Nor initiative and ambition. The impediment was an Act of Parliament passed more than 30 years before which curtailed speeds of 'light locomotives' to 2 mph (3 km/h) in the towns and 4 mph (6 km/h) in the open country. While such an outdated law existed the motorcycle seemed hardly relevant. However, in 1896 the Locomotives of Highways Act was passed following an active and vigorous lobby over many months by a number of pioneer motorists and supporters including Colonel H. C. L. Holden, who was later to design the Brooklands race track.

The Emancipation Run between London and Brighton on Saturday 14 November, 1896 celebrated the victory, though the jubilation, while symbolically significant, only marked the lifting of the speed limit to 12 mph (19 km/h). The gesture provided little additional incentive for manufacturers to embark on long-term engineering development plans. Nor did it, in terms of speed, lift the motorcycle much above the pedal cycle or the horse. But the repeal of the restrictive Road Acts of 1861 and 1865 meant that it was no longer necessary to have a person walk in front of a vehicle waving a red flag. And in those days that was progress indeed!

The art of riding a motorcycle at this time, even at such comparatively low speeds and on roads uncluttered by heavy traffic, was very much an adventure. With limited engine power and no variable gearing the rider had still to rely on pedalling to break the crest of hills, while the varied positions on the machine selected for the engine – from over or alongside the front wheel to over or behind the rear wheel! – made stability questionable at best. It was left to a couple of brothers, of French nationality but Russian extraction, to solve the problem of engine location once and for all.

Michel and Eugene Werner had originally been dealers in phonographs, but in 1896 an event occurred which was to change their direction and the course of motorcycle history. A colleague left a compact, high-speed, single-cylinder engine at their Paris workshops as a possible drive unit for their new-style kinetoscope which the Werners were set to launch commercially. Looking for an eye-catching method of drawing public attention to his new venture, Michel Werner fitted the engine to a pedal cycle ... and immediately saw the potential. The Werner 'Motocyclette' was the result, produced as nothing more grand than an experiment in economy transport. It was eventually to become an overwhelming success. At first they fitted the engine at the front, then at the back, and later, vertically, in front of the steering head with a flexible round leather belt used to drive on to a belt rim on the front wheel.

By this time Michel and Eugene Werner had abandoned their previous ambitions and negotiated a contract with Alexander Goven of Scotland for a supply of bicycle frames. A dozen Werner Motocyclettes were built and sold in 1897 and, following the sale of the British manufacturing rights to the Motor Manufacturing Company in Coventry, England, to provide much needed investment to improve the design, more than 300 were taken up in 1898. In 1901 more than 1000 Werner machines were sold.

The first Werner machines, exciting as initial examples of something new, had a too high centre of gravity, making them unstable on wet roads, and the tube ignition system proved unreliable. An electric system of ignition following the De Dion-Bouton principle was later used and helped to make the machine popular. By then the model was powered by a 217 cc single-cylinder, air-cooled engine with a 62 mm bore and 72 mm stroke. And by 1901 the Werner cycle had solved the problem of where to put the engine. By locating it centrally, low down in a diamond-shaped frame and between the road wheels, they lowered the centre of gravity and improved stability. While others might well

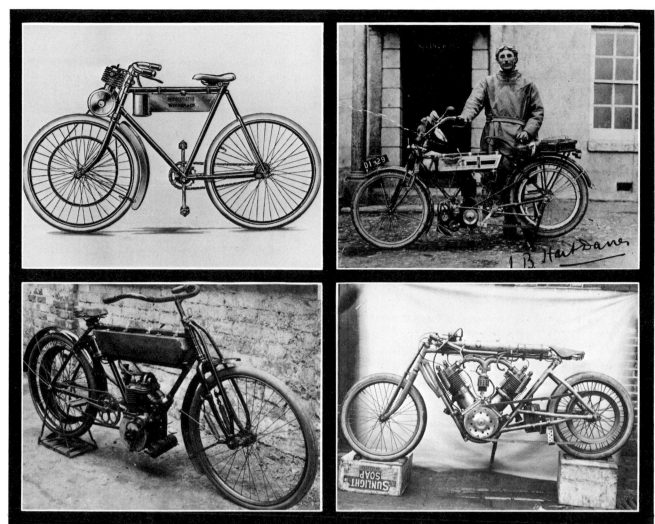

Top left : The Motocyclette of Michel and Eugene Werner, around 1898, with the engine mounted high up at the front (*National Motor Museum*). *Top right* : Triumph, a British motorcycle company of great tradition. This early model, with rider I.B. Hart-Davies, completed 886 miles (1426km) in 33hr 22min in 1909, finishing at the Lands End Hotel (*National Motor Museum*). *Above left* : The Werner twin of 1904 with the engine now located low in the frame between the road wheels. It solved the problem once and for all of where to put the engine! (*National Motor Museum*), *Above right* : The style of the times. This lean-looking 1909 NLG-JAP machine with a 90 degree V-twin JAP engine with 120 × 120mm cylinders (*National Motor Museum*)

claim to have arrived at this fundamental truth earlier, the Werners enjoyed much of the credit for the innovation, simply because they had the wit to patent their method of fixing the engine to the frame in this position. The positioning of the engine where once the pedalling gear had been located also improved the safety and the look of the machine.

These early Werner models are significant to the development of the motorcycle, being specially constructed with the engine unit built into the frame, thereby representing authentic ancestors of the motorcycle as we know it today. By this time the motorcycle idea was swiftly catching on. The French firm De Dion, Bouton et Cie had furthered the process significantly at the turn of the century with their prolific manufacture of 'over the counter' engines for all sorts of vehicles. Temperamental they may have been, but they were engines in an age when engines were beginning to mean

something, and they were readily available. Enthusiasts, many with more hope and energy than engineering skill, bought them to put into their own frames and it wasn't long before bicycle manufacturers woke up to the sales potential of adding engines to their models.

In Britain, firms including Raleigh, Matchless (founded in 1899), Royal Enfield (then known as Eadie) and Excelsior moved with the trend, as did Peugeot and Clement in France and Bianchi in Italy. Machines, constrained by the dictates of horsepower, were light and simple, and curiously at odds with the rugged roads which were available to them. Engine size began to rise, but after the flurry of ideas and experimentation which accompanied the first dawn of the motorcycle revolution, the inevitable 'shakedown' period that followed, settled for single cylinders, single speeds and belt drives.

During these years there had been other happenings too. In 1880 Hans Renold, a Swiss, introduced his roller chain, a development of the James Slater invention of 1864, and, four years later, a certain James Lansdowne Norton began business in Britain as a chain manufacturer. Sixty-five years later the brilliant machines bearing his name were sweeping Britain to worldwide racing supremacy. John Boyd Dunlop had developed his pneumatic tyre as early as 1888 and by 1903 the famous firm he founded was claiming in its advertising: '18,000 miles on a motorcycle fitted with one pair of Dunlop tyres'. In 1902 the sparking plug, and a year later the high-tension magneto system of ignition accredited to Robert Bosch, were soon to be in general use by all the prominent manufacturers.

Meantime, in the United States, the motorcycle revolution took longer to take off. After Sylvester Howard Roper's steam cycle experiments of the 1880s, came America's first production model, built by cycle manufacturer Albert Pope, but not until 1900. Other machines were also produced around this time and it was in 1901 that the Indian cycle company brought out their first motor cycle. Carl Hedstrom, who had come to the United States from Sweden, produced the engine, built broadly to the De Dion pattern, and George M. Hendee fitted it into one of his Indian bicycle frames. The single-cylinder, 1½ hp machine weighed only 98 lb (44½ kg). Indian went on to become the first big name for motorcycles in America while 1901 was also important because it brought together craftsman William Harley and pattern maker Arthur Davidson in the common ambition to produce a motorcycle. An early proto-type was promising and after moving into a wooden shed in the Davidson family's backyard in Milwaukee, the enterprise quickly moved ahead. Fifty motorcycles were produced by the partner-ship in 1906 and the Harley-Davidson company was incorporated a year later. Production went up to 150 machines in 1907 and within ten years had reached 18,000 as Harley-Davidson moved ahead to gain, over the years, the most famous name and the biggest and most enduring reputation of any American motorcycle manufacturer.

Back in Europe, the Humber Company, special-ists in tricycle manufacture, moved into motor-cycles in the early 1900s, as did Riley, Rover, Ariel, Singer, Rex, Triumph and Royal Enfield, among others. In Germany, NSU, who had been in the cycle business since the days of the Penny Farthing (about the 1870's), brought engines from Switzerland for their first motorised models, later building engines and frames themselves. Durkopp and Opel, also from Germany, Buchet from France, Puch from Austria and FN and Minerva from Belgium were among numerous companies which began producing motorcycles.

Until almost the mid-1900s the industry was not taken all that seriously by a lot of people and some even went so far as to state publicly that the new idea would never take over as a serious means of personal transport. It was only when the expediency of the motorised bicycle began to yield to the motorcycle, specially designed and built as such, that the motorcycle began to create its own identity. This led the way to more rugged models and everything got beefier – engines, forks, wheels. In Britain the speed limit was lifted to 20 mph (32 km/h), still well below the capabilities of many models, and on the roughly-surfaced, pot-holed roads riding a motorcycle was still an exciting adventure.

Technical progress was accelerated as racing began to take hold. The rawhide belt drive which had been good enough for domestic use stretched and broke in crucial races, leading to the introduc-tion of V-section, rubber-and-canvas or leather belts. Around 1905 several V-twins were in use and Werner produced an exciting multi with automatic inlet and mechanically operated exhaust valves. Sadly the Werner enterprise was almost at an end, for both Michel and Eugene died within a few years of one another and the enterprise finally collapsed in 1908. Increasing speed, par-ticularly in racing, brought the need for improved suspension and in 1906 Alfred Drew developed his front fork with side-linked compression springs, leading to better handling and steering. Five years later gearing became the major engineering chal-lenge as the TT races, in 1911, were switched to the formidable Mountain Course, including the six-mile (9½ km) climb up the Snaefell mountain. Variable gears now became essential. Multi-ratio, belt-drive systems were used by Rudge-Whitworth and Zenith from Britain, but the first three places in the most important Senior race were to be taken by American Indian V-twin four-stroke machines with their technically superior shaft transmission incorporating a clutch, linked to a drive chain and rear wheel sprockets, thereby dispensing with the belt drive system.

Earlier, domestic motorcycling had suffered its first minor slump. After an exhilarating and energetic phase, sales dropped during the two years from 1905, leading to hesitancy and nervous-ness and a slow-down in development: and as Douglas, who were to achieve considerable success in later years, brought out their first model late in 1907, the trade in the UK was lamenting a drop in sales of 25 per cent over the previous year. Before business revived in 1909, Alfred Scott had unveiled his twin-cylinder two-stroke to set new

A general view of the motorcycle show at London's Olympia in 1911. The cycle and motorcycle show moved to Earls Court in 1937, and in 1980 plans were made to move the modern equivalent to the National Exhibition Centre (*Illustrated London News*)

standards in smooth motor cycling. Until then most motorcycles had been powered by four-stroke engines – single-cylinder versions, V or parallel twins – but Scott's twin-cylinder two-stroke on which Frank Applebee won the Senior TT three years later was the first example of the two-stroke's potential in racing.

The first British Motorcycle show proper took place at Olympia in 1910 (until then motorcycles had been shown with cars), and names which were to create legends in motorcycle history were in their infancy. That year, for instance, the first BSAs appeared, as did the first Rudge-Whitworths. A year later, when Olympia opened its doors, 275 motorcycles were exhibited of which more than 80 per cent were offered with variable gears. That year also saw the 2-speed AJS. Later, Brough, whose founder William E. Brough had been building motorcycles since 1902, became prominent, and in the years leading up to the First World War motorcycling was booming. Sales in Britain rose almost three-fold in the three years from 1910, and by 1913 British bikes were sustaining a thriving export business.

Motorcycles played an important part in the First World War. Germany were said to have 20 000 machines available when war started, and in the combat areas and elsewhere 'despatch-riders' of both sides were essential in carrying messages from one area to another. Telephone communications were restricted and the motorcycle replaced the horse as a means of getting news from one place to another with all possible urgency. Popular with the Allies was the 499 cc side-valve Triumph single, later versions employing a Sturmey-Archer three-speed gearbox and final belt drive. A good many sidecar outfits were used, some as mobile machine-gun mounts, and were supplied by firms like Royal Enfield, Matchless, Sunbeam and others. Germany depended a lot on NSU models, and other motorcycles used during this war period were Zenith from England, FN from Belgium, Peugeot and Terrot from France and Bianchi from Italy.

Some promising designs which had been intended for civilian use were killed off because of the contingencies of war, but in 1918, with hostilities at an end, the world went motorcycle mad. Major firms which had built up large factories to cater for war contracts were anxious to switch their high production to civilian models. Throughout Europe hundreds of companies mushroomed in the hope of cashing in on what appeared to be an insatiable demand for motorcycles in those early days of peace. But with serious shortages of basic materials like iron and steel, rubber and sheet metal, waiting lists were long. Many firms in Britain and in Germany whose wartime production of armaments and other essentials like guns, ships and aircraft (including BMW, who had been building aero-engines) moved into motor-cycle production, BMW being probably the only notable example of a long-term survivor.

Improving supplies of raw materials and a dramatic rise in the cost of motorcycles combined to thin out the queues of waiting buyers as the industry began to settle down to a pattern much the same as before, with proprietary two-and four-stroke engines keeping the increasing numbers of assemblers happy.

As Europe moved gradually into what is now accepted as the Golden Age of the motorcycle for Britain, in the years between the wars, the United States industry, which had earned an international reputation for its superb and tough models from Indian, Harley-Davidson and Henderson, suffered a paralysing blow when Henry Ford got the price of his famous Model T car so low, leaving motorcycles little room to compete on a price differential. In Britain, in the 1920s, Brough launched what became known as the 'Rolls-Royce of motorcycles', the Brough Superior, and by 1922 the German industry had overcome post-war problems and was ready to expand and flourish. In 1923 BMW introduced their famous 500 cc flat-twin, four-stroke engine, which they supplied to many other manufacturers. It was about this time that Italy moved significantly into motorcycle production, with Garelli, Benelli and, perhaps most famous of all, Moto Guzzi, all finding their feet. Harley-Davidson produced a model specifically intended to capture sales in Europe, and in 1925 the death occurred in Birmingham, England, of James Norton who founded Britain's most famous motorcycle company of all time.

James Lansdowne Norton went into business on his own in 1898 forming a company which

Sedate, if not altogether comfortable. Early domestic motorcycling, three-wheel style (*Motor Cycle Weekly*)

produced parts for the two-wheel trade. After teaming with Charles Garrard, who imported the French-made Clement, Norton produced their first motorised bicycle in 1902. It was powered by the Clement four-stroke engine, mounted on the front down tube. Norton machines over the next thirty or so years gained an outstanding reputation all over the world and in the 1930s particularly dominated international racing, winning 14 TT races in the nine years leading to the outbreak of the Second World War. During that same period the Senior TT fell to Norton riders seven times.

Another famous British make, HRD, was seen for the first time around the mid-1920s and was quickly to gain a reputation as a 'bespoke' machine. Then in 1929 manufacture was taken over by Phil Vincent. At about this time Britain was reported to have more than 700 000 motor-cyles in use, more than any other country, and representing more than one-third of the world total.

Between 1918 and the economic depression of 1930, bringing dole-queues and hunger marches, motorcycles made remarkable progress thanks to the technological advances resulting from the dictates of war and design technology.

Stronger and more durable camshafts and valve springs became possible because of the harder steels now available, and aluminium was used to make pistons. Overhead valves operated by push-rods took over from side-valves and led, in the mid-1920s, to the overhead-camshaft engines. Racing, with machines employing great power and multiple gears, added to the technological advances for the domestic rider and the days of the hand-operated gear-change lever, crude and hazardous in use (certainly in racing), were numbered after Velocettes finished first and second in the Junior TT of 1928 using the positive-stop foot-gearchange mechanism invented by the factory's engineer, Harold Willis.

What could loosely be described as the 'modern motorbike' had, in basic concept if not in refine-ment, been produced before the outbreak of the Second World War in 1939. Scott and Vitesse had developed two-stroke engines with rotary valves, Moto Guzzi by 1930 had a three-cylinder, double overhead-camshaft four-stroke, and the four-stroke with four valves per cylinder instead of the custom-ary two was introduced by Rudge. Norton and BMW were among the first to use hydraulically damped telescopic front-wheel springs, bringing suspension in line with modern principles.

Ironically, when Britain led the world in a flourishing motorcycle sport, at home two of the most famous factories, AJS and Ariel, were to falter, creating concern and anxiety until reconsti-

James Lansdowne Norton (*left*) with his famous factory's Senior TT winning machine of 1924 with victorious rider Alec Bennett. Standing (*right*) is the firm's managing director of that time, Bill Mansell (*National Motor Museum*)

tution enabled their life to be extended. Enthusiasm for motorcycling on the Continent rose, and in Italy and Germany, encouraged by nationalistic policies, positively rocketed. By the early 1930s Germany had become possibly the most motorcycle conscious country in the world, with their DKW factory turning out machines at the rate of 20 000 a year.

Just a few years later Europe was once more thrust into war and the 'big four' in Britain – Norton, BSA, Triumph and Matchless – switched to providing personal mobility to a nation in crisis. In the six years of war over 400 000 motorcycles were supplied to Allied troops and in the immediate post-war years the British rapidly geared themselves up to cater for a phenomenal demand. Sales, which had declined from 1929 until the outbreak of war, when about only a quarter million motorcycles were sold, doubled within a year of peace returning and by the mid-1950s the

total number of machines in use in Britain stood at 1¼ millions.

Around this time Britain probably still led the world in motorcycle production, though in Germany the post-war 'economic miracle' had already started with volume production coming from factories like BMW, NSU and Zundapp. But if the British industry looked uncomfortably over its shoulder at the progress being made by Germany, it's fair to say that the world at large, including both Britain and Germany, were unsuspecting as a Mr. Soichiro Honda took a few curious machines to the Isle of Man in 1959 and somewhat surprisingly collected the Manufacturers Team Award in the lightweight class.

Within just a few years Honda was destined to extend the frontiers of motorcycle production in a way never before contemplated. Soon the once-proud British motorcycle industry would be in tatters, and Germany, Italy and elsewhere would wilt and wither as the small men from a long, long way away, branded first as nothing more creative than meticulous copyists, moved in to conquer the world of motorcycling, leaving little room for others.

17

Chapter 2

Racing into the Unknown

It wasn't long before the most intrepid of those stalwart motorcycle pioneers pulled their cloth caps firmly onto their heads, bent low over their primitive machines, and with an abandoned disregard for personal safety akin to those earliest aviators, raced off into the unknown. Bicycle clubs began to form motorcycle sections, and the earliest races pitted pedal against motor power. Not always did the motorcycle win! The *Horseless Vehicle Journal* as early as 1897 reported: 'W. J. Stocks on the cycle covered 27 miles 300 yards in an hour. Although the motor bicycle ran splendidly throughout, soon after the start the motor slowed down and the crowd jeered immensely, for they imagined its end had come. The cause of the pulling up, however, was that the rider thought from the shouting of the crowd that some mishap had occurred and he requested that they be kept quiet. Although at the finish the motor was 300 yards behind, it would be a bold man who declared that the cycle will always be able to beat the motor.'

When, exactly, the tide turned in favour of the motorcycle is not accurately recorded, but what *is* certain is that Continental Europe, and particularly France, was soon well ahead of Britain in motorcycle racing. The plain fact is that there was just nowhere in the UK for enthusiasts to race their machines. The authorities rigidly enforced the restrictive speed limits of 4 mph (6 km/h), then 12 mph (19 km/h) and later 20 mph (32 km/h), and legendary characters like the Collier brothers, Harry and Charlie, were forced onto cycle tracks to gain experience and test their machines. The Canning Town cycle track was a popular venue, along with Crystal Palace and Herne Hill, and fierce, abandoned racing on machines specially powered and prepared soon took top speeds up to around 60 mph (96 km/h). Harry Martin and his 2¾ hp Excelsior were a formidable combination and in 1903, with his soft cap turned peak to the rear, he did a standing start mile at the Canning Town track in 1 min 24 secs.

National racing and record breaking quickly led to international rivalry and it wasn't long before the famous French aces were making regular visits to Britain, these meetings being among the first to be organised on a commercial basis in England.

Harry Martin – the 'English Cannonball' – in action on his Excelsior machine at the Crystal Palace race track in 1902 (*Motor Cycle Weekly*)

Without encumbering speed limits, motorcycling on the Continent had stormed ahead. Those long ribbons of ruler-straight, deserted roads in France were ideal for testing machines to the limit and with no restraints to dictate compromise, the concentration was on the development of 'race specials' built for outright speed performance. France had also taken to racing her motorcycles round 'velodromes' and favoured events which had virtually no rules. This led to the development of grossly over-powered machines which in England offended good taste and were branded as monstrosities.

Enthusiasts in Britain gasped in almost disbelief at Maurice Fournier's 22 hp machine of 1903, for instance, for it was reputed to be capable of a top speed of 80 mph (128 km/h), had a 2340 cc twin-cylinder Buchet special engine, and was so brutal in concept that some people felt it to be incapable of being ridden with even the smallest margin of safety. The frame consisted of one tube of enormous diameter running from the bottom socket lug, down under the motor crank chambers and up to the seat lug. Tyres were 26 × 3½ in (660 m × 89 mm) and the machine weighed 360 lb (163·3 kg).

Fournier was an early visitor to England and in an event against the British rider Barden at Canning Town, in 1903, the five scheduled races

In the Brooklands Paddock in 1909 – the redoubtable Charlie Collier, one of Britain's most famous pioneer motorcycle racers (*Motor Cycle Weekly*)

carried a stake of £1000. Fournier won decisively, taking the first three races and eliminating the need for further competition.

Achieving success around this time was the French Griffon machine. The talented Genty rode it to make the best time in speed trials in 1903 at Nice, covering the mile from a standing start in 1 min 16.95 sec., an average of 61.5 mph (99.0 km/h), while Demester rode it to win the Circuit des Ardennes race.

In the continental inter-city marathon Paris-Berlin race of 1901 the French rider Rivierre competed on a Werner machine (*National Motor Museum*)

The epic inter-city marathons had started in 1895 and by 1903 had become alarming and frightening spectacles. Motorcycling's hero in these sensational affairs was the French ace Bucquet who rode a Werner machine. He had already won the Paris–Vienna race in 1903 and similar events and was again leading the motorcycle section of the infamous Paris–Madrid marathon when the race was abandoned in confusion, near hysteria and ignominy, at Bordeaux. These roaring, uninhibited races were brutish and crude as those monster motorcars of the period raced alongside motorcycles. Huge crowds lining the route for mile upon mile were near-fanatical in their excitement. This race, which was to shut the door firmly on these inter-city dramas, began at Versailles with competitors flagged away in pairs. Bucquet, fighting off a challenge from Demester, was first to complete the 119 km to Châteaudun, but even at this stage the motorcyclists were finding themselves becoming dangerously mixed up with the cars. A report of the day suggested that the British rider A. C. Wright had to pull up sharply to avoid running into one car, which was drawn right across the road. Safety became problematical as spectators, hypnotised by the incredible sight of these huge cars and over-powered motorcycles surging through enormous dust clouds as they roared over the primitive, pot-holed roads, pressed forward and spread themselves over the course in an attempt to catch an early sight of the oncoming vehicles.

Accidents involving motorcycles were rare, but the Paris–Madrid race was finally abandoned at Bordeaux because of the many accidents, some

with fatal consequences, involving the big cars. Forty-nine motorcycles took part with Bucquet being declared the winning motorcyclist, having raced 341 miles (549 km) at an average speed of 38·12 mph (61·35 km/h). Three million people were said to have lined the route for this final, searing drama, but with little organisation and hardly any control, the end was inevitable.

It was France again, however, which adopted the cause of motorcycle racing and, with the demise of the inter-city marathons, organised the first International Cup Race, a new form of racing round a closed circuit, in 1904. Austria, Denmark, France, Germany and Great Britain took part, but the race was shabbily organised and ended in confusion and chaos. Three riders competed from each country, but while the British team took the rules seriously, other competitors pushed the frontiers of gamesmanship beyond reason, riding machines which were heavier than the regulation 110 lb (50 kg), switching to machines, and using components, which had not been made in their own country; and even blanketing parts of the circuit with nails! The British team had so many punctures they were forced to retire, and in such utter shambles did the racing end that the French organisers annulled the results.

A second attempt the following year was more controlled, better organised and became recognised as the first motorcycle race of any major consequence. French and Austrian riders were favoured to win on the strength of their greater experience of riding at high speeds on roads similar to those around Dourdon, near Paris, where the event was held. Demester of France led the way, followed by Mueller of Germany, Campbell of Britain and Toman of Austria. Final rider to go, at number 12 and 24 min after Demester, was Wondrick of Austria. On the first lap Demester suffered a broken belt and punctures and the Austrian, Toman, crashed and was out of the race. Wondrick snapped up the advantage and on the third lap led Demester by 1¾ min. The Austrian, riding a Laurin Klement two-cylinder machine, broke all previous records for the Dourdon course, completing 270 km (168 miles) in 3 hr 5¼ min, an average speed of 54·5 mph (87·7 km/h). Demester's ill-luck persisted. He sustained yet another puncture on the fourth lap and was robbed of second place, being disqualified for changing a wheel. Joseph Giuppone, an Italian, on a Peugeot was the only other rider to finish the course, taking second place in spite of three punctures.

This second International Cup Race was a much more respectable affair though France 'bent' the rules by running their eliminating trials on the Dourdon course where the race was to take place.

In the meantime a new ruling body had been established, the *Fédération Internationale des Clubs Motor Cyclistes* (FICM), but as the race rules were unchanged, the race was not a favourite among British riders. The 110 lb (50 kg) maximum weight limit for machines, rigidly enforced by the organisers, encouraged the development of machines which were totally alien to the British emphasis on machines which were more akin to road-going models. While engine power increased, frames remained light. Wheels were undershod and design was stripped to the barest essentials – mini seats, no gears, rigid frames and inadequate brakes. It was the organisers' insistence on this crippling weight restriction which finally brought the extinction of the International Cup Race after 1906.

British riders were by now tired of competing on the Continent under rules they didn't agree with, which put them at a disadvantage, and were often 'interpreted' to their disadvantage, and a move for a British road race strictly for touring machines grew. By this time the Auto-Cycle Club, formed in 1903 and the forerunner to the present-day Auto-Cycle Union (A-CU), was finding its feet. They backed the idea and approached the authorities, but without success. Didn't they realize that Britain had a road speed limit . . . and no!, permission certainly could not be granted for certain roads to be closed temporarily while the race took place.

But the despair felt by motorcyclists at the authorities' decision led to what was perhaps the most fateful event in the entire history of motor-

Frank Appleby on a Scott races to victory in the 1912 Senior TT. He is seen at Kates Cottage (*Motor Cycle Weekly*)

cycle racing. Faced with a similar problem when they were about to select their team for the International Cup Race of 1905, the A-CU had successfully sought permission for the eliminating trials to be held on the Isle of Man. The Manx Government had been co-operative. They had no speed limit on their roads and had no objection to closing roads while racing took place. So attention was switched to the Isle of Man. Among the enthusiasts was the Marquis de Mouzilly St.

No. 22 – Rem Fowler's Norton twin (with Peugeot engine) of 1907, winner in the TT multi-cylinder class (*Motor Cycle Weekly*)

Mars, who not only encouraged others who were working out a framework for the Tourist Trophy (TT), but agreed to give a special trophy to the winner of the premier race.

And in 1907 the first TT Races took place on the Isle of Man, and the entire course of motorcycle racing took a new and historic turn.

At the same time in Britain the Brooklands race circuit was opened and together the TT Races and Brooklands were instrumental in giving British riders and manufacturers all the inspiration necessary to take them into the promised land.

The TT Races are studied in greater depth in Chapter 5, but Brooklands must be given further attention at this point since its impact was enormous over its relatively short life, and it captured a place in history as the world's first artificially constructed race track. Designed by Colonel H. C. L. Holden, whose four-cylinder motorcycle of 1897 was a talking point in the previous chapter, and paid for by Hugh Locke-King, a wealthy hotelier and owner of much of the land between Weybridge and Byfleet in Surrey, England, on which the track was constructed, the vision became reality because of Hugh Locke-King's passionate enthusiasm for cars. Building began towards the end of 1906 and by April 1907 the vast concrete circuit, almost oval and 2¾ miles (4.4 km) round, was complete. Though built principally for car racing, it soon became the obvious place for the high-speed testing of motorcycles. Organised racing quickly followed as Brooklands became known the world over. Features of the circuit like the *Railway Straight*, *Member's Bridge* and the *Byfleet Banking* became as significant to racing enthusiasts in

the early 1900s as *Druids Hill Bend* at Brands Hatch and the *Masta Straight* at Francorchamps were 60 years later. There was superior seating for 5000, further tiers of seats for 30 000 more and the whole complex incorporated workshops and garages, shelters and paddock facilities and, an important innovation, an electrical timing system.

The development of the British motorcycle industry owes much to Brooklands. At the time, British riders, on their basically standard machines, were no match for the specially-prepared race machines of their Continental rivals, and in particular, the French. If they were ever to compete realistically they needed somewhere close at hand and continuously available to develop their machines and racing techniques. The Isle of Man course was not the answer. It was too far away and the authorities couldn't be expected to be continuously closing its roads for racing. Brooklands plugged that vital gap.

The first official motorcycle race at Brooklands took place on 20 April 1908, with makes like Chater-Lea, Minerva, FN, NSU, Rex and Triumph all represented. A scratch race over two laps for machines not exceeding 80 × 98 mm per cylinder, the event was won easily by Will Cook on a 984 NLG Peugeot at 63 mph (101 km/h). A handicap race held a month later was even more popular among both competitors and spectators and was won by a relatively unknown rider, H. Shanks, on a 2¾ hp Chater-Lea at a speed of 42.3 mph (68.1 km/h). At this point Brooklands faced its first crisis as a motorcycle venue. Local residents, objecting to the noise at the track, sued

A 350cc Chater Lea at an early Brooklands meeting (National Motor Museum)

A 3½hp Triumph at Brooklands in May 1908 (National Motor Museum)

Locke-King in the High Court and he was ordered to pay £7000 costs, as well as being forced to build a new entrance road. Motorcycles were made the scapegoat – unfairly, because in those days racing cars made just as much noise – taking the brunt of the responsibility, and the British Automobile Racing Club (BARC), who organised racing at Brooklands, decided to discontinue motorcycle activities there, not relenting until the autumn of 1908. That year, on 8 October, Charlie Collier broke the world's one-hour record on a 964 cc ohv parallel-valved JAP Matchless V-twin, covering 70 miles 105 yards (112·8 km) with a fastest lap at 72·89 mph (117·30 km/h). A Test Hill was constructed and first used in 1909 and that same year the British Motor Cycle Racing Club (BMCRC or Bemsee) was formed with Brooklands as its headquarters. It was the first national club in the world formed solely for the interests of racing motorcyclists.

For 28 years Brooklands provided the only means on the British mainland for the long hours of testing of new ideas. As a racing venue it attracted the imagination and the presence of top riders from other countries as well as Britain. An early featured attraction which continued for a while were the Inter-varsity Meetings held between teams of riders from Oxford and Cambridge Universities. Then, in 1910, Harry Martin demolished the 500 cc flying-start kilometre and mile records on his 340 cc Martin-ASL-JAP. It was an outstanding performance and, with speeds of 68·28 mph (109·88 km) and 65·97 mph (106·12 km), was unheard of at that time for a 350.

It was the same Harry Martin, on the same machine, who won the first A-CU track-racing championship meeting – an open scratch race – when it was first held at Brooklands that first year. Until then this unofficial but widely recognised 'championship' had been held at ⅓ mile cycle tracks such as at Canning Town.

Towards the end of 1910 the stirring deeds of American racer Jake de Rosier began to percolate through to Britain and the news that he had covered more than 84 miles (135 km) in an hour on a 994 cc Indian machine was greeted around Brooklands with a degree of scepticism. The colourful American, however, was to show his talent in no uncertain way when he made his debut at Brooklands in 1911, prior to attending the TTs which that year incorporated the new Mountain Course for the first time, in a series of three races against the British ace, Charlie Collier.

The machines were in stark contrast. The Indian was chain driven and, with 28 in (711 mm) diameter wheels and thin tyres, looked lean against the more rugged appearance of Collier's Matchless, final drive of which was by belt. Jake's engine of 994 cc was fitted with auxiliary exhaust ports drilled in the cylinder, the exhaust pipes were only 3 in (76 mm) long and discharged straight into the open air. He chose his wider handlebars which he felt more suited to the bumpy nature of the Brooklands surface. Collier's 998 cc red Matchless had no auxiliary exhausts, but was fitted with long exhaust pipes and a newly-introduced Matchless spring fork was used. Both machines had magneto ignition and ran on petrol.

The riders' appearance also contrasted, adding to the interest and excitement of the occasion, de Rosier in tight-fitting brown leathers and helmet, Collier in riding breeches, a white pullover and leather flying-type helmet. You can sense the atmosphere and expectancy from this early report of the preparations: 'Harry Collier wheeled his brother's machine down to the far end of the bridge over the Wey and Garrett did the like with the Indian while the two rivals walked down together, chatting to one another. The starter's car was also there, and presently it was seen that all three motors, i.e. the car and the two motor bicycles, were coming nearer; faster and faster they went until, when the two competitors were dead in line, down went the red flag in the car and the race was begun.'

This first race was over two laps and Collier edged in front as they climbed the Members' Banking, but by the middle of the Railway Straight the Indian machine was level again. Collier pulled ahead once more, bent flat along the tank in contrast to de Rosier's more upright racing position, and unknown to the watching crowds the American was introducing a new tactic to Brooklands: the art of slip-streaming. In one of the most exciting races ever seen at Brooklands, the final spurt to end the race brought the advantage to Jake de Rosier by about a length at a speed of 80·59 mph (129·69 km/h). In the second race, over five laps, Collier roared once more into the lead from the start, only to see de Rosier by his rear wheel at the end of the first lap. The crowd held its breath on lap three when the Indian wobbled badly with the American struggling to retain control and went wild towards the end of the race as Collier swept into the lead. As the British rider raced on to win, there was no sign of the American. He limped in later with the remains of his front tyre dangling from the wheel hub and to the accompaniment of loud cheering. His front tyre had burst while he had been travelling at 80 mph (128 km/h) but with great skill he managed to keep control.

Now for the third and final race, over ten laps.

An historic picture of the bikes lined up ready for the start – the famous Brooklands banking can be seen in the background (*Motor Cycle Weekly*)

It was the decider, the Indian machine's slight advantage on speed against the more rugged qualities of the Matchless. After a couple of hiccups when it was discovered that Jake's machine had one or two loose nuts and someone had to go off in search of a spanner, and then that his magneto was broken, the final race was started with Charlie again moving fractionally ahead of the American. At the end of the second lap Jake crossed the starting line first and increased his lead, before Charlie, roaring through the Railway Straight, took the lead and was still ahead at the end of lap 4. Jubilant fans were now shouting for a British victory, but the American rejected any possibility of defeat. Racing round the high banking for the fifth time he was back in Charlie's slipstream, and the battle looked on again until the Matchless began to misfire. Collier looked down to see a high-tension wire adrift and as he struggled to remedy the fault, de Rosier rushed far ahead. With half a mile to pick up and now only four laps to go, Collier rode like a demon, but the distance was too great and he finished twenty seconds behind. Brooklands victory, and prize money of £130, went to the American and Jake de

Rosier had taught the old country a lesson in tactical racing, demonstrating that the astuteness of the rider was now becoming as important to the winning of races as courage, speed, strength and technical skill.

Brooklands had three main circuits and later a simulated road course called the Campbell Circuit. The complex reopened after the First World War

Testing Nortons at historic Brooklands. The rider is Dan O'Donovan on his well known Norton – 'Old Miracle' (*National Motor Museum*)

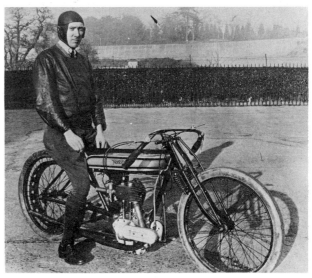

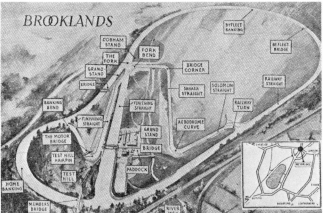

Above : The inspiration of Colonel H.C.L. Holden, who designed the circuit, and financed by Hugh Locke-King, the famous Brooklands race circuit under construction (*N.W. Lewis*)

Left : A plan of Brooklands, showing the layout and various features of the complex (N.W. Lewis)

Below Left : Norton machines were frequently at Brooklands. R.O. Lowe is seen astride No. 10 at a race meeting in the 1920s (*National Motor Museum*)

Below : Bob Dicker, winner of a three-lap handicap (classes C, D and E) on a Rudge Whitworth, at an early British Motorcycle Racing Club Meeting (N.W. Lewis)

in 1920 and remained in use until the outbreak of the Second World War. The British Motor Cycle Racing Club instituted the Brooklands Gold Star, a yellow medal award, which was presented to club members who at one of the club's meetings lapped the Outer Circuit at 100 mph (161 km/h) or more. Some 200 Gold Stars were presented, the first going to Bert Le Vack in 1922. Vickers-Armstrong took over much of Brooklands as an aircraft factory during the Second World War, and it was never used as a racing circuit again, except by the die-hard enthusiasts who even now continue to make annual pilgrimages to the once-famous track, the sweeped banking and stretches

1928 : GP start (*Motor Cycle Weekly*)

of crumbling concrete finding existence hard against the insistent encroachment of grass and overgrowth. Brooklands died with the Second World War, its comparatively short but glorious mission fulfilled.

As Brooklands and the Isle of Man inspired sporting hearts in Britain, motorcycle racing on the Continent continued to boom. The traditions of the classic Grands Prix began to take root and were soon to beckon the leading British riders of the day who left home shores on regular incursions to France, Belgium and elsewhere. The French Grand Prix of 1914, billed as the 'most important event of its kind on the Continent' attracted one third of its total entries from Britain, among them such revered names as Charlie Collier, Howard Newman and Cyril Pullin; but the event, to be run on 15 August, never took place. By then Europe was at war.

France held a Grand Prix again in 1920. The Belgian Grand Prix and the Italian Grand Prix were added the following year, and in 1922 there was also a Swiss Grand Prix. Germany followed suit in 1923, then Hungary, Holland, Austria and Sweden in the next few years. By the late 1920s, the 'Continental Circus' was established with top riders from Britain and other countries battling regularly at a series of Continental circuits in the style of the tennis pro circus today. By this time the nature of racing was changing. In the early days the men who raced were often the men who had constructed and developed their machines, but as specialisation took root and factories began to establish their own works teams, the motorcycle racer became a specialist in his own right. The origins of the Continental Circus were established by riders like Hubert Hassell, Vic Horsman, Graham Walker, Alec Bennett, Tommy de la Hay and Freddie Dixon on Nortons, Sunbeams, Indians and Douglases who often, at great expense to themselves, took the attack to their Continental rivals. As British motorcycles became supreme on the racing circuits there developed a truer appreciation of the commercial advantages to be obtained from racing success and factories like Norton, Velocette, Cotton, HRD, Rudge, AJS and Matchless began to marshall their own squads of 'works' riders, committed to full or part factory contracts. At first British competitive bikes were simply developed versions of roadsters, but in the 1930s factories began to see the potential in creating 'race specials' whose racing success could stimulate huge domestic sales.

Specialisation, advanced mechanical and technical development and almost every configuration was tried in a constant search for success – overhead valves, double overhead-camshafts, four valves per cylinder, four cylinders per engine, rotary-valve two-strokes, sleeve valve four-strokes. As the Second World War clouds hovered and the importance of racing success to national prestige grew, so the competition for the best riders, which only a few years before had been restricted to national boundaries, became an inter-Continental affair.

Even by 1939 the British motorcycle industry had seen most of its best days. When racing began to pick up the threads once more in 1947 the world-famous names of Norton, AJS, Velocette and Rudge, had but a few years left before wilting under the multi-cylinder machines from Italy and the superb NSUs from Germany in the smaller capacity classes and then, in the sidecar class, under the mighty BMW. Doom was comprehensive and conclusive some years later when racing machines from the other side of the world, led by Mr Honda, took motorcycle racing into a totally new and exciting era.

The first signpost to the British decline was perhaps set in 1939 when Germany and Italy, national prestige dictating a policy of enormous financial support for motorcycle racing, provided a grim hint of the future. While Norton, who had won 19 TTs and had supported the Isle of Man races every year since the first event in 1907, withdrew in 1939 to divert their entire resources to the production of motorcycles for the Services, Germany's Georg Meier on a supercharged BMW took the Senior race and while Stanley Woods kept an element of British prestige alive with victory in the Junior TT on a Velocette, the Lightweight event was won by the British rider Ted Mellors, but on the Italian Benelli machine.

Chapter 3

Bikes for all Reasons

Never has the motorbike rider had so much choice, the opportunity for so much fun. Motorbiking stretches from the low key motive of getting to and from work easily and economically to its serious challenge to the sports and performance car as an exciting, adventurous means of leisure travel or sport. Gone are the days of the dreary and dismal riding suits and the downgrade image. Colourful fashion clothing created specifically for riding has developed into a considerable industry in itself. 'Space age' helmets have added to the 'up market' acceptance of motorcycling, for both men and women.

There are models for all purposes and all tastes. They cost from a few pounds to a few thousand pounds. Motorcycling, unfairly, is often accused of being dangerous, when the problem more likely is that someone is riding a machine which is in excess of his capabilities or experience. So the sensible attitude is to choose the machine which is right for you – and if you've no road or riding experience, start small and work up. Leave the 1000 cc superbikes till later! Most of all, bikes themselves have been transformed and are now clean and gleaming in their chrome and distinctive individual liveries; sophisticated and civilised with flashing indicators, advanced instrument panels, rear-view mirrors and self-starters.

Broadly, the most popular motorcycles range from 125 to 500 cc with 250s and 350s in between. Anything below 125 cc is more accurately a moped or a development of the motorised bicycle and would not have the lines, equipment or performance to classify strictly as a motorcycle. The superbikes, of course, have the power and performance of many motorcars with their 750 cc upwards engines, and are gaining in popularity as the ultimate in 20th-century motorcycling.

Within virtually all classes nowadays the buyer will find a variety of machines available to him. While some factories gained their original reputations as specialist manufacturers – Honda for runabouts and small capacity models and Kawasaki for performance machinery, for instance – most now have broadened their marketing approach in an industry which is dominated by the Japanese – Honda, Suzuki, Yamaha and Kawasaki.

A 125 cc machine is ideal for town or city running. Small and sufficiently compact to retain the advantages of the motorised bicycle, like ease

The signs of the modern motorcycle rider – colourful one-piece leathers, space-age crash helmet, and a clean, sophisticated image (*Honda UK Ltd*)

of riding and manoeuvrability, it nonetheless has excellent acceleration and perhaps greater stability. It is easy to handle and in many circumstances is an excellent machine on which the beginner can gain experience.

More rugged and aggressive than the 125s, and

1 The Honda NC50K — a shopper's special with single-speed engine, automatic clutch and one of the easiest models to ride (*Honda UK Ltd*)

2 A modern sports moped designed as such, the Honda MB50 (*Honda UK Ltd*)

3 The Yamaha 125, basically a commuter machine but incorporating a sporting element (*Mitsui Machinery Sales UK Ltd*)

4 A mid-range motorcycle for the 1980s, the Suzuki GS250 (*Heron Suzuki GB Ltd*)

5 Introduced by Yamaha in 1980, this twin-cylinder watercooled two-stroke has a 347cc engine with a power output of 48hp at 8500rpm (*Mitsui Machinery Sales UK Ltd*)

6 Suzuki's GS550, an impressive king of the road (*Heron Suzuki GB Ltd*)

7 From Italy, a famous name, Moto Guzzi, and a superb example of 1980s engineering, the 850cc Le Mans

Smooth, clean lines of a modern superbike. The Italian Ducati 900cc Supersport in fashionable livery (*Coburn and Hughes*)

giving a more comfortable ride, the 250 cc models combine harmony in city traffic conditions with an ease of performance on the open road. The additional power of the 250 will also allow it to be ridden 'two up' with comfort and ease.

Machines of 350 cc are something of a hybrid. Generally no larger than a 250 they have the extra power which originally made them popular for town riders who preferred the additional performance of the 350 when riding on the open road during the weekends or on holidays. This still largely holds good in theory, but it is also true that some riders nowadays graduate directly from a 250 to a 500 cc.

Traditionally the king of the road, the 500 cc machine is every inch a motorcycle. It makes no concessions. It looks like one and performs like one. Plenty of power, acceleration potential which will leave many performance-cars behind. It is not altogether comfortable in heavy traffic, but on the open road has an unmatched exhilaration and sparkle.

The superbikes are the ultimate, designed as such and proud of it. Their rightful place is on the open road where their sheer power and additional speed finds the right environment. From 750 cc upwards, they are for very experienced riders only with their true passion for motorcycles.

Selection is a matter of personal choice and taste, but don't be misled into believing that all 250s, for instance, give the same performance. While this naturally is broadly true, machines have individual characteristics, and the industry is evolving all the time. For instance, at one time a Honda 250 would give a better performance than many 350 machines, but other than pure power, such features as the appearance of the bike, the way it 'feels' when you're astride it, the sound, controls and handling characteristics will all contribute to your ultimate choice.

The motorcycle dealer is the key figure in all this. He's generally an enthusiast himself and if you go round asking dealers' advice and guidance you'll be in a good position to make up your mind on the bike you want when the time comes.

Remember, if you're starting from scratch, buying the bike is only the beginning. You'll need to licence and insure it, and protective clothing and a crash helmet are essentials. Budget for them for they can add quite appreciably to the outlay.

Learning how to ride. An RAC/A-CU training session being put through the correct drill (*Auto-Cycle Union*)

Safety is the paramount consideration and in some countries excellent training schemes are now available for the novice or newcomer to motorbiking. The first essential is to know your bike thoroughly and a recommendation is to walk your bike round in a figure 8 so that you become thoroughly familiar with its handling. Riding a bike means controlling it, so it is essential that you get to know where each control is and what it does quite automatically. Movement on the twist grip, gear change and brakes must quickly become instinctive. In familiarising yourself with your machine and its controls, don't forget to enlist the aid of the owner's handbook. It is quite surprising how many riders hardly ever refer to the handbook. In Britain, the RAC/A-CU National Training Scheme has a reputation as perhaps the cheapest and most effective life-saver for motorcyclists. Started in 1947, it had 360 centres throughout the UK by 1979, the majority operated by local authorities. In 1978 more than 22 000 enrolled for the course which, on average, lasted ten weeks and cost around £12.

Motorbikes, like cars, have moved with the times. The days when you simply cocked your leg over and roared away into the distance are gone. The motorcyclist is as much a part of modern road discipline as anyone else so you have to use your mirrors and indicators and still, for the motorcyclist, hand signals are important and should be positive and direct. Much of sensible riding is acquiring a feel for the machine. Don't choose the busiest road in town on which to do your practising! On a quiet stretch you can safely experiment with the brakes, learning the essentials of blend between the use of the front and rear brake. This is particularly important in wet weather when additional care should always be exercised. Don't try to become a racing champion overnight. Never

be tempted to 'race' on domestic roads. Take it easy, progressing gradually so that by the time you are ready for more advanced riding you will have the experience, confidence, feel and downright commonsense on the bike to move on with safety.

Good riding is positive, confident riding, but that must never lead to a state of over-confidence where one's concentration might lapse, one takes risks by running too close to surrounding vehicles or becomes slipshod in anticipating distances and other potential hazards.

Safety on the road is a two-way business. Your own conduct is one side of it. Making sure you are seen by other road users is another. That's why colourful clothing is not just a fashion gimmick. It helps other drivers to pick you out. Of course, the professional racers with their sponsorship stickers and exotic outfits help to complete the showbiz mosaic which is all part of modern motorcycle racing, but racing leathers are still worn basically for the protection of the rider, with the protective additional padding around vulnerable areas like knees, hips and elbows.

The clothing you choose will depend on your ambitions and reasons for going biking. For the cost-conscious commuter, the long-distance touring enthusiast or the 'performance' specialist there is now a wide variety of clothing available and, again, you choose according to your needs. Always a point to bear in mind is that your riding efficiency is likely to lapse if you are uncomfort-

The paraphanalia of the modern motorcyclist – almost as important in the 1980s as the bike itself (*Honda UK Ltd*)

What the rider used to wear on his head (*left*), and what he is more likely to wear these days, the full face helmet (*right*) (*Motor Cycle Weekly* and *W Vero & Co. Ltd*)

able, cold or wet. So for your own safety, choose items which give comfort and are protective against the elements in all weathers. You'll need riding boots and gloves, and again you'll choose according to your needs. Rubber boots (or 'wellies') give protection in the rain while at other times the traditional motorcycle boots, now much more flexible, handsome and supple than they used to be, are still ideal. Made of reasonably thin leather, the rear zip makes them easy to put on and take off – but they might not be all that waterproof.

The traditional gauntlet is still essential motorcycle gear and worn with a thin inner glove, will keep your hands comfortable in wintry weather. You can also buy overmittens which can be carried in the zip pocket on the back of the gauntlets. In summer, a lightweight, unlined glove which covers the wrists will be more comfortable and will provide a degree of protection, should you fall off.

Again, depending on your needs and the reasons for being on a bike in the first place, you can economise on clothing by raiding some of the shops which still seem to do a good trade in army surplus clothing. A greatcoat is warm and protective, and from the same place you'll probably find cheaper overboots, storm coats which are waterproof, padded mittens and goggles.

Needs must not vary, however, when it comes to choosing a riding helmet. That's a choice which must be made as a priority. Your personal safety is the only consideration, so don't try to economise on this important aspect by buying a secondhand

helmet which doesn't give you the degree of protection you need. And never be tempted to ride even a short distance without wearing it properly.

The two main types in use are the full-face style and the older, open-face helmet. The full-face style appears to be growing in popularity. It is said to give additional protection over the ears, is less likely to be depressed laterally on impact, and its 'space-age' fashion gives more protection to the jaw and face. It has to be used with a drop-down visor and that can be a source of potential danger if it is not kept completely clean and changed immediately it becomes scratched. The visor can also mist up, especially when it's raining. Other disadvantages are that it is heavier than the open-face style, can become hot to wear in warm weather, and reduces peripheral vision. The open-face helmet is lighter and easier to wear and gives greater vision. It can be worn with either goggles or a visor and it is possible to have prescription lenses made. There is also free access to the face and the open-face helmet is somewhat cheaper. Clear, irrevocable decisions about helmets have not been made. Some feel that the full-face helmet might protect the face at the expense of the neck, though there is no solid evidence to support this view, or to disprove it.

It almost goes without saying that a helmet should be comfortable to the wearer – that means it has to fit correctly – but this is vitally important, particularly when you consider that far too many helmets come off in a crash, though whether it is the ill-fitting helmet that is at fault or the straps which give way is, again, not clearly known. When buying try the helmet on and do up the straps. The helmet fixings are very important and should be inspected at regular intervals to make sure there is no fraying or wear. If you drop your helmet, don't use it again. Many helmets have built-in pressurisation to absorb a once-only impact and would be virtually useless afterwards in the event of an accident.

In selecting the motorcycle itself it is a good plan to obtain the advice of an experienced rider friend and even to take him along when you are looking at various models, comparing his comments with those of the dealer. If you can afford only a secondhand model, then some mechanical advice, if you are not too technically minded yourself, is essential. If you are going to ride a motorbike at all, you must face the realisation that you are much more vulnerable than if you were driving a car, even when everything is in order, and you mustn't lengthen the odds by buying a bike which is in any way safety-suspect or which is going to cost you more than you can afford to put right.

Once you have taken delivery of your machine, don't economise on maintenance. Take pride in your machine. If you aren't qualified to maintain it yourself, let the experts do it for you. The increased dangers apart, nothing is calculated to spoil the fun and enjoyment you get from your bike than experiencing difficulty in getting it to fire, or if it doesn't sound or perform smoothly, or stalls at traffic lights. Regular attention to ensure everything is well is better than a massive blitz followed by a month or two of disregard.

Motorcycles continue to have two wheels, a frame, handlebars and a saddle, but beyond those easily identifiable and obvious points of recognition, you could argue that there is little to relate the glistening, chrome-plated Hondas and BMWs of the present generation with the far less sophisticated models of earlier years. Much of the credit for the transformation must go to the Japanese, who first came upon a new realisation of the lightweight motorcycle as a commuter-type, practical vehicle of enormous potential, and then, some years later, saw clearly the way the more expensive, powerful motorcycle fitted into the framework of a more leisured society.

Honda led the way, carving out a fortune for themselves and, through a phenomenally expanded market, giving opportunities to others to secure some of the action. In tune with its early, barnstorming image perhaps, the motorcycle industry has never been noted for the stability of its manufacturers. In fact, one estimate puts the figure of firms who have been tempted into making motorcycles in excess of 2000 and that more than a quarter of these were from Britain.

For years Britain led the world. Nothing could live with Nortons, Velocettes and other famous British makes on the race track; and for the technical brilliance of their motorcycle engineering, for the volume of their production, and for the number of manufacturers producing reliable and internationally reputable machines for use in export markets as well as at home, the British motorcycle industry was supreme.

Then came the Second World War. Historically, the warning signs had already been clearly emblazoned, for the background of motorcycling is littered with the relics of companies who have ignored changing times, keen and insistent competition, the need for machine development and the value of sporting success to promote their products. Rudge and Brough were among a number of British companies who disappeared at the start of the war, while others, including Sunbeam, failed to revive themselves successfully when hostilities ceased. Success went to those firms who had worked on war-time government contracts and were in a position to invest in post-war production. There is little doubt that in those early post-war years the initiative still rested with Britain as the market built up for the manufacture of proprietary two-stroke engines and lightweight bikes during the infancy of the motorised 'ride to work' revolution. Bigger firms like Norton, Ariel, AJS, Matchless, BSA, Triumph and Royal Enfield continued to design and build lightweight motorcycles powered by engines of their own design. Smaller outfits like Francis-Barnett, Greeves, DOT and Cotton used engines manufactured by firms like Villiers – whose 8E and 9E single-cylinder and 2T twin-cylinder units were to build big reputations – British Anzani and Excelsior.

As the BSA Bantam became the first really big success of the post-war years, there seemed little to disturb the quiet build-up of the British industry into pre-war proportions, and possibly beyond. Of considerable help were the claims made by British manufacturers on German designs on the basis of war reparations. The BSA Bantam was originally a DKW factory design and Ariel gained the rights of manufacture of the German Adler 250 cc two-stroke twin engine. In a specially designed frame of pressed-steel construction it was well ahead of its time. It's fascinating and, for British interests, depressing, to consider that the motorcycling public paused in amazement when the Japanese brought in flashing indicators many years later; and when Honda's phenomenal 1000 cc Gold Wing of the

Above : A respected British make from the past, the 2½ hp Ariel of 1903. The firm was established for motorbike manufacture in 1902 and was absorbed by BSA in the early 1950s (*National Motor Museum*)

Right : Motorcycles played an important part in the two World Wars. BSA switched its production to army needs, turning out machines like this 1940 model (*National Motor Museum*)

Below : The long-distance touring rider in action on the BMW R100RT (*BMW*)

1970s incorporated a dummy petrol tank, the real thing being situated lower down beneath the saddle, to improve low-speed handling by lowering the centre of gravity, the development was received as a typical example of Japanese ingenuity.

Yet the Ariel Leader introduced in 1958 had both flashing indicators and a dummy tank. In a fight for additional sales the BSA Bantam was restyled and the capacity was increased, but both it and the Ariel Leader were ultimately withdrawn. Towards the end of the 1950s the German NSU concern had virtually captured the market in small capacity machines as pedalling to work became an outmoded and unnecessary labour for thousands. Then came the scooter revolution, carrying the concept into totally new markets. Spearheaded by Italy, with their Vespas and Lambrettas, these 'civilised' machines – clean and easy and fun to ride, highly manoeuvrable in traffic and quiet in performance – brought motorcycling of a sort within the scope of the mass of the adult population. The 'step-through' design simplified the getting on and off, and even females wearing skirts found no embarrassment or difficulty. The front 'fairing' gave protection to the legs and you could ride without getting rigged up in special gear. Even ordinary shoes were right on a scooter.

The British industry woke up too late to this latest ride-to-work phenomenon and although models from Velocette, Triumph and BSA were later introduced they weren't as good as the Italian originals. When Alec Issigoni introduced the Mini car in 1959, the British motorcycle industry again suffered badly. Now you could buy a car for little more than a motorcycle would cost.

The promise of the post-war years had not been fulfilled but, ironically, the events which were to propel motorcycling into a totally new era, bringing enormous prosperity in future years, were to leave no room for Britain. The revolution began when a 40-year-old Mr. Soichiro Honda bought a batch of army-surplus two-stroke engines and started converting them so they could be fitted onto ordinary pedal cycles. That was in 1946 when, in post-war, bomb-torn Japan, public transport was virtually non-existent. Not surprisingly Honda's enterprise flourished. Within three years he was making complete motorcycles and within two more years brought out his first four-stroke motorcycle, the Honda Dream.

The young Honda company was ambitious. It's first objective was to capture the lion's share of the home market. Then it set out to dominate the world. It veered close to bankruptcy on a couple of occasions during those early years, sinking profits into massive re-tooling and investment, and cour-

age won the day. The Honda Cub, a utility 'step-thru' model, was introduced in 1952, to be followed by the Super-Cub, and then came the Benly 90 cc single cylinder four-stroke. Honda were making 1000 Benlys a month by 1953 and it was time to extend horizons. Mr. Honda visited the Isle of Man in 1954 and soon became aware that success on the race track would gain exposure for the Honda name and increased sales in the motorcycle showrooms of the world. He could also see the opportunities if he moved into Europe with small capacity motorcycles.

Honda's early machines, in many respects, were inferior to the British models of the day. Without damping they were uncomfortable to ride, tyres were of poor quality and a hazard on wet roads, and their road-holding qualities fell short of the average British bike. But their unorthodox looks, with angular finning and square-sectioned rear suspensions, captured curious attention at a time when the Honda name was beginning to make news on the Isle of Man and elsewhere. Most important of all, as an incentive to sales, were the 'gimmicks' of electric starters, toolkits, wing mirrors and flashing indicators provided, not as expensive optional luxuries, but as standard equipment at no extra cost.

The British decline began in the early 1950s, continued during the next decade, and was virtually completed in the 1970s. After the first serious inroads into the British home market were made in the 1950s by German, Italian, Austrian, Dutch and Spanish manufacturers, who captured significant sales of 125 and 250 cc machines as well as dominating the scooter and moped market, the door was wide open for Japan to move in. The British industry's apathy brought about its own death sentence and the success road of those little men from far away was littered with British factory fatalities – Ariel, Francis-Barnett and Royal Enfield being among a long list of familiar names to become only memories. For a while Britain continued to be prominent in the big-bike market, but once the Japanese began to have serious worldwide ambitions here – Honda by now having been joined by Suzuki, Yamaha and Kawasaki – the writing was on the wall for the British industry.

As competitors brought out bold new designs and adopted an innovative approach to the whole concept of motorcycling, Britain persisted with her vertical-twins and single-cylinder machines, content with minor modifications and cosmetic improvements. Their only armour seemed to be to close ranks and, at the start of the decline, they appeared too content, with Government urging in the cause of exports, to satisfy the present overseas needs for British machines when some time and investment would have been better allocated to planning for the future.

By 1961, approaching a score of European manufacturers were selling their machines in Britain, including such well known names as BMW, Bianchi, Guzzi, Gilera, MV, Jawa, Itom, Ducati, Bultaco, NSU, Puch and Zundapp, with Honda the only Japanese importer, while Britain's bigger vertical twins, which had sold successfully in the United States in the 1950s, were already under pressure there from German factories like BMW, Maico, NSU and DKW.

The British industry changed dramatically with many independents yielding to the business philosophy that unity and pooled resources were the only answer to overseas challenge. The process of amalgamation which was to be such a strong feature of the British industry's dying years, had started seriously as long ago as 1931 when AJS and Matchless had become linked under the umbrella of Associated Motor Cycles Ltd, (AMC). Five years later Sunbeam was acquired by AMC, before moving under the control of BSA, until BSA themselves were absorbed by AMC. By the 1960s, Ariel, Francis-Barnett, James, Villiers, New Hudson, BSA and even Triumph and Norton had been absorbed by the AMC conglomerate. The disaster was that by 1966 AMC themselves had run into such serious financial crisis that only a take-over by Manganese Bronze Holdings Ltd, saved the industry from what appeared to be total extinction there and then. On paper at least the new organisation, named Norton-Villiers Ltd, looked capable of stemming the decline and even if some of the famous names had to disappear for good, then perhaps that was a low enough price to pay for survival. The early mood of the new company was optimistic as the inevitable process of rationalisation began. James and Francis-Barnett, lightweight two-strokes with fine reputations, were the first to go, within only a few months, and in a year most Matchless and AJS models had been discontinued.

Norton, the most famous of all British makes, had joined AMC in 1952, though Norton continued to operate independently and retained its own identity. But as the overall sales of British bikes slumped, the inevitable decision to merge production facilities was taken and Norton's world-famous Bracebridge Street factory in Birmingham was closed down, production shifting to the AMC works in Woolwich. It wasn't long before the famous Norton name was compromised in the cause of survival as machines bearing the Norton tank badge began to emerge looking remarkably like Matchless models. Later all Norton single-

The little man who brought about a revolution in motorcycling, the Japanese genius Mr Soichiro Honda, founder of the Honda company (*Honda UK Ltd*)

cylinder models were discontinued, leaving the 650 and 750 cc vertical twins the sole survivors of a once-proud line.

BSA, Britain's one other remaining major factory, had meantime fared better. In 1951 they were probably the largest motorcycle manufacturers in Western Europe, having absorbed Sunbeam and New Hudson in 1933, Ariel in 1947 and Triumph in 1951. BSA were a vast group of companies with excellent financial resources and were in a stronger position to tackle the problems of the 1960s, with their own extensive BSA range, and Triumph and Sunbeam models; and at the beginning of the 1970s there was a degree of optimism about the British industry which raised hopes that perhaps the country which had for so long led the world did after all have some kind of future in motorcycles.

Britain saw that future in the production of the larger capacity superbikes where, in the United States particularly, a vast new market was opening up as a corollary to the new technological, highly prosperous, increasing leisure-conscious age of the 1970s. Italy particularly, and Germany too, through BMW, had also come to the same conclusion. Italy had originated the worldwide scooter boom with their Vespas and Lambrettas, which had led to a vast industry specialising in the production of lightweight machinery. But they more readily saw the danger as the Japanese launched their offensive into international markets and, as their overseas business in lightweights began to crumble, switched to higher-capacity machinery. Moto Guzzi, Ducati and Laverda all made the transition, as did BMW in Germany, who had been on the brink of closing down its motorcycle production in 1969, business was so bad.

So while the market in which the British industry saw its future was expanding significantly, the competition was keen and became intense once the Japanese, having now monopolised the lighter machine market, began to extend their interests into the 'superbike' class. For a time, however, Britain did well. By 1970 the

Norton-Villiers 750 cc Commando, a development of the successful 750 cc Dominator, which had made an impact on the American buyer, was selling extremely well in overseas markets while BSA's exciting three-cylinder Triumph Trident, released in the autumn of 1968, also seemed to be well on the right lines. Introduced at the same time was a BSA Rocket, basically the same machine except for its inclined instead of vertical cylinder block. Initially, these models did well, production racing success at Daytona and in the Isle of Man helping to boost sales, but a 750 cc road bike from Honda with five-speed gearbox, disc front brake, electric starter and a maximum speed in excess of 120 mph (193 km/h), was introduced within months, as were new competing models from BMW and Benelli, to claim enthusiasts' attention.

A British superbike which earned a big reputation – the 850cc Norton Commando (*Orbis Publishing***)**

Honda's vast motorcycle and car plant at Suzuka (*Honda UK Ltd*)

Some would say that, given a more astute management with a more sensitive understanding of the industry at that time and perhaps a tighter grip on the company purse, the BSA-Triumph Group might have prolonged its life, but the truth is that profits, which fell seriously in 1969 and 1970, were to plummet to a disastrous deficit of more than £8 million in 1971. The agony for British interests was heightened by two further body-blows as first Royal Enfield (end of 1960s) and then Veloce, whose classic Velocette machines had gained a reputation around the world, were closed down. Both had been in the motorcycle business for about 70 years and were the last two remaining independents of any real size.

Amalgamation was the only possible salvation and BSA-Triumph was joined to Norton-Villiers to form Norton Villiers Triumph, or NVT. By this time the Japanese had moved into the big bike market with a vengeance. Kawasaki, who had gained a toe-hold on a pronounced 'performance' image, followed their introduction of the fiery 500 cc three-cylinder two-stroke (the Mach III) with the formidable 900 cc four-stroke which gained numerous awards for its performance and refinement. That same year, 1972, Yamaha introduced their 650 cc ohc twin. While the Japanese manufacturers continued to gain ground throughout the world, the early promise of NVT faded and was ultimately lost under a sad and continuing saga of unrest and dispute. The Triumph plant at Meriden, just outside Coventry, was closed by NVT after much industrial trouble and was reopened some 18 months later as a workers' co-operative with Government sponsorship. NVT adopted a policy of further rationalisation, dropping production of the BSA twins in 1971, the Rocket 3 in 1972 and the 650 Triumph twins in 1975. The Triumph Trident and the Norton Commando were seen as the models on which to concentrate for the future, but in spite of enlarging the latter to 830 cc in 1973 and what seemed to be a respectable level of sales, the company continued to drop further into deficit. The Meriden co-operative came under more serious threat when, still losing money, a new government was elected in 1979, committed to cutting public expenditure and with a less charitable attitude to 'lame ducks'.

Production figures over the years show the extent of the British decline. In 1960 British manufacturers produced 194 000 machines. By 1965 the figure had dropped to 95 153 and in 1970 only 69 840 machines were produced by British manufacturers.

By comparison, Honda's production figures alone make staggering reading. Their first motorcycle was produced in December 1948. By 1962 more than 1 million Hondas had been made and in January 1968, less than 20 years after starting production, the 10 millionth Honda motorcycle left the assembly lines. Exports rose in spectacular fashion from 49 312 machines in 1961 to 142 552 in 1963. British exports in 1965 were 45 000.

The irony is that, in spite of the massive sale of Japanese machines, the number of makes and the variety of models available to the motorcyclist at the start of the 1980s continues to be exceptionally extensive. By the late 1970s more than 50 different lightweight machines were being manufactured in about 20 different countries and the real significance of the Japanese influence on the industry had been as much in their ability to expand by many times the total market for motorcycles all over the world as in their ability to secure the lion's share of that enlarged market for themselves.

They did this by turning the image of motorcycling upside-down. Previously, in the special type of clan-ship which had been a tradition among motorcyclists, there had always been an element of masochism which found expression in the oily, back-yard type of atmosphere where true enthusiasts were expected to tinker around endlessly with engines and wear heavy, drab clothing when out riding. This battered, down-trodden image was accepted without question as being part of the 'fun' of motorcycling. Honda changed all that, bringing cleanliness, chrome, sophistication, colour, glamour and a new kind of up-dated adventure to motorcycling which found expression in a changing, post-war world. Grimy hands and black finger nails were no longer the inevitable trademark of the motorcyclist. Nor was he a kind of second-class citizen – a motorcyclist because he couldn't afford a car, for by the late 1960s and 1970s many of the higher-powered motorbikes were costing more than some cars.

By the end of the 1970s two developments were combining to give motorcycling a further gigantic boost. Working men and women, with more sumptuous wage packets than ever before, were already enjoying more leisure time and were being urged to fill it with interesting, absorbing hobbies and activities. For many young men, particularly, growing up in this new environment, the adventurous appeal of motorcycling, stimulated by racing heroes like Barry Sheene and Kenny Roberts, found instant favour. The second development was the emphasis on fuel conservation as the world's energy supplies began to run out. Petrol prices soared and supply became haphazard. Reflecting these changing times was the International Motor Cycle Show at Earls Court in London in 1979. With sales of motorcycles booming, and with 210 separate exhibitors, it was the biggest bike bonanza for ten years with all attendance records for the event smashed as more than 154 000 walked through the turnstiles. Never had there been a wider choice of machines on display at the International Show, with something for every taste and every pocket, with an extensive choice for sport, both on and off the road, touring and commuting. There were 50 cc models right up to 1400 cc power machines and costing anything from £150 to more than £4000. The major exhibitors were, of course, Honda, Suzuki, Yamaha and Kawasaki, with huge display areas. Contrast this with the first equivalent show to be held at Earl's Court in 1937, the Cycle and Motor Cycle Show. Then there were 200 exhibitors, an overall attendance of 80 000, and the major exhibits were all British bikes – the BSA 500 cc M24 Gold Star, developed from Wal Handley's Brooklands' 100 mph (160 km/h) racer, the revolutionary Triumph 5T Speed Twin and the Brough Superior.

Technical evolution has had much to do with the more widespread public acceptance of the motorcycle, particularly since the Japanese brought a sharp understanding of the public needs in performance, reliability and appearance. It was they who promoted the idea that a motorcycle required no more maintenance than the average car. They produced a constant variety of models at competitive prices, handsome and sophisticated – Honda with four-stroke machines, Suzuki, Yamaha and Kawasaki with the rasping two-strokes. Less than 30 years ago the only overhead-camshafts were found on racing machinery, but Honda brought this technical innovation to the average buyer, on everything from 50 to 750 cc models. The 450 cc Honda had two overhead-cams and used torsion bars to return the valves. The development of modern materials combined with precision engineering to lift the Japanese makes ahead of their contemporaries.

Chapter 4

Today's Technology

In the two decades since the Japanese took over as world leaders, the design of roadgoing motorcycles has changed almost out of recognition. The overall effect is that today's machines are much more refined, luxurious and complex than their forerunners of the late 1950s. For example, whereas kickstarting was then the accepted way of bringing the engine to life, push-button starting is now the vogue and many models don't even have a kickstarter.

Similarly, front and rear winkers have greatly reduced the need for hand signals. Indeed, electrical equipment as a whole is much more sophisticated than it was, with powerful quartz-halogen headlamps and a cluster of fuses commonly fitted as standard.

These and other refinements – such as more effective silencers, larger seats, increased suspension travel, more gear ratios (usually five), lockable filler caps and helmet hooks – have inevitably pushed up weights, despite the offsetting use of plastics here and there to minimise the increase. To that extent, riders have had to accept a modest increase in weight as part of the price of progress. However, the trend got completely out of hand in the late 1970s with Japan's big-four manufacturers (Honda, Kawasaki, Suzuki and Yamaha) repeatedly upstaging one another to offer the most powerful and complex superbike (primarily for the American market), regardless of weight, bulk and thirst.

Twenty years earlier – once Britain's well-loved 1000 cc Ariel Square Four and Vincent V-twin had gone out of production – 650 to 750 cc was the top limit for a big roadster. Starting off at that capacity level with Honda's four-abreast CB750 in the late 1960s, the Japanese quickly progressed to such monsters as the Kawasaki Z1300 – a 120 bhp, water-cooled, shaft-drive straight six with a mammoth kerb weight of 700 lb (318 kg). Technically advanced though this design undoubtedly is – with electronic ignition, very refined carburation and an automatic afterburning system to comply with stringent Californian clean-exhaust legislation for years ahead – its bulk, weight and clumsy handling are for some a negation of what a motorcycle should be: light, lithe, easy to handle and manhandle, as well as economical to run.

Kawasaki were not the first with six cylinders, however. Italy set the ball rolling with the 750 cc

In the 1950s the British motorcycle industry had yet to experience the crippling effects of the Japanese drive for motorcycle exports. This picture shows plenty of activity in the competition department of Ariel Motors Ltd (*National Motor Museum*)

Benelli Sei and Honda were next with the 1047 cc, 24-valve CBX – both air cooled. All the sixes, though, are virtually status symbols or luxury toys rather than practical everyday machines. In a roadster with such a potential power surplus as the CBX, the complexity of four valves per cylinder is more of a sales gimmick than a necessity. But it was well known that Honda's phenomenal Grand Prix successes in the 1960s were based on four-valve cylinder heads (a design principle neglected in Europe for the previous quarter-century), so they were a powerful selling point once the superbike battle was joined – and Japanese factories are unbeatable at producing complex machines at competitive prices.

The extreme sophistication of modern motorcycle engineering – the driving power behind the Kawasaki Z1300cc six-cylinder supersports tourer (*Kawasaki UK Ltd*)

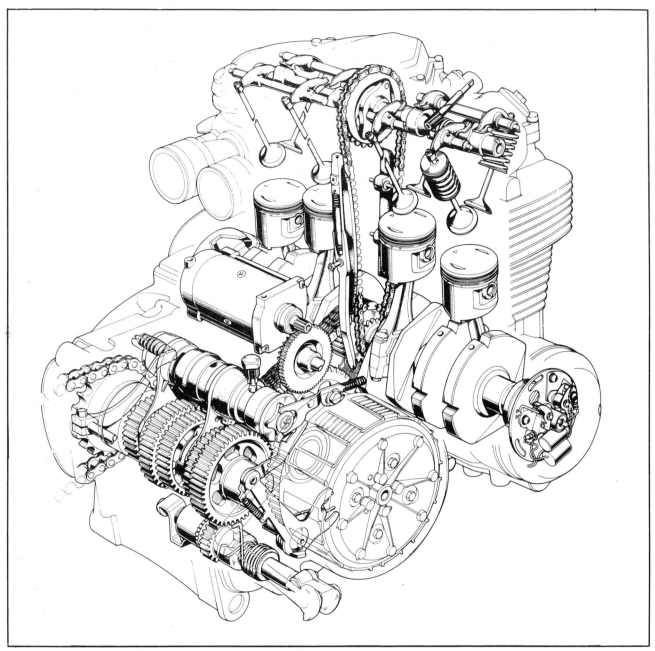

Four cylinder, 500cc and five speed. The Honda CB500 Four engine, a machine which achieved an equal reputation to that of the 750 for smoothness and reliability (*Honda UK Ltd*)

Lower down the capacity scale, where (in the absence of supercharging) higher engine speeds are unavoidable in the quest for power, paired valves have practical advantages as well as sales appeal – maintaining valve control at high rpm and giving deeper breathing for better pulling power. Examples are Yamaha's eight-valve XS500 parallel twin and Honda's CX500 water-cooled transverse V-twin – also, of course, with eight valves.

In the Japanese ranges, the CX500 is unique in operating the valves by pushrods rather than overhead camshafts. Otherwise, pushrod valve operation remains chiefly a European feature. It is found on all the BMW flat twins, the Moto Guzzi transverse V-twins and both the twin-carburettor and the single-carburettor versions of the Triumph 750 cc parallel twin – also on the massive American Harley-Davidson V-twins.

Four-valve cylinder heads got a further boost when manufacturers cottoned-on to the prestige value of success in endurance racing. There, engines have to be based on series-production units and competitive performance soon demanded paired valves. Hence the 16 valves in the four-abreast Honda CB900. Suzuki followed suit by switching from eight valves to 16 when they stretched their versatile twin-camshaft four for the third time, as the GSX 1100. And Laverda (in

Italy) kept Europe in the swim with the eight-valve Alpino parallel twin.

The Alpino and the Yamaha XS500, mentioned earlier, exemplify the two current methods of taming the vibration inherent in a four-stroke parallel twin. In the Yamaha, the pistons rise and fall together in the old fashioned way (360° cranks) and the large primary inertia forces at top and bottom dead centres (when the pistons have to be stopped and reversed) are neutralised by a counteracting balance weight on a separate shaft – a system pioneered by Dr. Fred Lanchester in the earliest days of the internal combustion engine. For the Alpino, on the other hand, Laverda adopted the crankshaft layout introduced many years earlier on the 250 cc Honda Dream. In this, the two cranks are spaced at 180°, so that the pistons always move in opposite directions, as in a parallel-twin two-stroke. Thus the primary inertia forces cancel one another at the cost of a much less troublesome rocking couple.

Except for the 850 cc Weslake parallel-twin racing engine, British designers always fought shy of this simple solution, afraid of the consequent uneven firing intervals (180° and 540° alternately). Hence many of their big parallel twins got (and deserved) an unhappy reputation for vibration. But the Japanese obsession with ultra-high engine speeds (by European standards) forced them to face up to the problem, and Honda proved that this fear was groundless.

With the demise of the British industry, integral construction of engine and gearbox (with primary drive by a pair of gears) is now practically universal. This development was long overdue, for only British manufacturers and one or two in Spain persisted with the anachronism of a separate or bolted-on gearbox driven by an adjustable primary chain.

The argument for a separate gearbox and primary chain used to be cheaper production. But the sheer volume and efficiency of Japanese production trims unit costs so much that specification standards no longer have to be sacrificed to price. This is evident in the near-universal adoption of overhead camshafts for four-stroke engines (abandoned in Britain to cut costs), even in small-capacity utility machines. Another traditional British feature (inherited from racing) that has gone into decline is the separate oil tank. Instead, the oil is most often carried in a crankcase sump, so dispensing with the need for a scavenge pump as well as a separate tank. The exception is on some machines used for endurance or TT Formula racing, where excessive oil temperature can be prevented only by a separate tank with an oil cooler in the scavenge line.

Initiative in design is by no means an eastern monopoly however – the Italians have shown plenty. After some outstanding racing successes in the late 1950s and early 1960s with a triple-overhead-camshaft system of desmodromic valve gear, Ducati incorporated the principle in their roadsters in simplified form (single ohc). In both cases, valve springs are dispensed with – the valves being closed as well as opened by cams and rockers, thus eliminating all possibility of valve float at high rpm. Moreover, while many big Japanese engines were growing embarrassingly wide, Ducati exploited their unique valve gear in an engine whose relative slimness makes it extremely attractive in a solo – a 750 or 900 cc L-twin with the cylinders spaced at 90° for exceptionally smooth running and first-class cooling.

Another example of Italian initiative is the 72° Moto Morini V-twin (250, 350 and 500 cc) with Heron cylinder heads (flat head face and combustion space formed in the piston crown) and the central camshaft driven by a toothed rubber belt. Heron heads were later incorporated in the 500 cc Moto Guzzi V50 transverse 90° V-twin.

Incidentally, the vogue in transverse V-twins arose almost accidentally when Moto Guzzi, short of novel ideas, took an engine designed some quarter-century earlier for industrial and military three-wheelers and adapted it for a motorcycle. Compared with a transverse flat twin, it has the advantage that the cylinder heads are less vulnerable, though the centre of gravity is higher.

The revolutionary and incredibly smooth-running Wankel rotary-piston engine has had a chequered career in the motorcycle field. Suzuki's attempt – the 500 cc water-cooled, single-rotor RE5 – flopped because the engine's performance was stifled by excessive weight, while the ignition and carburation systems were too complex. More successful was the light and lively 294 cc, fan-cooled German Hercules W2000 (marketed in Britain as a DKW), though its mechanical noise was above average and its six speeds were an unnecessary gimmick in view of the engine's exemplary spread of torque. It was left to Norton-Triumph to have the courage to go against the advice of the Licensing company (NSU) and tackle the daunting problems of cooling a 600 cc twin-rotor engine by direct airflow in the quest for a really high power/weight ratio.

After a long flirtation with four-cylinder four-strokes, even in a size as small as 400 cc (Honda), the Japanese revived the gospel of simplicity by producing a crop of medium-size parallel twins – and even a couple of British-style big singles: the Honda XL500S and the Yamaha SR (and XT) 500. Meanwhile, it is ironical that Italy weighed in with the smallest four of all, the rather uncompetitive 250 cc Benelli Quattro.

An offshoot of complex engine design has been a decline in home maintenance and the rapid growth of dealer servicing, using electronic diagnostic equipment. Whereas a talented amateur could tune and synchronise two carburettors on a twin, the same job with four or six carbs calls for vacuum gauges and an exhaust-gas analyser.

During all this time, one of the most remarkable features of the Japanese industry has been the rise and fall of the two-stroke. For many years, it was the mainstay of the Suzuki, Yamaha and Kawasaki ranges. And except for Suzuki's luxurious water-cooled GT750 three, the two-stroke roadsters were predominantly sporting air-cooled twins (Yamaha) and threes (Kawasaki and Suzuki) with throttle-linked pump oiling – another ancient European system resurrected.

Light weight and high engine torque, helped in some cases by reed-valve induction, gave them startling acceleration, while a rearward weight distribution made spectacular wheelies commonplace. But, for the most part, fuel consumption was disgracefully high (and often compounded by a ridiculously small tank), while the exhaust tended to be oily despite the automatic restriction of the pump feed at small throttle openings.

With world opinion increasingly hostile to the extravagant use of fuel, and with widespread legislation against noise and dirty exhausts, all three Japanese two-stroke makers brought in four-stroke ranges with an eye to maintaining sales long-term.

Mounting engine torque and tyre grip, together with the manufacturers' reluctance to enclose and lubricate the drive chain, have drastically shortened its life, and made adjustment a frequent chore on the more powerful bikes. Sealed, grease-packed links were an expensive stop-gap but shaft drive, such as BMW standardised from the outset in 1923, is now spreading rapidly, most manufacturers offering more than one model so equipped.

Automatic transmission, though, has made little headway for the simple reason that most foot changes are a joy to use. Both the Moto Guzzi V1000 and the Honda CB400AT have two overall ratios, drive and low - selected by pedal, and a hydraulic torque converter, so that speed control is simply a matter of throttle and brakes. But precious few Europeans with the *joie de vivre* to take up motorcycling are so lukewarm in their approach as to opt out of gear changing.

As to the design of cycle parts, one of the most notable developments has been the wholesale swing from drum brakes to discs, even on the rear wheel where the disc's advantages are at best marginal.

Chief virtue of the disc brake is its fade-resistance (as a result of better cooling) which is why it first took over in racing. A bonus is that, since it lacks the self-servo action of a two-leading-shoe drum brake, stopping power is directly related to control pressure.

Unfortunately, at town speeds, rainwater is not centrifuged off the friction surfaces well enough to prevent a delay in braking sufficient to embarrass the unwary, especially with the stainless-steel discs necessary to avoid unsightly rusting. For a while, the problem was mitigated by the use of cast iron, and perforations but the ultimate solution was the development of sintered-metal brake pads.

The widespread adoption of cast light-alloy and pressed-steel (Honda Comstar) wheels owes much to disc brakes. Since these wheels can be made much narrower across the hub than wire wheels, twin discs can be fitted up front without overwide spacing of the fork legs. Other advantages are truer running and freedom from the periodic need for expert attention to restore accuracy.

Since Japanese designers give much more thought to engines than chassis, frame design has virtually stagnated, tubes usually being wrapped around the power plant wherever there is room. There is a growing tendency, however, for the pivoted rear fork to be triangulated for torsional stiffness and attached at the apex to a single suspension strut above the engine. Though now given the exotic names of 'cantilever' and 'mono-shock', this arrangement is no different in principle from that standardised on the British Series D Vincents in 1955.

Rear suspension struts themselves have become more refined, however, with various schemes (including a pressurised gas chamber with a floating piston) to prevent aeration of the damping fluid and consequent fade. Regrettably, front suspension lags behind, many telescopic forks being deficient in stiffness and inadequately damped.

During the period under review, the major controls have been standardised, a welcome safety move. Unhappily, the American preference was chosen (brake pedal on the right) whereas using the right hand and left foot together (for braking), likewise the left hand and right foot for gear changing, is a much more balanced action, as in walking and running.

The once-popular sidecar – largely a British and German speciality – has become practically extinct, though there are signs of a revival with rather primitive models that resemble East European designs rather than the more refined western designs of yester-year.

Reflecting the popularity of cross-country racing (motocross) and trials riding, a new type of

lightweight has arisen — the dual-purpose trail bike. Fitted with the minimum equipment for street legality, trail bikes have the large ground clearance and knobbly tyres necessary for off-road riding. Naturally, such hybrids are neither fish nor fowl, so that their appeal is restricted.

In the lightweight and utility field, which probably accounts for the bulk of Japanese production, the scooter (practically a European monopoly) has given place to the step-through. This has the same attractions of an open frame and weather shielding, while the handling gives the beginner more confidence because of the larger wheels. And since most step-throughs are four-strokes, whereas most

scooters were two-strokes, it uses appreciably less fuel.

Its automatic (centrifugal) clutch is a further attraction for the timid. And though the foot change is generally a bit clonky, it is probably easier to master than the scooter's combined clutch and twistgrip gear change.

The ultimate in inexpensive power transport remains the 50 cc moped, where rear springing is a worthwhile advance within the obvious limits on weight. Here the two-stroke engine is unlikely to be displaced; high-compression four-strokes have proved too difficult for ladylike legs to start by pedalling.

Chapter 5

The Classic TT Races

Whenever racing enthusiasts talk together the subject will at some time almost certainly turn to the Isle of Man and the classic TT Races. The small island which hosts this unique festival of speed every year – and which, through motorcycling, has acquired a fame and reputation far beyond its natural means – is the ancestral home of British motorcycle racing. Yet the TT Races were born out of a desperate need in the hearts of racing men who, it must be said, settled for the Isle of Man as second best and who, given the choice, would have looked no further than the mainland on which to run their races.

In more contemporary times the once impregnable standing of the TTs has been chipped and challenged as the historic races stood shoulder-firm against a critical lobby which became increasingly vociferous as the casualty list grew and certain Grand Prix superstars boycotted the event. Then came the ultimate indignity in 1976 when the TT Races, a cornerstone of Grand Prix racing when the modern classics were instituted in 1949, were stripped of their world championship status. It was a time of crisis for the TTs and many observers doubted their ability to survive as a major racing event.

Yet the TTs have proved themselves to be more than just another series of races. They are a unique institution and have recovered from what, for many less historic events, would have been mortal blows. Despite all attempts to fundamentally change, coerce and even kill off the TT Races, they remain in the 1980s one of the foremost events in the racing calendar, attracting vast crowds and with lists of entries grossly oversubscribed.

In the 1960s they were harangued and boycotted by British riders like Derek Minter and John Cooper, perhaps with some justification, for offering too little financial incentive for privateers such as themselves. A decade later, world champions Giacomo Agostini (Italian) and Phil Read (British) were among a Grand Prix 'elite' who refused to ride in the races. They declared, and again many would have to agree, that increasing speeds had made the TTs too dangerous. But 70 years before, in the barnstorming days of motorcycling, the pioneers who rushed to the Isle of Man in the early 1900s had only one aim in life: to race. The TTs gave them that opportunity, for the first time in 1907.

Boy Scouts, from early times associated with the TT Races, hold the Isle of Man Tourist Trophy and the Junior replica at this civic reception held in Birmingham to honour the 1924 TT winners (*National Motor Museum*)

Motorcars were already racing on the Isle of Man over a course which went up and over the formidable Snaefell mountain, but motorcycles were hardly equal to such a test in 1907, so a shorter, less arduous course was chosen. Known as the St. John's circuit, it formed a triangle, starting

Frank Philipp on the Scott at the Senior TT of 1912 (*National Motor Museum*)

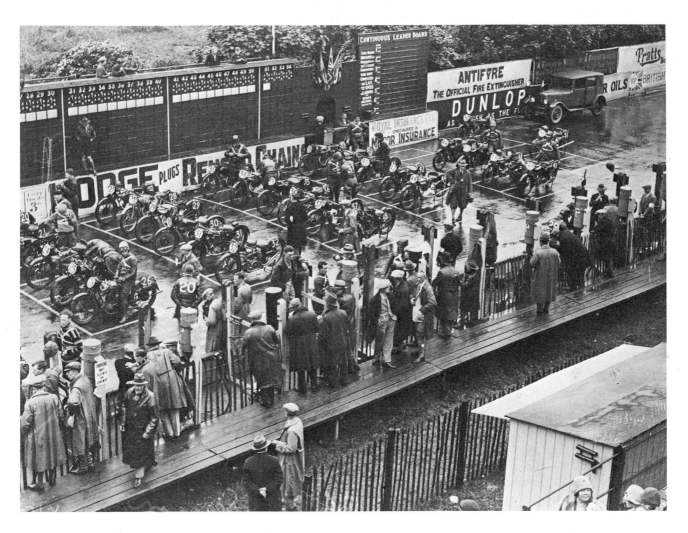

The 1928 TT Races with the 'Senior' bikes lined up on the start line. Charles Dodson was to win on a Sunbeam in a very rainy TT (*National Motor Museum*)

and finishing at St. John's and taking in places like Ballig Bridge, Laurel Bank, Glen Helen and Baaragarroo (names which were to become historic landmarks for racing men in the years to come) before turning south again at Kirkmichael and following the west coastline down to Peel. Each lap measured 15 miles, 1430 yards (25·442 km). May 27 1907 saw the start of it all as 25 riders collected together by the schoolhouse at St. John's, a cluster of onlookers waiting with a kind of resigned curiosity to see them away.

To appreciate fully those early regulations it must be remembered that the TT Races were born out of a disenchantment for continental-type racing and the desire of the British to give more emphasis to the touring aspect of motorcycling, hence the title, Tourist Trophy. So machines were obliged to be normal touring bikes and, again to emphasise the tourist element, there was a restriction on the amount of fuel which could be used. The outcome was to be judged on time, with competitors pushing

or pedalling their motorcycles away in twos at one-minute intervals. There were difficulties over the exact specification for a touring machine so in the end all the organisers insisted upon was that TT machines should have two brakes, a silencer, tool bag and a proper saddle. Two categories were chosen, one for single-cylinder machines which would need to be capable of 98 mpg and a second for twin-cylinder machines capable of 75 mpg.

Then, on a wet and blustery day, the 25 competitors were started and history was in the making. The task ahead was five laps of the St. John's circuit, an enforced 10-minute rest for refuelling and machine attention if necessary, then a further five laps, giving a total race length of 158 miles (254 km). There was a relaxed, fearless abandon about the whole affair, the lack of complexity and sophistication being in refreshing and fascinating contrast with the intensity of the modern race scene. The track-like roads were rutted and holed, while the unsprung bikes were indescribably uncomfortable and not easy to ride at speed. Spectators wandering deliberately onto the course to improve their view only added to the natural hazards of punctures, broken belt drives and straying animals; and at the end of it all, 10 men remained, to be helped, exhausted but proud, from their battle-scarred machines.

Hero of the single-cylinder class was Charlie Collier on his Jap-engined Matchless, who won at an average speed of 38·22 mph (61·15 km/h), taking 4 hr, 8 min and 8 sec to complete the race. Jack Marshall on a single-cylinder Triumph was 11 minutes slower to finish second, and Rem Fowler, third fastest overall, won the twin-cylinder class on a Peugeot-engined Norton at a speed of 36·22 mph (58·31 km/h). In fourth place was Freddie Hulbert on another single-cylinder Triumph. Fowler's twin-cylinder Norton, however, was much the fastest machine in the race, having reached an average of 43 mph (69 km/h) over one trouble-free lap but his overall speed fell short of that of Charlie Collier by 2 mph (3 km/h).

Collier received £25 and the almost 3-ft tall Tourist Trophy, a silver figure of Mercury, which had been presented to the A-CU by the Marquis de Mouzilly St. Mars, one of motorcycling's most avidly enthusiastic pioneers. Rem Fowler, for winning the twin-cylinder class, also received £25 plus a trophy, while second place winners were given £15 each. Riders finishing third each received £10. In the true tradition of the races, the early TTs were seen very much as a test between machines and of the personal skill and courage of the rider, rather than a rider-to-rider contest, and it was for this reason that a massed start was discounted, a tradition which has persisted for much of the races' long history.

Another well established TT tradition which began the following year was the swearing-in of race marshalls as special constables so they would have sufficient power to carry out essential duties like keeping the course clear. The world famous Mountain Circuit, 37¾ miles (60¾ km) of punishing test for even the most resilient of machines, was used for the first time in 1911, but before the end of this first stage in the development of the TT Races, several changes of note were to take place. It had been found in 1907 that the Triumph machines, surprisingly at odds with all the other entries in not being equipped with pedalling gear, were thus at a disadvantage, and it became a point of debate among groups of opposing supporters whether Charlie Collier might not have been beaten by Jack Marshall, had the former not been able to rely on the use of pedals on strategic sections of the course: and to support their claim that pedals should *not* be allowed, Marshall's supporters reminded the authorities that the event was indeed supposed to be a *motor*cycle race after all. To avoid similar argument in the future, the A-CU outlawed pedals from 1908 and that year also adjusted the petrol consumption allowance, singles now being required to average 100 mpg and twins, 80 mpg. The races were also moved from May to September and the event was even more popular with 36 starters, of which 21 were on twin-cylinder machines. As if to prove the pedalling gear theory, Jack Marshall reversed the 1907 decision, winning the 1908 race at an average of 40·4 mph (65·0 km/h) and recording a fastest lap of 42·48 mph (68·36 km/h). Charlie Collier on the Matchless was second, 48 seconds slower, and third overall was Reed on a DOT.

In 1909 two major changes took place. Since the twin-cylinder machines had not demonstrated any unreasonable advantage over the single-cylinder entries, it was decided that they should all race together, and the fuel economy regulations, in an age when petrol was cheap, were considered somewhat arbitrary and were dropped. Single-cylinder entries were limited to 500 cc and twins to 750 cc, but results showed that the single-cylinder machines had been unfairly handicapped and some adjustment became necessary for 1910. Entries rose to almost 60 and victory in this first all-in-one TT went to the other Collier brother, Harry, who also set the fastest lap at 52·27 mph (84·12 km/h). The last race over the St. John's Course, before the adoption of the Mountain Circuit, took place in 1910 and was an unqualified success for the Colliers. Charlie won his second TT in three years with Harry runner-up. Within four years the record average speed had risen from 38·23 mph (61·52 km/h) to 50·63 mph (81·48 km/h), the fastest lap from 42·91 mph (69·06 km/h) to 53·15 mph (85·54 km/h), and progress in the design and performance of motorcycles had been such that a more arduous test was now felt to be necessary.

The year in which the Mountain Course was first used also witnessed other significant landmarks in the history of the TTs, for it was in 1911 that: the races were first divided into Senior and Junior classes; the first time that a non-British machine won the event; and the first time that the top three places were all occupied by the same make of machine. The prospect of the 1400 ft (425 m) climb up the eastern face of Snaefell meant that variable gearing was now virtually essential. Royal Enfield used two-speed all-chain drive while the Douglases were fitted with two-speed countershaft boxes with chain and belt drive. The most popular interpretation, however, was the three-speed hub with direct belt drive, but in the Senior event the American Indian machines with their countershaft two-speed gears with chain drive to the rear wheel were supreme, finishing in the first three places. A team of five machines had been entered, led by the legendary American Jake de Rosier. Winner was Oscar Godfrey. Second was C. B. Franklin and third was A. Moorhouse – all of them British riders. The first Mountain Course measured 37½ miles (60½ km) (not 37¾ miles (60¾ km)) and road conditions showed enormous variation. Most of it was dirt and cart tracks and the climb up the Mountain and the Bray Hill descent were very rutted. Loose stones were a hazard, as were wandering goats, sheep and cattle – plus the gates along the Mountain road, which were often left closed! The Junior machines had to do four laps, the Senior machines five, and officially designated pit areas were at Douglas and Ramsey, the only places where additonal fuel could be taken on. That rule caused an upset for the redoubtable Charlie Collier, who finished the Senior race with the second best time, but was disqualified for taking on fuel unofficially. For the first time, it was against the rules to push or wheel a machine against the direction of the race and, sadly, the 1911 races are remembered for the TT's first fatal crash, Victor Surridge coming off his Rudge during practice on the Glen Helen section. The Junior race was won by P. J. Evans on a Humber with Harry Collier second on a Matchless and H. J. Cox third on a British Forward. The best overall lap speed was recorded by Frank Philipp on a Scott at 50·11 mph (80·64 km/h). The races in 1911 were held in June, thereby establishing another TT tradition, and the list of machines entered is interesting and a nostalgic reminder of some of the famous factories of the day. In the Junior race line-up were included six Humber twins, three New Hudsons, AJS, Royal Enfield, Matchless, Moto-Reve, Zenith-Gradua and three Alcyon singles from France. The Senior event included Triumphs, Rudges and Matchlesses.

Road conditions on that first Mountain race showed enormous variation. Much of the circuit was earth and stones rolled together and even the best sections were little better than minor roads. There was a record number of 104 entries, twice that of the previous year, though times, not unexpectedly perhaps in view of the punishing nature of the new course, were a little down on the previous year.

Within three years Europe would be at war, but in the meantime the TTs saw plenty of action of their own. The overall dominance of the twin-cylinder entries showed that the single-cylinder machines were too severely handicapped, and in 1912 the A-CU decided to have one engine size for each race, irrespective of the number of cylin-

The first winner of the Junior TT over the Mountain Course in 1911 was P J Evans, pictured here on his race-winning Humber (*National Motor Museum*)

ders, establishing a pattern that has continued up to the present time, with the Senior race for 500 cc machines and the Junior for 350 cc entries. That year's Junior entries had all moved up to near the 350 cc limit, though three Singers were classified at 299 cc. Lowest-powered machines in the Senior race were the Scott twins at 486 cc. For the first time in TT history the number of entries dropped, with 49 for the Senior event and 25 for the Junior, largely because of the elimination of class distinction on cylinders, but despite this the twin-cylinder machines were again supreme in both Senior and Junior races. Frank Applebee made history by becoming the first two-stroke rider to win any race with his 48·69 mph (78·36 km/h) average in the Senior on a Scott machine, also recording the fastest lap at 49·44 mph (79·56 km/h). The Junior race was won by Harry Bashall on a chain-driven Douglas, with another Douglas in second place and a Forward machine in third.

For 1913 a number of innovations took place aimed at increasing the attractions and popularity of the TTs. Major changes included substantially longer races with the events held over two days.

Above : Perhaps Britain's greatest rider between the wars, Stanley Woods, at Governor's Bridge on his way to victory in the 1926 Senior TT (*National Motor Museum*)

Below : A crowd scene at an early TT meet (*National Motor Museum*)

This complicated experiment permitted the Junior machines to complete two laps in the morning of the first day, Seniors to cover three laps in the afternoon, while on the second day the survivors from the earlier races (or 75 per cent of the starters whichever were the smaller) competed together, Junior machine riders in blue waistcoats and Senior riders in red. The machines were taken into custody overnight and no work was permitted on them until the start of the second day's racing. The races were re-dated to June 4/5. Altogether, the new ideas brought favourable results. There were twice the number of entries with 104 for the Senior race and 44 for the Junior, and 32 different makes of machine competed for the Senior trophy, 16 for the Junior.

In the final TT before the First World War, the complicated two-day system was abandoned, crash-helmets of an approved type were made compulsory, and by now the single petrol depot at Douglas had been equipped with pits.

Within eight years the TT Races had become the most famous motorcycle event in Europe, if not the world, for while the gruelling nature of the Mountain Course had been forcing the development of British machinery, interest on the Continent had dwindled. Immediately after the war they re-established themselves and with British interest high, the TTs soon became the standard against which all other circuits were judged. In the years between the wars British riders and British machinery were supreme, this golden age of motorcycling producing legendary characters like Tommy De La Hay, Howard Davies, Geoff Davison, Alec Bennett, Freddie Dixon, Wal Handley, Jimmy Guthrie, Graham Walker, Percy Hunt, Freddie Frith, Jimmy Simpson and perhaps the most famous of them all, the immortal Stanley Woods. This remarkable Irish rider entered 37 TT Races between 1922 and 1939, his impressive ten victories including Junior/Senior 'doubles' in 1932 and 1933 and a Lightweight/Senior 'double' in 1935, remaining an outstanding record until bettered by Mike Hailwood in 1967.

The redoubtable Jimmy Simpson showed scant regard for his machines, roaring to immortality as the first rider to lap the TT courses at 60, 70 and 80 mph. Appropriately the Jimmy Simpson Trophy, for the rider who each year is fastest round the TT circuit, was inaugurated in 1948. The quiet and respected Freddie Frith set the first ever 90-plus lap at 90.27 mph (145.25 km/h) to win the Senior event while the brilliant Jimmie Guthrie rode six TT winners, five Nortons and one AJS, and was so respected on the Isle of Man that a special memorial was unveiled in 1939, two years after he died racing in the German Grand Prix, at The Cutting above Ramsey, marking the place

Days of 'dustbin' streamlining, with Keith Campbell racing the 350cc Moto Guzzi (*B.R. Nicholls*)

In sharp contrast to the streamlined outfits of today, is this Norton/Hughes combination being driven by Graham Walker, with passenger Tommy Mahon, in the first 'Mountain' sidecar TT in 1923 (*National Motor Museum*)

where he retired in his last TT, the Senior event of 1937.

These were the halcyon days of Norton — who dominated the Island's racing in the 1930s with 14 victories in eight years — Sunbeam, AJS, Levis, Douglas, New Imperial, Cotton, Rudge and Velocette. Average speeds in the prestigious Senior race rose from 51.48 mph (82.85 km/h) in 1920 to 89.11 mph (143.41 km/h) in 1938. The first Sidecar TT took place in 1923, only to be dropped three years later. It reappeared in 1954 on the Clypse Course. In solo racing, the bespectacled Harold Daniell from London set a new fastest lap record of 91.00 mph (146.45 km/h) in 1938 — a speed not bettered until 1950 by the post-war hero Geoffrey Duke.

Over the years British riders on British machines had made the Isle of Man their spiritual home, largely beating off successfully the challenge of overseas competition, but soon after the war Germany and Italy, and later Japan, were to end the supremacy of the British bike. Warnings were sounded even before the war as, from about 1935, Italy led a continental challenge in the lightweight class with Guzzi and Benelli machines. Germany with the ear-shattering DKW supercharged two-stroke, took up the challenge, Ewald Kluge taking it to a roaring TT victory in 1938. Then, as Norton withdrew to concentrate on war preparation, Germany forced home their challenge with

Georg Meier winning the Senior TT of 1939 on a BMW. It was the first victory in the Senior TT by a non-British rider and the first 'all-foreign' win in the 32 years of island racing. Not until 1968 did another continental rider win the Senior TT – Giacomo Agostini in the supreme days of MV Agusta.

In the immediate post-war years Norton and Velocette continued their superiority in the Senior and Junior races, Guzzi and Benelli making the Lightweight TT their very own with wins shared from 1947 to 1953. The Italian tradition was continued when a 125 cc Lightweight race was

German rider Georg Meier on the way to victory on his 500cc super-charged BMW in the 1939 Senior TT (*Clive Gorman*)

introduced into the programme in 1951, Mondial machines taking the first three places that year, MV, and then the German NSU factory, and Mondial taking the honours for the remainder of the 1950s. In the higher-capacity classes Britain scored an impressive sequence of wins. Norton, through the rider talent of Harold Daniell, Artie Bell, Geoffrey Duke (who won three Seniors in a row and a Senior/Junior 'double'), Reg Armstrong and Ray Amm, won the Senior race from 1947 to 1954 inclusive. In the same period Velocette, Norton and AJS, through Foster, Frith, Bell, Duke, Amm and Coleman, secured the Junior title.

But in 1955 – with no 'works' machines available from Norton the writing was very much on the wall for British factories, and with the cream of British rider talent finding contracts with continental factories – Italy scored a resounding victory on the Isle of Man, winning Senior, Junior and both Lightweight classes. Germany rammed home the final nail in the British racing coffin with victory in the Sidecar TT, an event re-introduced only the year before and won then by Eric Oliver with the Norton outfit. Italy continued to dominate the solo classes until the arrival of Honda in 1961. After the withdrawal from racing of the Italian Gilera, Guzzi and Mondial factories at the end of 1957, MV Agusta alone kept the European flag flying until the advance of Honda, Yamaha and Suzuki in the 1960s. After Mike Hailwood and Phil Read had scored isolated victories on Norton machines in the Senior and Junior TTs of 1961, the Japanese won four solo machine categories on the Isle of Man for the first time in 1963, at the start of a new era of TT racing.

Post-war racing round the Island brought a number of changes. A Clubman's TT was introduced with great promise for roadster-based machines, but declining interest heralded its demise in 1957. The massed start, first tried out in 1924, was revived for the Lightweight TT of 1948, retained for 1949, and used again in 1953; there was the introduction of an Ultra-Lightweight race for 125 cc machines in 1951; and the adoption of the small Clypse Course in 1954 for the 125 cc race and the revived Sidecar TT. The Lightweight TT moved to the Clypse Course in 1955, the Sidecar event employed a clutch start for the first time in 1956, and the Races in 1957 celebrated their Golden Jubilee in sparkling fashion with an outstanding display by the great Scottish rider, Bob McIntyre. On 7 June that year, on a red and white Italian Gilera machine, 'Bob Mac' became the first rider to lap the Mountain Course at over 100 mph (160 km/h). In a Senior TT extended

Above : Flying high is the incomparable John Surtees, taking his works MV Agusta to victory in the 1958 Junior TT (*B.R. Nicholls*). *Right* : The two greatest TT riders of all time. Stanley Woods (*left*) and Mike Hailwood in 1967 after Mike had broken Stanley's record of 10 TT wins (*Mick Woollett*)

that year to eight laps, he took 3 hr 2 min 57 sec to complete his epic ride, which included four laps in excess of 100 mph (160 km/h), a new race average of 98·99 mph (159·28 km/h) and a new lap record at 101·12 mph (162·74 km/h).

The following year the 'dustbin' type fairing which had been a model of the successful Italian and German machines was outlawed as new rules cut back on streamlining because of the dangers and this slowed down the fastest machines. MV Agusta, however, performed a 'miracle', by winning all four solo TT classes. Allowing for the withdrawal of the only positive competition in the form of Gilera, Guzzi and Mondial, it has to be noted that MV's feat of winning all solo classes at any TT had never before been accomplished in the races' 51-year history. John Surtees achieved the Senior/Junior 'double', Tarquinio Provini won the 250 cc TT and Carlo Ubbiali the 125 cc race. Moreover, MV Agusta repeated their feat the very next year (1959) with substantially the

Tarquinio Provini on a 250cc Benelli in the 1964 TTs (*B.R. Nicholls*)

same riders, though with Luigi Taveri challenging strongly on an MZ and an emerging Mike Hailwood showing his paces on a Ducati, Ubbiali could do no better than finish in fifth place. MV's remarkable distinction was maintained for a second successive year through a Lightweight 'double' (250 and 125 cc) by Provini. In an astonishing run of success those four solo classes were won again by MV Agusta in 1959 and 1960.

In 1959 the A-CU added interest and excitement to the races by introducing a seeding system for the Senior and Junior events (on the Mountain Course) with the top seeds drawing lots to determine who should start first. The remainder of the field started singly at 10-second intervals. To counter accusations that the traditional 'touring' objectives of the races were being lost in deference to the interests of the major factories, with their greater concern to produce 'specials' which would give them a better chance of winning, the A-CU introduced the impressively-titled Formula 1 races in 1959 – one for 500 cc machines, the other a 350 cc machine class. These races were specified as being for 'standard production racing machines' and while in theory the idea seemed good and was obviously prompted by the most legitimate of motives, in practice it failed. The races lacked the sparkle and excitement present when more exotic machinery is being raced, the public showed little interest, and the experiment was not repeated the following year.

A new decade brought significant changes and a number of important milestones. For 1960 the Clypse circuit was finally abandoned, the two Lightweight races and Sidecar event joining the Senior and Junior classes on the Mountain

Course; TT Week was re-arranged into its modern programme with racing taking place on Monday, Wednesday and Friday, and with riders setting off in pairs at 10 second intervals; and that redoutable short-circuit character Derek Minter become the first rider to race a TT lap at more than 100 mph (161 km/h) on a single-cylinder machine. It was also in 1960 that motor-cycle racing, the TTs included, witnessed the first, largely impotent, signs of the Japanese revolution which was soon to overtake and engulf it. Honda had made an exploratory mission to the Isle of Man the previous year and although in 1960 they again failed to make an impression on the results, it was a totally different story in 1961. That year Mike Hailwood took Honda to victory in both Lightweight TTs, and their total command was such that in each class they filled the first five places.

With Honda soon to be followed to the Island by Suzuki and Yamaha, the 1960s became a breathtaking period for the TTs as Japanese creative technology and unbounded motorcycle ambition combined to lift racing into a completely new era. A 50 cc class was introduced in 1962, to be dominated immediately by Suzuki, who took the title for the first three years. Production events were added in 1967 and a Formula 750 cc TT in 1971. By this time the free-spending, exotic days of the Japanese full works teams had gone and the lobby condemning the TT Races as being unacceptably dangerous in the light of modern machinery and higher speeds had become more vocal. The Italian rider, Agostini, refused to ride again in the TTs, his last appearance there being in 1972 when he won his fifth consecutive 'Senior' and recorded his fourth Senior/Junior TT 'double'. He became a major critic of the races from afar. Racing's new glamour boy, Barry Sheene, also made no secret of his dislike for the TTs, and the criticism also found support from former World Champion, Phil Read.

To begin with few doubted that the TT Races, so historic and so full of racing tradition, would not be able to weather the storm. After all, the TTs had been criticised in some way or another almost from the start, and despite everything had emerged as the greatest series of races in the world. So in the meantime, the A-CU kept themselves busy with other things. The tiny 50 cc class, which Suzuki and Honda, with their magnificent twin-cylinder racers, had made their own, was abandoned after 1968 and the last 125 cc TT was run in 1974.

Speeds continued to rise and in 1976 Tom Herron won the Senior TT at a race average of 105·15 mph (169·22 km/h) with a fastest lap at 112·27 mph (180·68 km/h), a new lap record.

Unfortunately, the catalogue of victims of the demanding Mountain Course, which its critics condemned because, among other reasons, they felt it too long for riders to get to know sufficiently well before racing, also continued to rise and in the end the FIM heeded the pressure and withdrew the TTs from the world championship Grand Prix series. In its place was a new class of races for Formula 1, 2 and 3 machines. The controversial atmosphere in which the new class was born was not helped by the authorities' misguided though well-intentioned decision to grant it the status of a world championship. Thus, Phil Read, who had been one of the TT's strongest critics, made a surprise return to the Island and in winning the Formula 1 event on a Honda, the only race in that category during the year, automatically became a surprise world champion yet again.

In the late 1970s the TT Races, despite everything, seemed to have lost none of their power and

influence among motorcy
Prix circus continued to
Mike Hailwood in 1978
than made up for any d
the TTs drew enormous
introduction of Formul;
sponsored Classic 1000 c
sound of the prodigiously fast Superbikes to the Island, creating a new brand of excitement and new records. In 1978 Mick Grant on a 750 cc Kawasaki rode the fastest TT in history to win the Open Classic event at a race average of 112·4 mph (180·9 km/h), and set up a new absolute lap record of 114·33 mph (183·99 km/h), breaking through the twenty seconds barrier for the first time.

On the Isle of Man, Mick Grant and the Kawasaki have been supreme for speed, setting up a new absolute lap record of 114.33mph (183.99km/h) in 1978

Off-Road Riding

Motorcycling doesn't only take place on the road. Off-road riding and racing has a long tradition and in the past 20 years has gained enormously in popularity. Speedway, first known as dirt-track riding, is now very professional, solidly structured into leagues of opposing teams, and enjoys widespread public support. In Britain, for instance, it is said to be second only to the national game of soccer in its fan following. As an evening spectacle under floodlighting, and with its dazzling broadsiding and close rider-to-rider combat, it has become a completely separate sport in its own right.

More akin perhaps to the truer traditions of motorcycling are trials riding, motocross and enduros. Trials draw from the rider the greatest skills of all. Fine balance, a delicate sense of unity with the machine, and the sensitive ability to manoeuvre the bike slowly over terrain which was never really meant for motorcycles – and all without dropping a foot to the ground or permitting your machine to falter – are essential in this most original of all the off-road sports. Motocross developed out of trials and was known at first in England, where it originated, as scrambling. As Continental Europe adopted the sport with commendable relish the French-styled motocross became the new, universal label, even in North America where the sport enjoyed the beginnings of a major boom from the mid-1960s, with the Japanese manufacturers

recognising the commercial opportunities inherent in motocross and introducing special models. What motocross might lack in fundamental rider skills, when compared with the more classical trials riding, it makes up for in sheer excitement, energy and enthusiasm. For many, the greatest thrill in the world is surging through mud or dust, leaping over rocks, charging through streams and gulleys and exerting every ounce of physical strength and courage to finish first in a motocross race. Enduros, longer than motocross races, are the most arduous of all.

Different versions of speedway are grass-track, ice and sand racing. The rules are similar, but applying them to grass, ice and sand has created interesting new forms of motorcycle sport. Grass-track racing, in fact, has a longer history than speedway and most of the latter's top riders were grass-track enthusiasts before switching to speedway. There is a home-spun atmosphere about grass-track racing. Though lacking big-time glamour and substantial commercial support, it appeals to a growing number of enthusiasts who are doers rather than watchers and who enjoy the close contact and friendly, club-like atmosphere which is so important to grass-track racing. Ice racing and sand racing, spectacular and dramatic to watch, are modern-style derivatives of speedway and though still cinderellas of the sport, have established themselves strongly in some countries; ice racing in Scandinavia and the USSR and sand racing in North America and Australia.

Overall, off-road riding provides for the amateur and beginner as well as for the professional of many years experience and is now important as both a spectator and participatory sport. Special machines, considerably different from road machines built for pleasure or racing, have been developed and riders have found fame, and sometimes made their fortunes, in off-road motorcycle competition.

In the booming motorcycle years of the 1970s – as the United States took to motorbiking in a way it had never before contemplated and Europe began to re-adopt the motorcycle, but this time as part of the new leisured society – riding 'off road' for pleasure and not in competition became a new fashion and the trail bike was born. This new, non-competitive hobby allows enthusiasts to explore the countryside in two-wheel fun and comfort, suitably encouraged by the major manufacturers who now produce special trail bikes specially for the purpose.

Similar in appearance to the trials bike, the domestic trail machine has large wheels to give additional grip over non-tarmac ground and has good ground clearance to cater for uneven terrain. Wide handlebars are fashionable and the most modern trail bikes are suitable for use both on and off the road. Most major manufacturers now include this new type of domestic bike in their ranges, the power choice being wide, from 50 cc two-strokes to formidable 500 cc four-stroke versions.

The maximum power of the trail bike, because of its purpose, is located higher up the rev scale and because it is a non-competitive bike, the need to keep down overall weight is not all-important. Thus it is generally fully equipped with comprehensive instrumentation including flashing indicators, dipped headlights and tachometer. More recently the trend has been for manufacturers to produce an all-purpose machine suitable for trail riding, cross-country, enduros and motocross.

Off-road riding, whether for fun, sport, leisure or professional competition, has come a long way in the last 15 years and is now important in a new, revitalised, more sophisticated and up-market motorcycle leisure scene – its influence having spread throughout the world.

The excitement of motocross. Riders roar away from the start of the British Grand Prix at Farleigh Castle in 1971 (*Mick Woollett*)

Chapter 7

Motocross: Racing over the Rough

There is a taut kind of discipline about road racing. For motorcyclists who prefer their excitement in more exuberant style, modern motocross is often the answer – it is essentially a speed event, the fastest rider between two points, riding over rough ground. Established in Britain when a group of trial riders unshackled themselves from the confines of what was at that time the most popular off-road sport – and charged unashamedly through mud and muck in an abandoned attempt to be the fastest – it has become second only to road racing in popular acclaim. Enthusiasm for the sport in America substantially increased its influence and standing at an international level, and colourful characters like Pierre Karsmakers and Brad Lackey added a further dimension by leaving the United States to compete against the top European stars like Heikki Mikkola from Finland and Roger de Coster from Belgium.

The first scramble took place on 29 March, 1924 over a 30-mile (48 km) course at Frimley near Camberley, Surrey, England. A well-established British event in those days was the Scott Trial which, like most reliability trials, included observed sections, but it was also timed. It was the time factor which appealed to a group of enthusiastic riders of the Camberwell Club who wanted to run a similar event to the Scott, but concentrating on a timed trial section. When the regulations were submitted for approval the Auto-Cycle Union pointed out that unless the event included observed sections, it could not be classified as a trial. Nonetheless, the clubmen went ahead with their race across some of the roughest terrain they could find and in attempting to put a name to the kind of event they were running, one of them described it as 'a rare old scramble'. The name stuck, scrambling was born, and motocross was on its way.

Rough Rider Scrambles had earlier been held in Northern England, but in this first, historic, documented scramble at Camberley there were 80 competitors, the race being decided on the fastest time over two heats. Almost half the riders retired. The winner was A. B. Sparks on a Harley-Davidson. The appeal was obvious and before long

scrambling was well identified from other forms of motorcycle trial by clearly defined regulations and, later, by machines specially built for the sport. Although famous names like Norton, BSA, AJS, Greeves, Velocette, Ariel, Metisse and others all built special trial bikes before the Second World War, it was the British rider Brian Stonebridge who introduced the first real motocross bike, the historic 500 cc machine on which he was to achieve so much success. For 15 years scrambling was unknown outside Britain, where the new sport was dominated by brilliant all-rounders like Alfie West, Len Heath and Bob Foster.

The prestigious Motocross des Nations, an annual competition between teams of riders of national teams selected and entered by each country's motorcycling federation (only one per country), was started in 1947 and by the 1950s motocross was booming on the Continent, particularly in France and Belgium. As the sport advanced and opportunities increased, enthusiasts began to specialise in racing over the rough. Top British riders like Les Archer and Brian Stonebridge were attracted by the spectacular progress made by motocross in continental Europe and went off to compete in events which, by the mid-1950s, were attracting crowds in the region of 50 000 and were run on well-established, permanent courses. So strong was the interest in motocross on the Continent at this time that gradually the French name for the sport, motocross, became almost universally adopted.

In Britain, where it had all started, motocross was to receive a phenomenal boost when it was televised experimentally and was so enthusiastically acclaimed that it became compulsive viewing for thousands. For a number of years it made astonishing impact on the small screen and this continuing national exposure generated enormous public interest in the sport.

In the beginning, scrambles were raw, uncomplicated and exhausting. Normal road bikes were acceptable and on arrival at a meeting riders would strip their machines of weighty and unnecessary items like lamps and mudguards and simply take to the rough. The rider who finished first was the winner. On the Continent they developed a much more complicated system based on heats, time scale, finishing positions and marker boards, but neither rider nor spectator took to the system, and in most countries amendments were made.

At first manufacturers ignored motocross, but once it gained ground support was forthcoming and factory involvement increased. Riders became specialists, the structure of the sport was established and the number of competitions increased. Bikes carrying motocross adaptations developed into models specially designed and marketed for the sport.

In the first Motocross des Nations, teams from France, Belgium, Holland and Britain competed on 500 cc machines. For five years Britain and Belgium shared the results, three-to-two in Britain's favour, but in 1952 Britain took the initiative to win the title for the next three years, before Sweden emerged as an exciting outsider to claim their first victory in 1955. Sweden, and Britain particularly, stood high above all competition for the next decade or more, until the USSR won the Motocross des Nations for the first time in 1968. Czechoslovakia performed a similar feat in 1975, between times Belgium recapturing something of their former glory by taking the honours in 1969.

At first British large-capacity, single-cylinder, four-strokes dominated motocross. For such a tough, punishing spectacle nothing less powerful seemed right. Alone, in the Sidecar class, has tradition prevailed and Robert Grogg of Switzerland has taken his Norton-Wasp combination to the title in 1976, 1977 and 1978. A 250 cc class existed, but with much less status. It gained considerable prestige, however, with the introduction in the 1960s of a new generation of 250 cc two-strokes produced by Sweden, Britain and Czechoslovakia. High-level recognition of its mounting importance came when the FIM, in 1961, established a competition similar to the Motocross des Nations, but exclusively for 250 cc machinery. Called the Trophee des Nations, this new competition was dominated by Britain for the first two years. Sweden then took over, but from the late 1960s, and all through the 1970s, Belgium were in a class of their own, winning the Trophee des Nations for 10 years running, up to 1978.

The modern formula for both competitions, which are for solo machines only and where the emphasis continues to be on team performance, was set in 1963. There are two separate races, and points are awarded on a sliding scale to all riders who finish the course. The nation with the three highest scorers in each race wins.

The first Motocross International had taken

Showing the style of a champion. Torsten Hallman riding Husqvarna in the Trophée des Nations in the 1960s (*Motor Cycle Weekly*)

place in 1939 at Romanville, just outside Paris, and motocross showed so much promise post-war that it was inevitable that for its top exponents an individual contest should transpire. In 1952 the FIM established a 500 cc European championship, the Belgian rider Victor Leloup on a Belgian FN machine gaining that first title. A parallel 250 cc European championship, developed out of the European Cup, was added in 1957 and at the same time the 500 cc class was given world championship status. Sweden's Bill Nilsson on a British AJS machine was the first-ever 500 cc motocross world champion. When the 250 cc European series was itself up-graded in 1962, it was Sweden's Torsten Hallman on a Husqvarna who became the first 250 cc motocross world champion. A European championship in the 125 cc class was forthcoming in 1973 and elevated to a world championship just two years later when Gaston Rahier of Belgium on a Japanese Suzuki took the title; but a 750 cc European Sidecar championship set up in 1971 had to wait until 1980 before being upgraded to a world competition.

The visual impact of motocross is nerve-tingling and, at times, alarming. It's a breathtaking sight as riders, in long line abreast, surge from the start line with a thunderous roar, mud flying high in all directions. The physical demands imposed on the rider are greater in motocross than in any other form of motorcycle sport – and a firm will, coupled with strong mental resolve, is essential. In the early days races were far too long, being unnecessarily gruelling for the riders and unimaginative for spectators. Nowadays, rider pressures are more intense and the excitement less contain-

Dave Bickers in his heyday, riding the CZ in the style that made him perhaps Britain's most famous 250cc motocrosser (*B.R. Nicholls*)

able for the many thousands who regularly follow the sport.

To be first off the line in motocross means that you immediately avoid a number of the immediate hazards. You've no fear of being hemmed in, dust or mud isn't thrown up into your face from the rear wheels of faster riders, you're in a position to exert some control on how the race will be run, and you don't have to think about the difficult manoeuvre of hazardous overtaking – when, where and how. The only trouble is that all other motocross riders have the same idea!

Cornering reveals a rider's true skill for he must enter it as fast as possible, taking the correct line and leaning over just enough so that he is able to emerge on the straight with as much power as possible. Climbs and descents provide different kinds of problems and will highlight a rider's inexperience or unfamiliarity with his machine. Climbing long stretches successfully means extracting the maximum pulling power from the bike with precise timing of gear changes important to keep the machine going as fast as possible, and downhill runs call for a cool head and lots of experience if they are to be negotiated safely and competitively. Prolonged descents make the bike increasingly difficult to control because of the inertia forces and too much throttle can create problems at the end of a descent, particularly, as is often the case, if there is an immediate corner or S-bend. Typical of motocross is the spectacular jump . . . with the rider standing high on his pedals and delicately shifting his balance so that the machine lands correctly positioned. Jumping requires courage and skill and whether witnessed factually at a meeting or through the remoteness of film or television, never fails to make an enormous impact with the dedicated fan and casual

observer alike for its sheer daring and exhibitionism.

All these factors together would seem to be more than enough for a motocross rider to contend with, but it must also be remembered that the surface – always rough and often heavily ridged or angled awkwardly – can vary from thick mud to almost sheer dust, from hard compacted soil to part-gravel, and that the rider's technique must relate to these conditions. During the course of a race even the surface conditions can change quite dramatically.

Protective clothing might add to the charisma and drama, but is not there for that purpose. Crash helmets are obligatory and international regulations also call for the wearing of goggles. Nowadays the top riders are like creatures from outer space in their full-face protective masks, and 'body armour' includes chest and shoulder guards and special pads for vulnerable parts like knees.

If it's tough on the rider, motocross verges on the irresponsible in its treatment of machines. Pierre Karsmakers, who built an international reputation for his hostile treatment of his race-winning Hondas, reckoned that to be a top man in motocross you had to ride so hard that your machine was virtually worn out at the finish of a race.

Radical change in the character and appearance of motocross machines has been apparent over the years. General purpose 'war-horses' have given way to highly tuned 'specials' which, for all their relatively stark and uncultured looks, are scientifically right for the job and can withstand enormous battering. Gut power and brute force used to be enough to win the day, but as the big four-stroke Nortons, Matchlesses, AJSs and BSAs of the 1950s gave way to the lighter two-strokes of the 1960s from Greeves, Husqvarna and CZ, motocross stepped over into a new age. Until then the smaller capacity bikes, lacking power and mobility, were only useful to the beginner, but the new breed of 250s were so fast and controllable that they were soon a serious threat to the bigger capacity four-strokes. Once the lightweight manufacturers began to bring out 350 cc versions to circumvent a hurried-through FIM ruling which outlawed the 250s in 500 cc races, the impact was enough to send the four-strokes reeling into a decline in motocross from which they have never really recovered. As the Norton, AJS and Matchless four-strokes became obsolete, only the development skills of Jeff Smith – who in more than 20 years (until Graham Noyce's success in 1979) was Britain's sole motocross world champion – and Vic Eastwood, for a while kept BSA in the picture. Once BSA axed their motocross team at the end of

Jeff Smith rode to fame in the days when the sport was still known as scrambling. He became one of the most successful riders of 500cc motocross machinery (M. Carling)

Joel Robert, the outstanding Belgian motocross rider, competing in the Spanish Grand Prix on his Suzuki machine (*Mick Woollett*)

the 1960s, the four-stroke as a major influence in motocross was at an end.

With the lighter and more economical two-strokes came a tremendously exciting upsurge of interest in motocross. Replicas of works machines produced for general sale at competitive prices added charisma as unfamiliar names jostled with the established manufacturers for a share in the new prosperity. CZ and Husqvarna from Czechoslovakia were still there, but by the mid-1960s the choice had widened to include Maico from Germany, Puch and KTM from Austria, Montesa, Ossa and Bultaco from Spain. Once the vogue spread from Europe to the United States and the enormous potential of the North American market stood revealed, it wasn't long before the major Japanese manufacturers, having conquered the world in the manufacture and racing of road machines, moved into motocross.

Suzuki plotted the course. Combining remarkable engineering flair with a highly-expensive crash programme of development and a kind of sixth-sense knack of identifying market requirements, they rounded off the whirlwind package by signing the two biggest names in the business, Joel Robert and Roger de Coster. It brought sensational

results and Suzuki, through Robert, secured the 250 cc world championship for three consecutive years from 1970 and, through de Coster, the 500 cc world championship for four years out of five from 1971.

The other major Japanese manufacturers – Honda, Yamaha and Kawasaki – were to follow Suzuki into motocross, becoming heavily committed at the highest competitive levels both in Europe and in the flourishing American sporting scene. Much of their effort, and that of their European rivals, went into improving frame design. Springing and damping became increasingly important. Yamaha came up trumps with their ingenious triangulated rear fork. Engine power is all very well, but in motocross unless it can be linked to extreme flexibility in the frame section, it loses much of its race-winning potential. This basic principle influenced the design of motocross machines almost from the start. In fact it wasn't until telescopic front forks and hydraulically-damped swinging arm rear suspensions were introduced – which gave that essential stability when the machine was ridden at high speed over rough ground – did motocross really become a more spectacular and serious sport.

Above : The 500cc motocross Husqvarna as ridden by Rolf Tibblin to gain the world championship in 1962 (*Motor Cycle Weekly*)

Right : Heikki Mikkola, one of the most successful motocross riders of all time, competing in the British Grand Prix of 1975 (*B.R. Nicholls*)

Below : The 1980s motocrosser – Honda's CR125R Elsinore with a new frame wrapped around a works-type centre post engine, 'claw-action' tyres and new, low weight (*Honda UK Ltd*)

Yamaha's idea, which incorporated a pivot system and a king-sized damping unit, allowed significantly more movement at both the front and rear. This meant that even over the roughest ground the wheels could maintain contact, giving the rider greater control and more adhesion together, incidentally, with an increased element of comfort in riding at speed. With this 'mono-shock' racer Yamaha captured the 250 cc world motocross championship through the Swedish rider, Hakan Andersson, in 1973.

The modern motocross machine looks considerably different from the trials bike from which it was derived. Its major eccentricity is the exceptionally wide clearance between wheels and mudguards. This grew from the need to accommodate deep wheel movement and the effects of elaborate rear suspension systems which enable the machine to absorb the violent vibrations as the bike is ridden at top speed over exceptionally rough ground. Motocross machines have also grown lighter over the years through the use of plastics and alloys. Even until well into the 1950s heavy machines from the British factories and FN in Belgium weighing around 375 lb (170 kg) were

the natural motocross machines, but within ten years or so the liberal use of lightweight materials and titanium for the frame and engine have got the overall weight of championship motocross machines down to around 135 lb (61 kg).

Despite their enormous investment and characteristic zeal and diligence, the Japanese couldn't enforce a total capitulation from their European rivals and at the top rung of the motocross ladder the fight continued during the 1970s. After Suzuki's phenomenal run when they swept aside all opposition to take six world titles in four years from 1970, Husqvarna were able to capture the 500 cc championship through the 'Finnish Flyer' Heikki Mikkola in 1974, though for the remainder of the decade the Japanese factories dominated with two championships each for Suzuki and Yamaha, and one for Honda, in 1979. Honda's success was significant in two ways. It was their first ever world title in motocross and it was won for them by the British rider Graham Noyce. Not since 1965, when Jeff Smith topped the championship on a BSA, had a Briton been successful. Only through Dave Bickers and Greeves in 1960 and 1962 has Britain (though the inventor of the sport), through a rider or a machine, been successful in the 250 cc premier motocross championship where, interestingly enough, the Japanese have made far less impact, particularly in the late 1970s. The Soviet Gennady Moisseev on a KTM achieved a breakthrough in 1974, following Hakan Andersson on a Yamaha to the 250 cc title. Harry Everts of Belgium, riding an Austrian Puch machine, was successful in 1975, then came Mikkola on an Husqvarna (1976), Moisseev again on the KTM (1977 and 1978) and Hakan Carlqvist of Sweden on a Husqvarna in 1979.

When motocross began, events were basically cross-country marathons run for the enjoyment of riders. Little thought was given to spectators. But shorter races round circuitous courses now bring the action almost to the feet of the watching enthusiast and it is this close contact and personal involvement which gives motocross its attraction as a great spectator sport. It is less remote than road racing. When the United States took to motocross in a big way the final sanction had been declared with motocross truly 'arrived' as a major international motorcycle sport.

For all its vigour and bluster motocross is a far less dangerous sport than road racing. One reason is that speeds are much lower, another that when a rider parts company with his machine he generally lands on soft mud or earth instead of the uncompromising rigidity of tarmac or concrete. Motocross events at all levels are relatively less expensive to run. You don't have to lay down a highly formalised circuit, nor set up elaborate stands or spectator facilities. This means that there is generally plenty of money available at the end of the day for the most successful riders, who do extremely well financially since motocross has become so successful.

The international stars of motocross are nowadays true professionals, facing a demanding programme of events in the world series which begins in the spring and extends through the summer into the autumn. There are 12 rounds held in major European centres and with so much interest in motocross in Eastern Europe, countries like Poland, the USSR, Yugoslavia and Czechoslovakia are always strong candidates for inclusion. Similarly, the United States has now been brought into the series. There are two races in each round and points are scored as follows: 15 for first place, 12 for second, 10 for third, with other points being awarded in descending order: eight, six, five, four, three, two and one. An aggregate of points from the two races determines the overall winner and the championship is decided on an accumulation of points; the rider with the most wins.

The most successful motocross rider of recent times has undoubtedly been Roger de Coster, the brilliant Belgian who amassed five world titles and six national titles in Belgium. He won his first world championship in 1971 and brought Suzuki five 500 cc world titles in just six years. In 1974, when he relinquished the championship to Heikki Mikkola, he went to America and won the lucrative American Trans-AMA motocross championship. In spite of a near-fatal crash before the start of the 1978 season, he still managed to finish a remarkable third.

Taking over from de Coster as the acclaimed 'king' of motocross was the flying Finn, Heikki Mikkola, up to the end of the 1970s still the only rider to claim world titles in both the 250 cc and 500 cc series. Mikkola is a quiet, solitary figure who sets about his work as a professional motocross rider with a ruthless dedication. His partnership with the Husqvarna factory which started in 1964 spanned 13 successful years, and on the famous Swedish factory machine he snapped up the 500 cc world championship in 1974 and the 250 cc title two years later. When Husqvarna cut back its racing programme in 1976 Mikkola signed for Yamaha to spearhead their challenge to Suzuki in the 500 cc world series, bringing them the championship in 1977 and 1978.

The only motocross champion to emerge from East Germany is Paul Friedrichs, who won the 500 cc title three years running in the 1960s and may well have made a much greater impact had he not become a political pawn in the sensitive East–West relationships of those disturbed times. Up to the beginning of the 1980s he was still the only rider to win the 500 cc world championship three years in succession. Friedrichs' competitive career began on a 125 cc MZ in 1958, but he only began to make an impact internationally after joining the CZ team at a time when the Czechoslovakian factory was giving strong support to motocross, and developing their larger-capacity machines. His first full season in the Grands Prix was in 1965 and he became world champion for the first time the very next year. Friedrichs was possibly the fastest motocross rider in the world and his machine control was exceptional. Had the East German authorities allowed him to compete more freely in international competition he might well have made an even greater impact.

Although John Draper on a BSA and Les Archer on a Norton won the 500 cc championship when it had European status, only two British riders won the world title up to the end of the 1970s – Jeff Smith on a BSA in 1964 and 1965 and Graham Noyce in 1979. Smith put an end to a five-year reign by Swedish riders and for two years this exceptional exponent of motocross tech-

Suzuki signed Belgian ace Roger De Coster when they led the Japanese advance into motocross competition. *Inset* : De Coster after signing for the Suzuki factory (*Mick Woollett*)

Torleif Hansen, impressively airborne, on the Japanese Kawasaki during the 1977 British 250cc Motocross Grand Prix (*All Sport*)

nique, riding his 440 cc and 480 cc BSAs, set Britain firmly, if fleetingly, at the top of international motocross. Noyce's championship on a much different and more sophisticated Honda motocross special of the late 1970s, was secured before a 30 000 crowd at the Belgian Grand Prix at Namur. His third place gave him a total of 217 points for the season to put Britain back on top after 14 years in the shadows.

In the 250 cc class Dave Bickers, riding Greeves machines, was Britain's most successful rider during the days of the European championship between 1957 and 1962, when Rolf Tibblin and Torsten Hallman also made their mark. But although Hallman was to go on to win the 250 cc title three more times after it had gained world status, the most successful rider in this competition has been the wildly exuberant Belgian, Joel Robert. He took the title first in 1964 on a CZ

machine and dominated the class so profoundly that he won the championship five more times, from 1968 to 1972. His last three titles were won on a Suzuki machine. Robert, born 1943, became the youngest world motocross champion in 1964 when he was still four months short of his 21st birthday. A fine showman and one of the greatest crowd-pullers in the business, Joel Robert was an incredible performer – individual, temperamental, tempestuous and audacious.

The man who led the American motocross invasion into Europe was the colourful Pierre Karsmakers. Born in Holland, Karsmakers had competed in the traditional Grand Prix rounds before being tempted to America where, if he was to temporarily relinquish his chance of a 'world' title, he enjoyed the consolation in the early 1970s of becoming one of the highest paid motocross superstars in the world.

Karsmakers' style caught the attention of Yamaha American team boss Pete Schick when the Dutchman competed in the Trans-AMA series and considered him ideal to show the American riders the ropes. In 36 US starts in his first season Karsmakers collected overall honours 17 times and won the National Open Championship. With Yamaha Karsmakers became a top celebrity, but he switched to Honda in 1975 to spearhead their assault to capture sales in the vastly expanding American motocross market. For a while Honda kept him busy riding in the United States, where his presence and winning performance could have the most effect on the world's biggest market, and when they let him return to Europe to contest one or two world series rounds he was not notably successful, finally shifting back to Yamaha and, eventually, back to the United States.

Another American to make an impact on European motocross up to the end of the 1970s is Brad Lackey, who took over from Karsmakers in the Honda team and came second to Mikkola in the 500 cc world series of 1978.

In the more recent 125 cc world class Suzuki have dominated, winning the title in all five years up to 1979. Gaston Rahier of Belgium brought them the title in 1975–77, Akira Watanabe – the first Japanese rider ever to win a world motocross title – won in 1978 and Harry Everts of Belgium in 1979.

Motocross is perhaps the most cosmopolitan of all motorcycle sports. Many developments and improvements have taken place in its 60-year history, but the basic elements of being close to the action and the exhilaration of fast riding over the rough are as hypnotic for the spectator and rider today as they were in the less commercial and contrived 1920s.

The evolution of the motorcycle. *Left:* a replica of the historic Werner of 1903 with the motor positioned low between the wheels (*National Motor Museum*). *Below:* the 1928 BSA 493cc 'Sloper' with a 1925 BSA 2½ hp 249cc model in the background (*National Motor Museum*). *Below left:* the high technology of the 1980s is seen in this sophisticated 1300cc superbike from Kawasaki (*Kawasaki UK Ltd*). *Below right:* a pre-Second World War 500cc racer from the famous Gilera factory (*All Sport/Don Morley*).

Chapter 8

Trials and Enduros

A motorcyclist puts his basic skills and techniques more on the line when he takes part in a trial than in any other form of motorcycle sport. His performance must be sensitively controlled, being observed over various sections, his balance impeccable, and he must display a kind of divine unity with his machine which keeps him in the saddle and his feet off the ground as he manoeuvres and negotiates round boulders, through streams and over rocks. Speed is not of prior importance. The essential elements are to keep going, keep your feet off the ground, and stay mounted.

It's like a circus act, as finely balanced as that of the high-wire walker, as intriguing as that of the down-to-earth juggler. Riders haul, encourage, coerce and restrain their machines across terrain which incorporates all the impediments and obstacles imaginable. It's a man-sized test of a rider's ability and at once a training ground and launch-pad for a career in most other branches of motor-cycle sport.

The trial is as old as motorcycling itself and developed from the competitive urge for a rider to test his machine against those owned by others, and to establish manoeuvrability, reliability and hill-climbing performance. As early as 1903 the Auto-Cycle Union (then the Auto-Cycle Club) organised a 10-day, 1000-mile reliability trial based on London, and the idea spread to France the next year with a long-distance event from Paris to Bordeaux and back. Italy also organised a number of inter-town trials. By 1906 motorcycle manufacturers were supporting a one-day event based on southern England, and interest in trials developed to such an extent that three years later a five-day event in Scotland attracted 33 riders and was to be the forerunner to the famous Scottish Six-Days Trial, now an outstanding classic event in the trials calendar and incorporating almost 800 miles (1300 km) of road and rough riding and some 180 odd sections.

These special 'observed sections' became necessary as machines grew more capable. Early events were uncomplicated affairs. Riders who finished the course, usually over roads and hills, within a certain time received an award. But as machines improved and rider technique advanced a tougher test was necessary. Observed sections were added in which points were lost for stopping and other infringements, and over the years these sections

Above : Checkpoint Ross-on-Wye in the 1907 Auto-Cycle Club 1000-mile trial. *Left to right* : timekeepers George Reynolds and J.W.G. Brooker, Teddy Hastings and W.H. Wells, who competed on a Vindec (*National Motor Museum*)

Below : The incomparable Sammy Miller competing in 1963 on his beloved 497cc Ariel (*B.R. Nicholls*)

were made progressively more difficult to stay ahead of the additional skills of riders and the technical progress of their machinery.

Even before the outbreak of the First World War it was usual for many motorcyclists to go trials riding and it was the popularity of trials riding as a recreational sport that led to the inauguration of the now famous Scott Trial, which began as an annual closed event for workers of the Scott motorcycle factory in Yorkshire, England in 1911. The Scott was made an open event in 1920 and was to grow into one of the toughest and most demanding trials in Britain. The now classic 'Scott' is also historically significant because it introduced observed sections over rough country where before they had been accommodated within road sections and a time element was an important factor so that the event became a time and observation trial. This led in turn to a further adaptation by a group of Scott employees who dispensed with the observed sections in a breakaway race which was the forerunner (see previous chapter) of the more modern sport of motocross.

Still important within the trials calendar, the Scott is a one-day event run over more than 60 miles (95 km) of rugged terrain and is held exclusively across country. It traverses a complex route incorporating some 60 observed sections and because of the time element makes exceptional demands on a rider's skill and his reading of the event.

It was in Britain that trials riding gained most of its early impetus. It developed seriously after the First World War after the potential of the motorcycle over rough and muddy terrain had been demonstrated by war-time despatch riders. Civilian enthusiasts started competing against each other on rough roads and up and down hills, and it was through the enthusiasm of the British motorcyclist, and the aegis of the Auto-Cycle Union (A-CU), that the first moves were made to place trials riding on some kind of international footing. As early as 1910 trials had become so popular that regional centres were set up and team events were taking place between different clubs. A six-days trial organised by the A-CU led to the first International Six-Days Trial (ISDT) held in Britain in 1913. It was a team event with member countries of the Fédération Internationale Motorcycliste (FIM) competing for the International Trophy.

This kind of endurance test was chosen to demonstrate and promote the motorcycle as a reliable means of transport and to get manufacturers to build long-suffering and highly-dependable machinery. National teams had to ride machines built in their own country. This soon became a hardship for some countries whose motorcycle production was meagre, so in 1924 a secondary competition was introduced into the ISDT allowing three-man national teams to compete for a Silver Vase Trophy and on foreign machinery if they wished. The original ruling for the main trophy was abandoned after 1970 and now, for both awards, teams are able to ride whatever machines they want, though the choice must be within a specified cc framework.

Standard road machines were used for the ISDT at the beginning, but as special tests and more arduous cross-country sections were introduced, machines became more specialised. Early teams included sidecar combinations. The ISDT, although developing from the traditional basis of reliability, is now unique, being an inter-nation contest over an incredibly tough course, but based purely on time. In this respect it is akin to motocross or the traditional car rallies. By no means do all competitors finish, and while machine capacity is important, lightness and handling are more vital than sheer power.

The ISDT is held in a different country each year and nowadays six-man teams ride for the premier Trophy and four-man teams for the Vase. There are manufacturers and club team awards, and gold, silver and bronze medals for the best individual riders. Over the six days competitors are allowed only a few minutes each day to maintain their machines and at night the bikes are locked away in a special enclosure. All competitors are required to start the next morning within a specified time or points are lost. The ISDT competitor must be an expert mechanic as well as a skilled rider and be capable of doing his own running repairs from the tool kit he carries. Covering an overall distance of up to 2000 miles (3200 km) in the six days tests both rider and machine to the limit. Physical exhaustion is not uncommon. Half the machines never make it to the end.

Considerable national prestige is at stake in the ISDT and being a team event there are many demonstrations of personal courage in the face of gross discomfort or untreated injuries in order to keep faith with the common effort. Britain produced the most successful teams in the early years, winning the Trophy eight times out of fourteen. Memorable battles in the years before the Second World War were between Britain and Germany, and in the years after, between Britain and Czechoslovakia who, by the mid-1950s, were the strongest country. East Germany were supreme in the 1960s winning the Trophy six times in seven years, before the 1970s saw the re-emergence of Czechoslovakia, whose riders secured the Trophy

Above: Mike Hailwood in action in the 1965 Senior TT. His machine battered after a fall, and with no windscreen to gain protection, he nevertheless raced on to a glorious victory *(All Sport/Don Morley).* Right: Possibly the greatest festival of speed on earth. The Tourist Trophy races on the Isle of Man and a lone rider makes his way round the famous 37¾-mile course *(All Sport/Don Morley)*

Right: The famous Ballaugh Bridge on the Isle of Man Mountain Course where riders take to the air. Showing how it's done is Alex George *(All Sport/Don Morley)*

Left : More recently the Americans have moved into international trials riding. Talented Marland Whaley of San Diego, USA, is seen competing on his 350 cc Montesa (*John L. Clarke*). *Centre* : Showing the fine art of trials riding as only a champion can. The demonstrator is Finnish specialist Vrjo Vesterinen (*P. Christie*). *Right* : Britain's Malcolm Rathmell hardly making a splash as he negotiates the Ricany course in the Czechoslovakian round of the World Championships on his Montesa trials special (*John L. Clarke*)

five years running from 1970. The East European teams have also done well in post-war years in the Vase competition, with Czechoslovakia in the vanguard. Britain took the Vase, however, in 1948 and 1950, Holland in 1951, 1954 and 1956, but during the 1960s and 1970s, Czechoslovakia and East Germany have dominated the results, though Italy took the Vase for the first time in 1968 and the United States in 1973.

Despite its undoubted importance and prestige as an international event, the ISDT is not typical of trials generally. Both the ISDT and the Scottish Six-Days Trial are really enduro events. The majority of trials are one-day affairs and are held over a course of about 30 or 40 miles (48 or 64 km), divided into a number of sections. As he rides through the section, the competitor is observed closely and marks are put down against his name if he loses his balance and puts a foot to the ground, if he stops or falls over, or if he moves outside the marked route. If he puts a foot down to steady himself he loses one mark; three are lost if he uses his feet or legs while still in the saddle and he forfeits five marks if the motorcycle stops, goes off course, or fails to complete a section. At the end the rider with the least number of penalty marks wins. Speed is not important, the rider only having to make sure he completes the event within a fairly generous time scale. Trials are all about the rider against the natural hazards of rocky streams, mud, stones and gravel, tree stumps and boulders. After successfully travelling through a special section, a rider moves on quickly to the next one, sometimes over public roads, where his skills are once again tested and observed.

For many years trials riding was very much an amateur sport with little reward, other than personal satisfaction, for the best riders. Not until the

1960s did trials riding move into the modern era, gaining ground and increased attention with the big-money international events. Nowadays the best trials riders are rewarded handsomely for their success. For a long time, however, the FIM failed to recognise the increasing importance of trials and only in 1963 were the first moves made towards the establishment of an individual world championship. Two years before the Belgians had run an international contest to be decided over a number of rounds, but run on a team basis. It made little impact until the FIM decided, following pressure, that one of the rounds would count towards a new, individual title. It was named after the great Belgian trials enthusiast, Henri Groutars, and the Henri Groutars Prize became accepted as an unofficial European championship. But not until 1964 was a European championship made official, and trials lacked an individual world championship of its own until 1975. British rider Don Smith was the first European Trials champion on a Greeves. Sammy Miller took the title in 1968 on a Bultaco and Smith, having joined the Spanish Montesa factory, recaptured the title in 1969 on his new machine. Another Briton, Mick Andrews, was the first rider to win the European championship two years in succession, gaining the distinction for the Spanish Ossa company in 1971 and 1972 on a machine he himself designed.

Roadsters were plenty good enough in the early days of trials riding. Even into the 1950s the most successful machines were the British 350 cc Matchless, AJS and Ariel. These still relied on traditional thumping power to carry them over the rough terrain and were still basically little different from road machines, though by now exhausts had been raised well clear of the ground, petrol tanks had shrunk to conserve weight, and knobbly tyres had, of course, become standard for extra adhesion.

But once the importance of lightness and good handling qualities had been accepted, the traditional 350s gave way to the ultra-lightweight and by then powerful enough, 250 cc two-strokes. For a time Britain retained its premier position through purpose-built trials machines like the Cotton, Dot and, particularly, the successful Greeves, which used the Villiers proprietary engine, but these were later eclipsed by the superb Spanish Ossa, Montesa and Bultaco models. Later still the Japanese factories, encouraged by the increasing interest in trials riding in the United States, became interested and Honda, Yamaha, Suzuki and Kawasaki all now produce trials machines for the average rider as well as being interested in the upper echelons of the sport. The sport was helped enormously in the United States following demonstration tours there by both Sammy Miller and Don Smith.

There are no regulations governing the cubic capacity of a trials machine, but the 350 cc two-stroke single seems to have settled down as the most popular and gives the right kind of power–weight ratio for rough country riding. Throttled down there is still plenty of power though it is possible to ride a trials bike at 1 mph (2 km/h) without stalling the engine or touching the clutch. The modern trials bike is a specialised beast. Structurally, it must combine toughness with a degree of flexibility and since the machine is not built to travel fast, its centre of gravity can be high, allowing many essential parts to be raised for necessary ground clearance. Total weight is about 220 lb (100 kg), and the knobbly tyre at the rear is only partially inflated to gain extra grip. It's all highly skilful and good fun as competitors squelch through mud, splash across streams and gulleys, shudder and shake over ridges and cavort and lurch round rocks and boulders.

The legendary king of trials riding is the Belfast-born Sammy Miller, who reversed the usual trend by specialising in trials after a successful career as a road racer. That was in 1958, when he began to build up an impressive list of successes. He collected 11 British titles in 11 years, two European titles, and won the important Scottish Six-Days Trial five times, the Scott seven times and the British Experts competition on six occasions. Miller's earlier successes were on the famous 500 cc Ariel, but he left BSA, Ariel's parent company, at the end of 1964, signed for Bultaco and became equally successful on the 250 cc two-strokes. After an impressive riding career, Miller stayed with Bultaco to help design and develop their Sherpa machine which took Bultaco to a near-monopoly in trials competition. In 1974 he

was signed by Honda, by then actively interested in trials, to help produce a trials machine and run a team of riders. In two years the 306 cc Honda four-stroke trials machine which Miller developed had made an impressive name for itself in what was by then a highly-competitive sport.

As in motocross, Suzuki had been the first Japanese manufacturer to show interest in trials, developing single-cylinder machines from their road bikes. When Miller signed for Honda he was merely following a trend. Earlier Mick Andrews and Don Smith, both exceptionally gifted riders, had been taken on by Yamaha and Kawasaki respectively to help give them the impetus they needed to move them into the trials market. The Japanese, however, found the Spanish factories by no means easy to dislodge and Bultaco, through their gifted Finnish rider Vrjo Vesterinen, continued to dominate the world championship series. British rider Malcolm Lampkin rode a Bultaco machine to take that very first individual world championship in 1975 and in an impressive demonstration of skill and strength, Vesterinen captured the title in 1976, 1977 and 1978 – always riding Bultaco machinery.

Said to have the same intense dedication as Sammy Miller, Vrjo Vesterinen is a supreme exponent of top-class trials riding. He is utterly composed, has deep concentration and that fine sense of balance and coordination which is so important. After a career which began on trial mopeds, he was the Finnish junior champion in 1969 and joined Bultaco in 1972. He turned professional in 1974 after serving in the Finnish Navy and although he scored more wins and amassed more points in the world series in 1975 he finished second in the table, since only the seven best performances counted. He made sure of his first world title the very next year.

Among other riders who in the 1980s may make an impact in trials are Malcolm Rathmell, Malcolm Lampkin, Mick Andrews, Ulf Karlsson and Bernie Schreiber.

The world championship has now matured into an important prestigious competition. Twelve rounds in different countries are held each year with 15 points being awarded to the winner of any round, 12 for a second place and 10 for a third place, and other points in descending order. All rounds count.

For all its adult stewardship in the 1980s, trials riding still generates enormous appeal at grass roots level and continues to be the sport which many riders turn to first when they start a competitive career. It is comparatively slow, relatively safe, yet as a challenge to one's ability as a motorcycle rider, trials riding is supreme.

Left: Massive crowds and an exciting sport. Gennady Moisseev (USSR), world 250cc motocross champion in 1977 and 1978, climbing high on his KTM machine during the Motocross des Nations *(All Sport)*. *Below:* Honda riders both and two of the world's best. American motocross star Brad Lackey leads Britain's ace Graham Noyce to the top. Noyce became world 500cc motocross champion in 1979 *(All Sport/Mark Moylan)*

Left: The 'togetherness' of motocross. No. 35 is Britain's Vaughan Semmens, 250 cc Bultaco; no. 16 is Eugene Rybalchero (USSR), 250 cc CZ *(All Sport/Tony Duffy)*

Left: The International Six-Day Trial (ISDT) is an incredible test of skill and stamina and is punishing on both rider and machine. Note the body protection showing through this Maico rider's jersey as he splashes through the water *(All Sport/Don Morley)*. *Below:* A fine sense of balance and mastery of your machine are essential for success in trials riding – generally accepted as the most skilful branch of motorcycle sport. Britain's Martin Lampkin is seen on his Spanish Bultaco *(All Sport/Steve Powell)*

Chapter 9

Grass Track Racing – Ice and Sand

Grass-track racing lacks the big-time glamour of speedway and the heavy sponsorship and investment to be found in road racing or motocross, but it is this very lack of commercialism – as well as the excitement of the racing, of course – that creates such a strong appeal to the grass-track enthusiast. He enjoys the friendliness of it all, its disarming 'low profile', and will be quick to point out that the comradeship which was once a feature of road racing, evident in the help of one competitor to another when a spare part or extra pair of hands is needed, is still to be found in grass-track racing.

Grass-track races take place over closely marked circuits of varying lengths with solo machines running in an anti-clockwise direction, sidecars clockwise. As many as a dozen or more solos go at the same time. For sidecar competition there are four or perhaps even six competitors to a race. The minimum width of a grass track is 25ft (7.6 m) in Britain.

Broadsiding, power sliding or side-slipping (it is called all these things) is a feature of grass-track racing as it is in speedway, and it would be wrong to suppose that the former is simply a tamer version of the latter. With four-lap heats and finals and machines taking the bends at perhaps 60 mph (95 km/h) – and reaching speeds of 80 mph (130 km/h) on the straights – grass-track racing can be spectacular and demands its share of bravery and courage from the rider.

The special machines used for grass-track racing are generally 350 or 500 cc single-cylinder inverted singles. The JAP engine was for years the main power-source for grass-track solo machines, but more recently the British Weslake unit, with the four-valve head, has made enormous impact. Frames are built to twist and to accommodate the contortions of broadsiding and incorporate mini-fuel tanks designed to take no more methanol-based petrol than is necessary to see them round the standard four laps. Unlike speedway machines, which have virtually no suspension or brakes, grass-track bikes incorporate some rear suspension to absorb bumps in the ground, and are equipped with a moderate braking system, though sliding on the corners provides most of the necessary braking. Riders wear masks over their faces as a protection against flying stones and a special iron protector on the riding boot which they constantly dig into the ground as an accepted means of controlling the skid.

While it's true to say that riders were probably racing over rough grass-tracks even before speedway became established in its original form of dirt-track racing, both grass track and ice racing are now generally looked upon as offshoots of speedway. This view is encouraged by the unusual number of speedway riders who acquire their early experience and technique racing on grass. All three share common origins, being invented in America at the turn of the century when riders found fun and excitement in racing round dust and dirt tracks on their machines. Under the influence of the British and Australians who respectively popularised grass-track racing and speedway in Europe in the late 1920s, the sport moved in different directions. Ice racing began in Sweden in the early 1920s when the basic American idea was adapted for use on frozen lakes and has since become one of the most spectacular of all sports.

Grass-track racing gained considerable ground in Britain in the 1930s with the formation of the Brands Hatch combine and its influence at club and regional level spread throughout the country in the 1940s, leading to the establishment of a National Championship in 1961. A year later the Auto-Cycle Union introduced their Grass-Track Stars Competition, a forerunner to the British Championships which were introduced in 1965. Eric Oliver, four-times world road-racing sidecar champion from 1949 to 1953, was a well-known grass-track racer in the 1930s, regularly reaching speeds approaching 60 mph (95 km/h). Jack Surtees, father of the famous John Surtees, the only man to win a world championship in motor racing and motorcycle racing, was also well known for his grass-track exploits on a 1000 cc HRD, travelling well in excess of 50 mph (80 km/h).

All the thrills of grass-track racing with acknowledged expert Chris Baybutt on a Sieger showing the way (*B.R. Nicholls*)

Monty Banks, Austin Cresswell, Arthur Stuffins and Reg Luckhurst were among grass-track racing's popular figures in the 1950s with one of the most famous characters in the sport, Don Godden, gaining prominence in the 1960s. He collected his first national title in 1965 and in an outstanding career was successful against most of the European aces. Famous sprinter Alf Hagon gained National Championship 350 and 500 cc 'doubles' in both

Plenty of mud flying as Chris Baybutt manages to hold on to the lead in this all-action picture which typifies the excitement and energy of grass-track racing (*B.R. Nicholls*)

1959 and 1962. The first official grass-track British Champion was Dave Baybutt, who won both 350 and 500 cc titles in 1966, and it was brother Chris who stamped his name on the sport after a 250 cc class had been added by taking the title three years running from 1972.

Grass-track racing achieved additional status in 1978 when a European championship was established, thus giving riders a formal structure beyond national competition. Reigning British champion Chris Baybutt claimed the title on a British Weslake machine in a dramatic meeting held in the UK at Hereford. Former speedway star Peter Collins ran him close with two initial wins, one against Baybutt, but a protest by Don Godden claiming that Collins' machine contravened the stringent noise test levels, was upheld and the former speedway champion was disqualified. With West Germany, Holland, Denmark, Britain and Sweden all represented in this first European championship, Britain dominated the top positions. Apart from Franz Kolbeck of West Germany on a Jawa, who came second, the next three positions were all occupied by British riders. Don Godden and Mike Beaumont, both riding Weslake machines, were third and fourth with Trevor Banks on a JAP machine finishing joint fourth.

In recent years grass-track racing has developed into a popular junior sport and youth riding, well structured under the aegis of the Auto-Cycle Union, flourishes in Britain.

Motorcycle racing on ice is a phenomenon which has gradually gained ground in the colder countries of both Eastern and Western Europe. Early races saw riders in pairs competing against the clock and before the adoption of standard 400 metre ovals, tracks would often be 800 metres long and occasionally extend to almost four times that distance.

The coming of spiked tyres and the speedway type of trailing leg technique produced more dramatic and spectacular racing and stimulated increasing interest. Even before the Second World War some machines were being designed and built specially for ice racing. After the war Russia was attracted by ice racing and it was their rider, Gabdrakham Kadirov, who became the first European title holder when a Championship was established in 1963. From then until 1970 the Championship was dominated by the Soviets, and particularly by Kadirov. Ice racing gained world status in 1966, but the Soviet stranglehold was broken when the Czechoslovakian Antonin Svabb took the title from Kadirov in 1970. The only Englishman to make any kind of impact in ice racing is Andy Ross, though the Czechs have increasingly been strong contenders for the title.

Showing how it's done on three wheels – Roger Measor and Peter Dullalee on their BMW outfit (*B.R. Nicholls*)

Don Godden in action (*P. Simcode*)

Ice racing is exceptionally dangerous. The needle-sharp spiked tyres, now standard at 105 spikes on the front and 86 on the rear, give remarkable grip on the ice and machines can be banked over to an alarming degree. Races are now held on specially refrigerated tracks, both indoors and outdoors. The riders' knees scrape the ice and sections of tyre are strapped on to cover the left knee and lower leg for essential protection when cornering. As races are run in an anti-clockwise direction, the spikes, more than 1 in (2·5 cm) long and often sharpened by hand before a race, are positioned more on the nearside wall of the tyres rather than on the crown to give maximum grip when the machine is banked over. In the near-arctic conditions in which ice racing is popular, the machines have often to be warmed up with a

Top: Ice racing is one of the most dramatic and dangerous of motorcycle sports *(All Sport/Don Morley)*

Above: The mud is flying and the 'wheelies' much in evidence at the start of another grass-track meeting at Lydden Circuit in south-east England *(All Sport)*

blowlamp to get them to start.

Sand racing is also a derivative of speedway and is closely allied to grass track racing. In Britain the beach racers gained recognition in 1976 when the Auto-Cycle Union backed a six-round national series. Bob Hamilton on a JAP machine secured the coveted 500 cc title with former grass track and ice racing star Andy Ross in second place.

Chapter 10

Speedway Scene

Speedway owes its origins to America, much of its early development to Australia, and its international acclaim to a crowd-oriented spectacular which is unique in motorcycle sport. Its enormous impact has made speedway an entertainment in its own right with a massive fan-following which, but for its commitment to speedway, might otherwise show little interest in motorcycling. For in speedway the machines are relatively unimportant. It's the excitement of the racing, the atmosphere, the riding heroes and the tension which pulls in the crowds. Even in the early 1950s, while soccer was still struggling to break down national barriers, the superstars of speedway were already sportsmen of international standing, known and admired far beyond their native shores.

Speedway is a gripping spectacle. The format has been developed over the years to provide the public with exactly what it wants: breathtaking action at close quarters and plenty of it. Four riders in line abreast form up at the start gate, crash-hatted, elbows widely spread and bodies leaning forward heavily, the weight on the handlebars. Colourful caps, tunics and leathers help the crowd to pick out their favourites. Tension mounts as engine power surges to a peak, then up goes the barrier and the four machines hurtle from the start with almost freakish acceleration, each rider grappling desperately in a fearless effort to be ahead on that all-important first bend. Races are run anti-clockwise and, with machines equally matched, are always close, the riders racing round terrifyingly near to one another as they battle for the lead four times round that quarter-mile (400 m) shale track. The bikes have no brakes, hardly any suspension, and are hurled forward without mercy. The action is fast, furious, noisy and dirty, as riders 'broadside' round corners, their reinforced left boot digging into the surface of the track and sending up showers of loose shale.

It's brash, but skilful. As a rider deliberately lets the back wheel slide out on corners and slings the bike into opposite lock, it's the coordination between speed and balance which counts; and all the time throttle control is vital if he is to avoid being overtaken or crashing into the safety fence.

Speedway is organised into teams, like football, with league matches normally running to 13 heats, two riders from each team riding in each race. A race consists of four laps. There are generally

A line-up of dirt-track riders at London's White City track in 1928 (*Illustrated London News*)

seven men in a team and two reserves and racing is arranged so that riders are paired differently each race. Scoring is three points for the winner of a heat, two for a second place and one point for finishing third. Individual points are totalled towards a team score and the team with the most points wins. Teams have home venues, closely identified with towns, and generally use sports stadia. Their regular supporters follow their progress up and down the league tables. At the moment there is no promotion and relegation system but, like football, riders can be switched from one team to another. A lot of speedway takes place in the evening, under lights, which adds to the atmosphere.

In Britain speedway is now the second largest spectator sport with an average weekly attendance at league meetings in excess of 170 000. Almost 40 teams compete regularly in the two national leagues.

At an international level speedway attracted official recognition for the first time in 1936, during a period which is generally recognised as the sport's barnstorming days, when a world championship was held under the auspices of the FIM at Wembley, London. Riders from America, Australia, New Zealand, Sweden, Germany, Canada, Britain, Denmark, Spain, South Africa and France took part. After tying on points the Australian, Lionel van Praag, won the run-off against Eric Langton of Britain to take the title. Jack Milne of the United States and Bluey Wilkinson of Australia became world champions in 1937 and 1938.

Floodlighting adds to the atmosphere of speedway *(Alf Weedon)*

Although these pre-war events were classified as world championships, in the absence of any other claimant to the title, it wasn't really until speedway settled down after the war that the championship became officially recognised as a 'world' competition. Britain, through Tommy Price, took the first post-war world championship in 1949. A team world championship was inaugurated in 1960 with Sweden taking initial honours. In the first ten years Sweden won the title five times, Poland four times and Britain once, in 1968.

The big names of contemporary speedway include the brilliant Ivan Mauger (pronounced Major), Ole Olsen, Jerzy Szczakiel, Ove Fundin, Barry Briggs, Anders Michanek and Peter Collins. In the later 1960s and 1970s the New Zealander Ivan Mauger was the most successful rider in terms of individual world championship results. Born in Christchurch in 1939, Mauger won the European championship in 1966 and finished fourth in the world championship. He holds the distinction (early 1980s) of being the only speedway rider to win an individual world championship for three consecutive years – 1968, 1969 and 1970. He added further world titles in 1972, 1977 and 1979 to bring his record to six. The next best speedway rider at the start of 1980, with five titles was the Swede, Ove Fundin, in 1956, 1960, 1961, 1963 and 1967.

Fundin was a contemporary rider of Barry Briggs, another popular New Zealander who gained his first world title in 1957, the year after

New Zealander Ivan Mauger demonstrates the style of a champion. Mauger was world champion for the first time in 1968 *(Alf Weedon)*

Speedway is an outstanding spectator sport. At the starting gate *(left to right)* at Wimbledon in 1975 are Malcolm Simmons (hidden), Ray Wilson, Peter Collins and Jimmy McMillan *(All Sport/Tony Duffy)*

Speedway's World Team Cup Champions of 1968, Martin Ashby, Ivan Mauger, Barry Briggs, Nigel Boocock (team manager R. Greene) and Norman Hunter (*Motor Cycle Weekly*)

Fundin won his first championship. Briggs repeated his success the very next year and added two more championships, in 1964 and 1966, before retiring from international speedway. His 1957 championship was won after a run-off with Ove Fundin. In 1958 he collected the title with maximum points and in addition to his four world titles he was runner-up and third placed rider on numerous occasions to become one of the all-time popular speedway greats.

Scandinavia has been well represented in speedway, in contemporary times by the outstanding rider from Denmark, Ole Olsen. He rode in his first world championship final in 1970 and made the title his own the following year. He won it again in 1975 and once more in 1978. He was the first Dane to win the speedway world championship and has achieved much success in major events all over the world.

Anders Michanek, who won the title in 1974, was born in Stockholm in 1943 and took the championship by the largest margin (up to that time) of four clear points, scoring a maximum of 15 points to Ivan Mauger's eleven.

While Poland has been strong in team world championship speedway, it wasn't until the outstanding performance of Jerzy Szczakiel that the Eastern European country figured in the individual championship. Szczakiel secured his world title in 1973 – and in more than 40 years of the championship and until the 1980s, he was still the only Polish rider to hold such a distinction, though fellow countrymen Antoni Woryna in 1966 and Edward Jancarz in 1968 had reached third place.

When Peter Collins won his world title in 1976 it was the first success in this competition by a British rider for 14 years, Peter Craven then securing the title. Collins' success was achieved in Chorzow, Poland, when he was only 22, and he became the youngest world champion for 21 years. Peter, one of four speedway-riding brothers, is a popular champion and took his title by one point from fellow English rider, Malcolm Simmons.

Graduating from fairground-type beginnings to a sophisticated professional sport, speedway was first known as dirt-track riding. It began when motorcyclists started racing their machines around the horse-trotting tracks and dirt ovals of the

Even in the earlier days of speedway the excitement was obvious as the riders lined up for the spectacular start (*Alf Weedon*)

United States. In the 1920s the sport was popular in America with the big Harley-Davidson and Indian 1000 cc V-twins being hurtled around established circuits. This was before the days of power sliding, and racing with such overpowered machines, the sport was hyperdangerous at this stage. Only after serious accidents, including some fatalities, were restrictions imposed limiting machines to 500 cc. To get more speed the broadsiding technique caught on. A demonstration of a closed-circuit race by American riders at Maitland, Australia, at the New South Wales Agricultural Show in 1925 was an instant success and the Aussie stars who until then had ridden on grass tracks and concrete took to it immediately. They laid out special cinder tracks, a third or half a

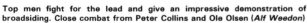

Top men fight for the lead and give an impressive demonstration of broadsiding. Close combat from Peter Collins and Ole Olsen (*Alf Weedon*)

mile round, for the first original races. The visiting American rider Cecil Brown introduced the leg-trailing, broadsiding technique to the Australians and the new sport received a further spectacular boost when, on the loose cinders, a rider called Billy Lamont, from Australia, showed that, by maintaining power and thrusting the rear wheel into a continuous slide, it was possible to drift round the corners in one all-action movement. It changed the face of dirt-track riding.

Speedway was first seen in Britain in 1927 when a dirt-track meeting of sorts was held on the military ground on Camberley Heath, Surrey.

It departed from the Australian pattern by being staged on an undulating, sandy course and with riders racing round in a clockwise direction, but sufficient had been seen of the new sport for further tracks to be set up around London, leading to the now historic meeting at an old cycle track at High Beech, Epping Forest on 19 February, 1928. It was an enormous success and although it would certainly have been outlawed under the present regulations governing speedway, it set the seal on the sport's development within Britain. About 3000 spectators had been expected, but more than ten times that number flocked there, blocking roads and causing traffic chaos for miles around. Spectators not only thronged the outside of the track, but were lined up along the *inside* as well, and so keen were they to catch sight of every bit of action that once the riders had raced past they spilled over the track and had to push themselves back off the track as the machines came round again. It's a miracle no one was killed, but the full programme was completed and the Australian Billy Galloway, present to give a public demonstration, astonished and thrilled the crowd with his spectacular broadsiding technique.

At first in Europe it was the visiting American and Australian celebrities who captured all the attention, but gradually home-produced riders were appreciated for their skill and bravery. The sport developed its own characters. Still remembered from the early post-war years is Split Waterman, who turned to speedway in 1947 after sand racing. His skill on the track was obscured by his cavalier personality and although he won many honours he missed a world title. He was closest in 1951 when Jack Young of Australia beat him. Peter Craven was another British rider of note from the earlier years. He secured the world championship in 1962 and was killed the following year while racing in Scotland. The sport has had its ups and downs. In the late 1960s weekly attendances in Britain reached 350 000 at some 40 tracks, after a temporary decline during the 1950s.

Unlike most world championships which are decided over a series of events, the speedway world championship is won and lost on the outcome of one event.

The first evening meeting under floodlights to be held in Britain took place at Stamford Bridge on 5 May, 1928, and the first speedway leagues were formed the following year with 25 teams competing in two leagues.

In the early days of the sport the machines used were virtually road models stripped of all unnecessary equipment and with handlebars turned down for visual impact. Bikes with a low centre of gravity were most suitable, but in post-war years specialisation has become apparent, as in all other branches of motorcycle sport. Frames were designed exclusively for speedway and are now virtually standardised and change little one decade to another. They are light and spindly and incorporate a modest degree of suspension at the front and none at the rear. Combine these features with a short wheelbase and you have the characteristics of a bike which is ideally suited for sliding round the bends on maximum power.

Speedway machines are powered by principally rather old-fashioned 500 cc single-cylinder four-strokes which combine flexibility with ample torque. A second gear is unnecessary since these quite low-geared singles will move from a standing clutch start to maximum revs within the initial straight. They run on alcohol fuel and display dazzling acceleration. A modern speedway bike will weigh about 190 lb (86 kg) and reach a maximum speed of about 80 mph (130 km/h). For around 30 years the natural choice of engine was the British JAP four-stroke, but challenge came in the 1960s from the Czechoslovakian ESO 500 cc four. The Eastern European factory found a way of increasing both power and flexibility in a strong, simple engine with a somewhat shorter stroke, and within a few years the ESO, which was later to become the JAWA, had largely taken over in speedway. Britain came back strongly with the remarkable Weslake speedway/grass-track engine, 500 cc single-cylinder but with four valves, and it made a dramatic impact, capturing much of the speedway market. JAWA countered with a four-valve unit and the Swedish ERM company have also been active, but Weslake engines continue to be very successful in both speedway and grass-track.

The gaunt appearance of the modern speedway machine – the 1980 Weslake (*Alf Weedon*)

Speedway in the 1980s — exceptionally competitive and dramatically exciting (*Alf Weedon*)

Chapter 11

Fastest in the World

In motorcycle sport one achievement stands supreme. That is the honour of being the fastest rider in the world. But unlike road racing, moto-cross or speedway, there are no world titles. The only prize for a record-breaker is the extreme satisfaction of knowing that nobody else has trav-elled faster on two wheels.

A world record can be held by only one rider – there are no ties – and new claims must be significantly faster (by at least one per cent) to take preference. In this respect, record-breaking is more critical than racing where world champion-ships are won on results – the speed of a race is irrelevant.

Although regulations describe both as 'motorcy-cles' there is no comparison between a modern racing machine with its need for precise cornering and braking, and a record-breaker, which is required to run only in a straight line. The specialised needs are totally different and both requirements have drawn apart as races and records have become increasingly faster.

But this did not apply in the early days when conventional machines were the basis of all forms of motorcycle sport. Road-racing machines, with only minor modification, were used for world record attempts until 1956 when a German NSU, designed originally for road racing in 1938, reached a speed of 211 mph (340 km/h). From that point onwards, it was the record-breakers who broke away from established design. Although road-racing machines have little in common with standard touring machines, their general appear-ance has remained essentially similar.

Conversely, with wind-resistance being the greatest barrier to attaining speeds beyond 200 mph, (322 km/h), when stability is also a difficulty, record-attempt machines have become long, low, torpedo-like projectiles with minimal manoeuvrability. It was different during the 1920s when speeds were around 100 mph (161 km/h) and riders had the advantage of various tracks and roads which could accommodate such performances.

Nonetheless, even 60 years ago, it was soon apparent that engine development was progressing far more rapidly than frame design. Manufac-turers gave little thought for steering, handling or comfort and regarded the frame simply as the means of suspending the engine between the wheels, with virtually no thought for the rider.

When motorcycle sport got moving again after the First World War, the top-speed target was 93·48 mph (150·44 km/h). This had been set by a British rider, Sydney George, on an American 994 cc Indian V-twin at Brooklands on 2 May, 1914. To break this record and set the 'world's' first 100 mph (161 km/h) performance was the ambition of all speed-aspirants, but while Britain's speedmen were battling away at Brooklands, built in 1907, an American, Eugene Walker, took a mass of records and beat Britain for the first 'official' 100 on the Florida sand at Daytona Beach. Walker, riding a works-prepared 1114 cc ohv V-twin Indian attained 114·71 mph (184·61 km/h) on 16 February 1920 – along with 103·77 mph (167·00 km/h) on a 1000 cc engined version.

Curiously, although the publication *Motor Cycle* stated: 'The tests were officially observed by the AAA and the M & ATA (America's then ACU/FIM equivalent) and as members of the FICM (FIM) may be taken as correct' – no credit was given to Walker's 114 mph speed in Europe.

This was probably due to the faster machine being above the FIM's maximum limit of 1000 cc – and it was his 103 mph performance only that was regarded. For this same reason, speed claims by various American riders using big engines were always ignored in Europe and this included the aircraft pioneer, Glen Curtis, who fitted an aero engine into a frame and was said to have achieved 136 mph (219 km/h) in 1907!

Controversy over engine capacity was a major factor which influenced America's decision to withdraw from the FICM in 1920 – an unfortu-nate state of affairs which remained until the United States Motorcycle Club joined the FIM in 1963; and the subsequent American Motorcycle Association affiliation in 1972. But even after this, the matter of maximum capacity limits for record-breaking persisted and several irrefutably accurate performances did not receive FIM ratification.

British riders gained prominence in 1921, but only by riding American machines which at that time were the world's most advanced.

Britain's Douglas Davidson (not related to the American manufacturer) hit 100 mph (100·76 mph) (162·16 km/h) at Brooklands on 27 April 1921, on a 989 cc side-valve V-twin Harley-Davidson. Despite European belief that this was

Pioneer record breaker Claude Temple on his 996 cc British Anzani with which he lapped Brooklands at 101.23 mph (162.91 km/h) in May 1923 (*Motor Cycle Weekly*)

the world's first-ever 100 mph record Walker's performance at Daytona, in 1920, is fact.

Harley-Davidson, of Milwaukee, had sent over two machines to be ridden by Douglas Davidson and Claude Temple, for the sole purpose of achieving 100 mph on British soil for the first time. Temple opened with 97·26 mph (156·52 km/h) in one direction (there were no two-way averages in those days) and was immediately followed by the Harley-Davidson team's only serious rival, Bert le Vack, riding a 1911, 994 cc ohv Indian V-twin with four-valve cylinder heads, who responded with 98·98 mph (159·29 km/h)! It was then Davidson's turn and despite having his saddle come loose, he set his already mentioned 100·76 mph. Davidson's 'record' stood for less than 24 hours. For the next day le Vack wheeled out his old Indian and, having done nothing more than slacken the tappets, achieved a speed of 106·52 mph (171·43 km/h), breaking Walker's record and setting a new world's fastest.

Le Vack's engine had been fitted with the then new and experimental KE 965 steel for its exhaust valves and these expanded more than anticipated. Had they been sufficiently loose the day before, le Vack would probably have set the first-ever British 'ton' with a world-record breaking performance.

These performances were all set in one direction, but subsequent 'official' record attempts required a two-way average speed to cancel-out any advantage gained from running only one way, i.e. from a tail wind or gradient. The point of this can be seen from the 102·8 mph (165·5 km/h) performance which le Vack set on an ohv 998 cc Zenith-Jap on 31 October 1922 – this was taken as the first FICM (it became FIM in 1945) world record.

With the introduction of mass-produced cars, popularity of motorcycles in the United States fell away and development was soon overtaken by the British industry which had Brooklands and the Isle of Man TT races to aid development.

However, as speed increased, it was soon apparent that Brooklands was no longer suitable for all-out speed and riders began to look elsewhere for long, straight roads. This was impossible in Britain where, except for the Isle of Man, the law forbids the closure of roads for motorised sport. But this did not apply in Europe and Freddie Dixon took advantage of this in September 1923, by rushing up and down the Bois de Boulogne at 106·8 mph (171·9 km/h) on a V-twin American Harley-Davidson.

The last world record to be achieved at Brooklands came with Claude Temple's effort on 10 November 1923 when he set 108·48 mph (175·58 km/h) on his famed 996 cc ohc OEC-Temple-Anzani, designed by Hubert Hagens. Bert le Vack tried to beat Temple, but realised this had become impossible at Brooklands where, apart from having insufficient space, engine performance was restricted by the obligatory use of silencers. Le Vack went over to France and set 113·60 mph (182·82 km/h) on a Brough Superior-Jap, at Senart, on 27 April 1924. Knowing this was within instant striking distance by several rivals, le Vack returned to France (Arpajon) on 6 July to increase his own record to 119·05 mph (191·59 km/h).

But this only delayed his rivals and Claude Temple subsequently responded on 5 September 1926, with 121·41 mph (195·39 km/h). This was Temple's peak performance with the Anzani-

Joe Wright made a number of attempts at the 'world's fastest'. Here he is seen, with a natty line in headgear, at Southport in 1933 (*Topical Press Agency*)

engined machine which, totally without streamlining and weighing 500 lb (226.8 kg), was said to produce 58 bhp.

Temple's record stood until 25 August 1928 when Oliver Baldwin made the trip to Arpajon, south of Paris, France, to set 124·62 mph (200·56 km/h) on a 980 cc ohv Zenith-Jap.

Bert le Vack set his final speed swan-song exactly a year later on 25 August 1929 by hoisting the record to 129 mph (207 km/h) with a 980 cc Brough Superior, during the same Arpajon Speed trials. His record failed to last a month and the effort which followed not only closed the golden era of the 1920s, it brought a totally new approach to record-breaking aspirations.

Until that time most attempts had been held within a club-like atmosphere – riders were rivals with the fastest gaining the laurels from competitive meetings – such as the annual Speed Trials at Arpajon. But on 19 September 1929 BMW of Munich wheeled out a supercharged ohv 750 (735 cc) twin on to a nearby autobahn which had been closed for the occasion and Ernst Henne proceeded to dash all earlier efforts with an astonishing 134·68 mph (216·75 km/h).

Apart from the innovation of its supercharger, this machine was also the first of the 'streamliners' for the engine was cowled over and Henne wore a shaped helmet which flowed along his back. The performance, mainly from the surprise of its secrecy, caught all British riders napping and to be beaten with 134 mph (215 km/h) from a 750 was alarming. First to respond was Claude Temple who fitted a supercharger to his newly-built 996 cc OEC-Jap and arrived at Arpajon with Joe Wright as his jockey to challenge Henne on the spot at the annual record-attempts meeting. Because the British machine failed to run effectively, Henne was so confident that his existing record was safe that he didn't bother to run and took the BMW home. What he and BMW failed to appreciate as 'new boys' to the sport, was the experience and determination to succeed on the British side – and Temple made a 'secret' arrangement to hire the Arpajon road after everybody, except the timekeepers, had gone home!

The big Jap chimed in at 6.30 a.m. on 31 August 1930 and Joe Wright claimed Henne's record with 137·32 mph (221·10 km/h). This obviously hurt the German team, for within a month Henne spent two days rushing up and down the local Bavarian autobahn before finally managing to break Joe's speed by just 0·34 mph (0·55 km/h).

With the advantage of using their blown British 1000, against the German 750, Temple and Wright remained confident against Henne's small

improvement and they went over to Cork, Ireland in November 1930, where, after problems with the OEC, Joe regained the record on a 'spare' Zenith-Jap with a magnificent 150·70 mph (242·53 km/h) along the now legendary Carrigrohane Road.

This marked the end of all British success until 1936 when the lone effort of Eric Fernihough was to fleetingly regain the honour.

The depression which hit the early 1930s affected the British motorcycle industry badly and a great many manufacturers closed down. Among these was AJS, of Wolverhampton, who built a 1000 cc twin for a crack at the world record. This was a V-twin with overhead camshaft gear from the 500 cc road-racing single, but despite supercharging and the occasional hint of 150 mph performance, poor reliability prevented any success.

A similar project was built by Excelsior in 1931 with a supercharged Jap engine, but again, and despite attempts to provide an element of streamlining with stainless-steel cowls which gave it the name 'Silver Comet', this too was just another shooting star, although it did reach over 160 mph during one run at Tat in Hungary.

Temple and Wright's confidence from 1930 stood until 1932 – it presumably took until then for BMW to raise the power of their 750 to speed it over 150 mph – for when it next appeared, at Tat, Henne regained the record with 151·86 mph (244·39 km/h).

The world's speed record then became Henne's and BMW's exclusive property and they proceeded to break their own record four times until Henne achieved 169 mph (272 km/h) on a fully-streamlined machine. This performance, set on 12 October 1936, along the Frankfurt autobahn, was most significant, for he did it on a 500 cc (493 cc) machine. The 750 cc engine had been developed from an ohv roadster, but the new 500 was an ohc designed with a supercharger as a racing unit.

A deserted stretch of road and a lone rider – a typical scene of pre-Second World War record breaking attempts before the days of the Bonneville Salt Flats. Ernst Henne on his BMW in 1937 (*Motor Cycle Weekly*

Eric Fernihough, one of Britain's leading contenders for the 'world's fastest' honours, on his streamlined Brough Superior (*Motor Cycle Weekly*)

Although British factory interest was minimal, there was one serious challenger – Eric Fernihough, a Cambridge MA, who was helped to some extent by Brough Superior and J. A. Prestwich Ltd (Jap) with his 996 cc engines.

Eric had witnessed Henne's performance in 1936 – and was not impressed by the antics of the streamlined machine as it weaved along in the wind; and it gave him grave doubts about total enclosure.

Eric nonetheless realised the essential need to cheat the wind as velocity began to climb towards the 200 mph target, and he chose to enclose his Brough Superior entirely, except for the front wheel, along with remaining totally exposed himself as he rode it.

It was in this form that 'Ferni' took the 'Bruff-Sup' to Gyon, Hungary, on 19 April 1937. After tests he removed the fairing and set his first 'naked' run at 175 mph (280 km/h) when the Jap engine shed its driving sprocket. With this replaced, he returned along the road with a new record average of 169·78 mph (273·23 km/h), to beat Henne by a whisker.

Eric's record stood until 21 October when a fresh aspirant appeared in Italy. It was Piero Taruffi with the 500 cc supercharged, four-cylinder Gilera-Rondine, which then produced about 80 bhp. This was one of the original 1935 road-racing machines fitted with full-enclosure streamlining, and Taruffi attained 170·5 mph (274·5km/h) along the Florence *autostrada*. Versatility of this machine was such that Taruffi also ran up and down the *autostrada* slowing and turning at either end, to set the 'Hour' record at 121 mph (195 km/h)!

German prestige was then at stake for having had an Englishman and then an Italian beat their record, the lines between Berlin and BMW must have buzzed hot, for soon Henne was out·on the Darmstadt autobahn and seemingly without effort

– there were certainly no delays – he zipped up and down to reach 173·67 mph (279·49 km/h) on 21 November 1937.

Fernihough was determined to wrest back the record for Britain, but as a privateer with virtually no support, compared with the factory backing for Taruffi and Henne – whose countries also aided them by closing nearby roads, it was a costly business.

Eric prepared his Brough Superior with a totally new shell and made the long trek to Hungary in his Ford van. It was just before Easter, 1938, and on arrival the weather was hopeless with high winds. He came home.

He returned a few weeks later to Gyon (Hungary) where the road was closed for him at a fee of £150. Everything seemed perfect and he set off. Eye witnesses stated that the engine sounded superb and the machine was accelerating to astonishing speed – estimated at 180 mph (290 km/h) – when it went into a massive wobble and weaved to the side of the road where Eric was flung off and killed.

Following the 1939/45 War, first to go for Henne's record was Britain's Noel Pope. This was a scheme which had lain dormant from 1939, for Pope had followed Fernihough's wheel tracks very closely during the late 1930s. Pope also preferred a Brough Superior and had the 1931 Ted Baragwanath model which he bought on the latter's retirement in 1933.

Pope's subsequent improvements included a later and more powerful 8/80 model Jap engine which, with its supercharger, gave about 120 bhp, and he set the ultimate and never-to-be-broken solo record around Brooklands at 124 mph (200 km/h) in 1939. With this same machine, Pope, with the support of Surrey motorcycle dealer, Teddy Comerford, began preparing for an attempt at the world record soon after the war and his target of the late 1940s was to reach 200 mph.

A new world speed record of 290 km/h (nearly 180 mph) attained by Wilhelm Herz in 1951 on his 500 cc NSU (*Popperfoto*)

The machine was totally enclosed in an aluminium shell like a bulbous egg, and the Bonneville Salt Flats, Utah, was chosen as the venue. Regrettably, the shell was damaged during the journey to Bonneville and despite repairs it remained distorted. This was presumed the reason for Pope, then 39, going out of control and crashing during his abortive attempt in 1949.

However, from more than 30 years ago, it is more likely that the very shape of the 'streamlining' was wrong and probably suffered from the fact that it was inspired by aircraft design, for motorcycles are not intended to take off!

Although Pope was not seriously hurt and his machine was later repaired, the cost of another trip prevented him from ever going for the record again.

Next to try was a South African, Vic Proctor, with a brand new unblown 1000 cc Vincent Black Lightning, in 1950, but this effort too ended in a heap at the roadside. Also worthy of note was the effort of American Rollie Free, whose disregard for streamlining included shedding his own clothes and, wearing only swimming trunks and lying prone along the machine, achieved 150 mph (240 km/h) on another Black Lightning at Bonneville, to mark America's new post-war interest in two wheels.

Incidentally, up to 1950, the fastest motorcycle speed in America was set by Joe Petrali in 1937 when he reached 137 mph (221 km/h) on a semi-cowled Harley-Davidson, at Daytona Beach.

By comparison with Pope and Proctor, the next and successful attack on the world's fastest figure went ahead with such ease that it made the challenge seem no more involved than wheeling your own machine from its garage for a Sunday afternoon spin.

Behind it, however, was the full effort and resources of the German NSU factory who planned, prepared and carried out the operation with typical Teutonic precision.

Wilhelm Herz, then 38, seemingly did little more than trigger off his 350 cc supercharged NSU, before the timekeepers announced that his speed was only 0·2 mph (0·3 km/h) short of Henne's 500 cc record! Then, with the double overhead camshaft 500 cc twin, reputed to develop 110 bhp, Herz pushed the absolute record to 180 mph (290 km/h) This engine was designed in 1935 – with the 350 cc version following in 1938.

Herz declared afterwards that 200 mph (322 km/h) could have been exceeded if a greater distance had been used; but this was not done because the eddying effect when passing beneath two bridges may have upset the steering.

Following this, the London based publication

Motor Cycle offered a prize of £1000 to the first British rider of a British machine to regain the record, and while this caused considerable interest, the surprising outcome came with the news of it being won by a New Zealander, but this was not until 1955!

Adding nothing more to his unsupercharged Vincent Black Lightning than a fairly compact streamlining, Russell Wright achieved 185 mph (298 km/h) along a normal road at Christchurch, New Zealand.

But from that point on, the FIM's record book was knocked sideways, for over on the Bonneville Salt Flats, with little knowledge of the FIM (and more especially of its rules), was an American team which had fitted an unblown 650 cc Triumph engine into a machine that is best described as a cigar-shapd projectile. Long and low with the 'pilot', Johnny Allen seated inside the cockpit, the 'Devil's Arrow' set a speed of 193·72 mph (311·89 km/h). The FIM did not dispute this, but, because it had not been set under FIM administration, it remained 'unofficial' and was disregarded.

However, NSU did not disregard it and in a blaze of confident publicity which included brochures with spaces to write in the new records, arrived at Bonneville in 1956 totally confident of breaking 200 mph (322 km/h). The machine was virtually the model from 1951 and fitted with 350 and 500 cc engines, first built in 1935.

Russell Wright was also on the Bonneville salt lake, but try as he did, he just failed to reach 200 mph (322 km/h) with the still unblown Vincent and he withdrew from all further contests.

Doing just what they set out to achieve, Herz opened proceedings for NSU with the 350 cc machine and zipped back and forth across the Utah salt at 189 mph (304 km/h). Then, just two days later on 4 August 1956, the huge machine was wheeled out with its 110 bhp, 500 cc engine in place and Herz repeated his ride to the tune of 210·64 mph (338·99 km/h) – and NSU went home to Germany in a blaze of glory, not suspecting that any rival could approach them.

But that was only from the point of view of using a 'conventional' motorcycle; for incredibly, it was NSU themselves, under Gustav Baumm, who had developed long, low, torpedo-like projectiles with minimal frontal area, and one of these had achieved well over 100 mph (161 km/h) with a 50 cc engine during 1954.

Texan Johnny Allen returned to Bonneville barely a month after the NSU attempt and with a 650 cc unsupercharged Triumph engine, with about 65 bhp, burned across the salt at 214 mph (344 km/h). He had timed his attempt precisely from knowing that it was then too late in the year for NSU to return and make a counter-attack; the salt lake is at its best in September and the weather then closes in. (At 100 mph (161 km/h), 98 per cent of engine power is absorbed to overcome wind resistance. Only 2 per cent is required to counter rolling friction.)

Then followed the biggest dispute record-breaking had ever known. The FIM disallowed Allen's performance on the grounds that: 'although the accuracy of the timing equipment was not questioned, it did not have the FIM seal of approval.'

Allen appealed. Triumph, of Coventry, sued the FIM – and were subsequently suspended for a time from all FIM competitions – and finally, with the FIM accepting the validity of the questioned timing apparatus, they said it could be used only for *future* attempts and Allen's record was not accepted!

NSU never returned to defend their record, but the quest to go faster continued and Triumph did eventually gain the honours when another American, Bill Johnson, achieved an FIM approved speed of 224.57 mph (361.41 km/h) in September 1962 with another unblown 650 cc engined projectile.

This record stood 'officially' for several years, but following the Allen affair, the United States paid little heed to the FIM and were content in knowing they were accurate and no less accepted around the world with attempts under their own American Motorcycle Association regulations.

It was under these circumstances that Bob Leppan, of Detroit, ran his 'Gyronaut' projectile to a 245.67 mph (395.37 km/h) AMA 'world' record in 1966. His machine was fitted with two 650 cc unsupercharged Triumph twin-cylinder engines.

Next step up came in 1970 when Harley-Davidson prepared a massive 1850 cc V-twin engined contender as a challenger to Leppan, along with Californian, Don Vesco, who fitted his

Johnny Allen with his 650 cc Triumph which in September 1955 took him across Bonneville Salt Flats at a record breaking speed of 193.72 mph (311.89 km/h) (*Popperfoto*)

home-built streamliner with two 350 cc TR2 Yamaha two-stroke engines.

Vesco made the first attempt, but malfunction caused the machine to veer off course and roll over at some 250 mph (400 km/h). Even at this speed, Vesco was only shaken and the machine so little damaged that he was able to run again after on-

The impressive 'Spirit of America' in which Craig Breedlove of the United States cracked the outright speed record with 527.34 mph (848.67 km/h) in 1962 (*Motor Cycle Weekly*)

the-spot repairs and he claimed the AMA title with 251·92 mph (405·43 km/h). As this was achieved during the Bonneville Speed Week, Cal Rayborn went next and he too crashed with the machine flipping several times; but he also was unhurt and on the re-run set a speed of 265·492 mph (427·268 km/h) over the Measured Mile – as opposed to the shorter kilometre distance favoured by the FIM.

Leppan went next and he also crashed, at about 270 mph (435 km/h), but in this his left arm came out of the cockpit and was so severely injured that he was never able to race again.

From this, however, big capacity machines found recognition from the FIM with the provision of a 'special vehicles' category which came into being after 1962 when American Craig Breedlove built a massive three-wheeler machine 'The Spirit of America' which was ostensibly the fuselage of a jet aircraft – and he took the world's absolute record at 527·34 mph (848·67 km/h).

It was under these regulations that Cal Rayborn's motorcycle record was accepted by the FIM. However, subsequent to this, Rayborn was killed in a road-racing accident and during the 1970s, only Don Vesco remained active.

The massive Honda organisation, through their subsidiary in the United States, moved on stage effectively in 1971, though murmur of a Honda interest in the ultimate speed record had been circulating for some time. In September 1971, they announced details of the Honda Hawk. This breathtaking projectile was more than 21 ft (6.4 m) long and had a wheelbase of more than 13 ft (4 m). The turbo-charged machine weighed 900 lb (408·6 kg) and was powered by two 750 cc four-cylinder engines to give 280 bhp. The chassis incorporated a semi-monocoque centre section, alloy steel bulkheads and an aluminium double skin.

With Harley-Davidson's current record standing at 265·49 mph (427·26 km/h), Honda's aim was the 300 mph and 500 km/h barriers. Piloted by Jon McKibben, the Hawk flashed through the speed traps at 286·567 mph (461·185 km/h), well in advance of the record, but on the return journey it crashed spectacularly at 180 mph (290 km/h), sliding on its side for more than 500 yards, though McKibben was unhurt.

Honda maintained their ambition through 1972 and into 1973, but as success eluded them and in the face of what must have been quite monstrous expenditure, the project petered out. An attempt had been made in the autumn of 1972 when the Hawk broke loose at 270 mph (435 km/h). The incident is described in *The Story of Honda Motor Cycles* published by Patrick Stephens: 'After swerving first left and then right, the projectile reared skywards before crashing down on to the salt, the two braking parachutes having been released by McKibben keeping the streamliner stable. When the skidding and movement stopped, McKibben stepped out without help and walked away!'

It was reported early in 1973 that the Hawk had made runs at Bonneville fitted with special gearing which gave it a theoretical maximum speed of 366 mph (590 km/h), but after two years the promise was still beyond realisation.

Meanwhile, Norton and Yamaha made strong bids and then Don Vesco, having rebuilt his machine with two 700 cc four-cylinder Yamaha engines, raced to 302·66 mph (487·08 km/h) in 1975 and then rebuilt the same machine with two 1000 cc four-cylinder Kawasaki engines for his next attempt.

Fitted with turbocharging (a form of supercharging) Vesco covered the course at 318·598 mph (512·734 km/h) on 25 August 1978 – to leave the world's fastest motorcycle record at its peak as motorcycling moved into the 1980s.

A number of factory-sponsored attempts have been made to secure the outright speed record in recent years. Kawasaki invested heavily, as did Norton with their special streamliner pictured here. But after a number of attempts in 1974 the record was still beyond them (*Motor Cycle Weekly*)

Top : Acknowledged king of speed in the late 1970s is the Californian Don Vesco, who piloted Yamaha's gleaming projectile to repeated success (*Mick Woollett*). *Below* : Vesco in action on a record run late in the evening in the isolation of the Bonneville Salt Flats. The American later switched to Kawasaki and again took the outright speed record — pushing the speed to more than 318 mph (512 km/h) in 1978 (*Mick Woollett*)

Chapter 12

Sprints and Drag Racing

Sprinting from a standing start to maximum speed over a short distance must be the oldest form of motorcycle racing – for it is more than likely that this was how the first-ever machine was tested; and the second machine built was raced against it.

The relationship which existed in the early days between sprinting and road racing is easily appreciated, for acceleration and speed were more essential for winning races than the later need for superlative steering and brakes. As performance and reliability improved – and this took many years – the specialised requirements for road racing drew the sports apart, but sprinting kept its connection through track racing, notably at Britain's Brooklands, the Surrey speed-bowl which existed from 1907 until 1939.

Famous riders from those days, especially the 1920s, included such legendary names as George Dance, with his 'sprint' Sunbeams, Bert le Vack, who used Jap engines from 250 to 1000 cc in many different makes of machine, Freddie Dixon, on Indian, Brough Superior and Douglas twins, Vic Horsman, with his Triumph, Dougal Marchant with the 350 cc Chater Lea, little Bert Denly, who rode Norton and AJS and Bill Lacey, on his gleaming nickel-plated 500 cc Grindlay Peerless-Jap.

Successful as these and many others were, the first machine built specifically for record-breaking was probably the supercharged 736 cc ohv BMW ridden by Ernst Henne in 1929. Built predominantly to attack the world's maximum speed record, successfully gained at 134·25 mph (216·05 km/h) and 136·8 mph (220·2 km/h) for the flying-start kilometre and mile, Henne also set new standing-start (sprint) records with 23·8 seconds (93·5 mph (150·5 km/h)) and 33·8 seconds (100·5 mph (161·7 km/h)) for the mile.

Henne reduced the 750 cc record to 23·75 seconds in September 1930 along with a 500 cc record of 24·45 seconds, in April 1932. He and BMW dominated the world record-breaking scene during the early 1930s, but Britain's leading privateer, Eric Fernihough, subsequently gained the absolute standing-start kilometre with 22·615 seconds (98·9 mph (159·2 km/h)), on his 996 cc Brough Superior-Jap, in October 1936. Italy's Piero Taruffi also improved the 500 cc

record on the supercharged, four-cylinder, Gilera-Rondine, with 24·05 seconds, in October 1937.

This was the position with the major capacity classes when World War Two broke out in September 1939.

First to improve the pre-war sprint kilometre record was Germany's Wilhelm Herz, who set 22·00 seconds (101·84 mph (163·90 km/h)) on a 500 cc NSU supercharged twin in 1951.

British manufacturers had lost all interest in sprint activity and records generally during the 1930s, and what there was rated no higher than club-level sport. Best known of these events was the Brighton Speed Trials and in 1946, Bob Berry set FTD (Fastest Time of the Day) with 79·5 mph (127·9 km/h) for the standing-start half-mile on his 1000 cc Brough Superior.

This still existent event continued with limited appeal until 1954 when Roy Charlton won with a run of 22 seconds over the longer kilometre course to 'equal' the world record and set the first 100 mph (161 km/h) run in Britain.

Charlton's performance, on his self-prepared 998 cc Vincent, instantly revived this 'forgotten' sport. It clearly indicated that world record sprint performances could be achieved by private riders on comparatively cheap, home-built and prepared machines.

Several clubs began to hold regular meetings; particularly popular was the Sunbeam motorcycle club's quarter-mile event at Ramsgate, Kent, and the National Sprint Association (NSA) was formed in 1958 to help advance and develop the sport.

From a competitive aspect, quarter-mile events were strongest. This was not entirely due to the greater availability of 440-yard courses, but more to the influence from America where the similar sport of drag racing was strongly established and extremely popular.

The essential difference between sprinting and drag racing is that a sprint is where machines run individually and are timed to determine results. A drag is where two machines race against each other and first across the finishing line is the winner – irrespective of elapsed time.

Despite the growing interest in the quarter-mile, the standing-start kilometre remained as the predominant FIM world record distance – which requires machines to run in both directions of a

Flying the flag for Britain. The 'father figure' of British sprinting for so many years, George Brown, on his famous record-breaking machine, Super Nero (*B.R. Nicholls*)

course, with the time determined by the two-way average.

Wilhelm Herz's record from 1951 stood until 1956 when the late Dickie Dale (British), riding the unsupercharged V-eight-cylinder Moto Guzzi road-racing machine, returned 21·90 seconds (102·5 mph (165·0 km/h)).

This was considered astonishing as the machine was in virtually road-racing order, running on petrol and with narrow racing tyres.

This stood for just one year until Alfredo Milani, achieved 20·9 seconds (106·71 mph (171·73 km/h)) on an unsupercharged, four-cylinder Gilera. This machine was modified slightly from road-racing order. It featured a more enveloping streamlining than for racing and the engine ran on an alcohol-based fuel.

Popularity for quarter-mile sprinting through the NSA led to the establishment of national records in Britain and the first competitive meeting for this was at Wellesbourne Mountford, near Stratford-on-Avon, in 1961.

Standard for the future was set by George Brown with his 1000 cc Vincent 'Nero' with 10·48 seconds; fastest 750 was Reg Gilbert, with 12·18 seconds on an unsupercharged 650 cc Triumph. Best of the 500s was Alec Bascombe, with 12·95 seconds on a 500 twin-cylinder

Triumph. Basil Keys, riding a Norton, was top of the 350s with 14·18 seconds, while George Brown also clinched the 250 title with 14·32 seconds on an Ariel Arrow.

Interest in the standing-start kilometre prompted the NSA to move this annual event to Chelveston, Northants, where Fred Cooper set 24·51 seconds on a 500 cc supercharged Triumph

Conqueror of the drag racing scene in America, Tom Christenson, in action on his famous 'Hogslayer' at Britain's Santa Pod Raceway (*Roger Gorringe*)

twin. World status came to this meeting in 1965 when it moved to Elvington, Yorks, for the first time and the NSA riders broke 17 world record figures.

Most dominant of British riders was unquestionably George Brown – he died, following a heart attack, in March 1979. Riding his own Vincent-based machines, George was a leading sprint and record-attempt rider for more than 20 years.

Although sprinting and record breaking attracted very little trade support, George Brown's professional approach to it attracted not inconsiderable assistance. Most important was his development of the original Avon Slick rear tyre in 1960 which went far towards bringing all sprint times down when these tyres went into production. Factors such as this brought considerable improvement to performances – for winning sprint runs are determined by thousandths of a second!

The introduction of supercharging to boost power still further beyond the bonus provided by nitro–methane based fuels was probably the most significant time reducer between two points set 440 yards apart. But allied to this came the need for the design and construction of purposeful machines built solely to dash between two points in a straight line.

Sprinting and world record-breaking was most certainly the one motorcycling sport where British riders and machines were supreme during the 1960s – mainly due to the fact that other countries paid no attention. Co-operation with the NSA saw British riders cross over to Holland, and this subsequently determined strong Dutch interest, led by Henk Vink, whose personal activity brought him world prominence.

However, interest in sprinting with its total lack of competition against rival riders, saw drag racing take precedence. With professional promotion, accentuated by occasional appearances of American riders, drag racing, unlike sprints, drew spectating crowds and brought financial rewards to the riders which has resulted in the development of machines which are possibly more specialised, for their single line purpose, than any others in any form of motorcycle sport.

For popular appeal, drag racing scores over sprinting because of its competitiveness. The spectator interest factor present at the sight of a motorcycle covering a straight, measured distance from a standing start, is substantially increased if you put two such missiles side by side and make a race of it. While it is true that drag racing sprang from sprinting and to that extent had its origins in

Britain, it was in America in the late 1940s that the sport was re-born in its new form, developing from the popular speed trials of the day. Illegal public highway performances also contributed to its development as American youngsters tested their courage, and the prowess of their machines, by racing one another as the traffic lights flashed to green.

In essence, a drag race is a contest between two riders who set off at the same time from a standing start to see who can complete a quarter-mile dash in the shortest time. They race against each other and not, as in sprinting, simply against the clock. Mechanical development and the somewhat weird appearance of modern drag racers only add to the exotica which has built up around the sport in recent years, as speeds have gone higher and crowds have got larger. Tension and excitement build up as these remarkable machines nowadays reach speeds approaching 180 mph (290 km/h) – with the finishing line only 440 yards (403.3 m) from the start pad. Races proceed during the day on a knock-out basis, the whole event reaching a climax in the final run-off.

Curiously, though the sporting element is still the root of drag racing, performance figures and plain speed has in recent years gained prominence. This led the Americans to question whether terminal speed might not be more a measure of what they wanted from the spectacle than elapsed time.

During the 1950s drag racing gained momentum though there was still a traditional 'feel' about the sport. Machines consisted of specially lightened frames into which were slotted all kinds of roadster engines, but the bikes still held a familiarity with road-going models. These were very largely the days of non-special fuel, the main method of gaining extra speed being to reduce the weight of the machine. Developing emphasis on drag racing brought keener competition, so it wasn't too long before supercharging was used along with methanol fuel. Now there was much more basic power, but without some means of converting that into practical traction on the tarmac, it was of little use, the rear wheel merely spinning rapidly as the clutch was dropped at the start. Tyres provided the solution, Avon's special wide, flat-sectioned 'slick' being used to push speeds higher. These no-tread tyres with their soft, pliable exterior produced such additional road adhesion that dragster machines had to be made longer to counter the 'front lift' risks which came with the extra propulsion resulting from the use of slicks.

Britain's Alf Hagon furthered the cause by dispensing with a gearbox – since they had the tendency to fail after the introduction of the wider slick tyres which fed additional power loads to the transmission – and with his 1300 cc JAP V-twin supercharged motor, he rocketed over the standing quarter mile in less than 10 seconds, with a terminal speed of 160 mph (256 km/h).

When you further consider that drag racing machines now need to incorporate two or three highly tuned, multi-cylinder high performance engines to be successful at the highest level of competition, it's not surprising that their appearance has grown spectacularly apart from that of the normal road-going machines, or indeed, road-racing 'specials'. They are custom-built and to that extent their success or failure is largely established in the workshops. For just a few seconds' performance-burst, the backroom-boys will devote long hours of painstaking nurturing and tuning. All the top performers now use potent fuel mixes which possess a high proportion of nitro-methane. Incongruous to the purist eye they may well be, but for the technically minded, drag racers must hold an hypnotic attraction. Created by dedicated designer-builders whose task is to build a machine which incorporates incredible acceleration and exceptional speed over a quarter-mile straight distance, the races are merely a public measure of their success – or failure.

Visually, there is little doubt that drag racing is sensational. Riders stretch forward, bodies flattened horizontally against the bike's superstructure, fingers stretching for the handlebar controls. A series of coloured lights flash their warning to competitors to get ready, the green signifying the start. The sequence is red, three amber lights and the final green. The lights' superstructure is situated between the two riders and a rider will watch the light change closely, for a keen anticipation of the green light will give him the chance to release his clutch at the earliest moment, giving him a starting advantage. Unsilenced exhausts send noise levels soaring. There is smoke from the tyres as the bikes scorch away in an almost unbelievable demonstration of full throttle fury. Wonder and tension are held at a peak for a few awe-inspiring seconds, then it's all over, the incredible machines stilled and spent like a deflated balloon. Timing has to be extremely precise

Top to bottom : Third member of Britain's traditional trio of sprinters in the 1960s, along with George Brown and Fred Cooper, was Alf Hagon, seen on his supercharged JAP (*B.R. Nicholls*); The modern drag racing scene with plenty of burn out, USA style, as Joe Smith makes tracks (*Jim Reynolds*); David Lecoq making short work of a quarter-mile distance with the elegantly engineered Drag-Waye (*Motor Cycle Weekly*); One of the most successful of European drag racers, John Hobbs of Britain, is typical of the sport's engineer racers (*Kenneth Cole*)

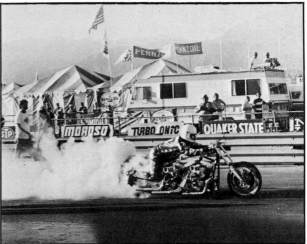

The wonder man of drag speed, American Russ Collins and his world famous, twin-engined Sorcerer special

because of the exceptionally high speeds achieved in drag racing, and electronic equipment is used with bikes breaking light beams linked to photo-electric cells.

Split seconds decide issues in drag racing. When American Joe Smith crashed through the 9-seconds barrier in 1971 on a 1700 cc Harley-Davidson it was an amazing feat. Another American, Russ Collins, whose firm tunes Honda engines in Los Angeles, took his spectacular 858 lb (389 kg)

monster, said to have cost more than £10 000 to build (around 21 000 dollars), through the quarter mile in under 8 seconds, and then the race was on to get down to the once-thought unbelievable time of 7 seconds. In 1978 Collins, with his new 2000 cc eight-cylinder *Sorcerer* clocked 7·62 seconds and 199·55 mph (321·14 km/h), and as drag racing roared into the 1980s Collins was strongly fancied to be the first to break through that 7-second barrier.

Unlike ultimate world record speed attempts, drag racing (and sprinting too) is a one-way-only event. Restrictions, kept to a minimum, are against the nature of the sport and almost any kind of engine is permitted, up to 3500 cc or 2000 cc if supercharged. The attendant organisation contributes to the spectacular nature of drag racing, the best tracks being of special construction as an additional means of contributing to performace, and the preliminary 'burn out' on the start line – the tyre being spun deliberately to bring it up to the best temperature for racing, in water or bleach – contributes to the 'show biz' atmosphere of drag racing, flames and smoke creating visual impact.

Probably Russ Collins' best known contemporary is the American Tom Christenson, who wrote drag-racing history in 1973 when he introduced the slipper clutch, devised by his friend, John Gregory. Before this innovation the fastest drag bikes had single-gear transmissions and depended on wheel spin to get away quickly from the start. With the slipper clutch the rider could rev to maximum, gaining improved grip and extra speed right from the getaway. This new approach combined with multi-engined units to drop the times below the 9-second mark. Tom 'TC' Christenson himself, with his renowned *Hogslayer*, (so named because of its prowess over units powered by Harley-Davidson engines – known as hogs) powered by two Norton engines, went on to conquer the drag-racing scene in the United States and became almost certainly the most successful exponent in the sport's history. In 1973 he clipped half a second off the existing record time for the quarter mile, (an appreciable margin in a sport which is determined in hundredths of a second) and eventually got down to 7·93 seconds and a terminal speed of 176 mph (283 km/h). Christenson went on to win virtually every major drag-racing event.

Another American to gain recognition on the drag-racing strip is Boris Murray. After Joe Smith had rocketed through the 9-seconds barrier, Boris Murray followed suit later that same year, 1971, on a double-engined Triumph machine. He was also the first to be timed across the finishing line at more than 170 mph (274 km/h).

In Europe two of the most popular drag racers have been Britain's John Hobbs and the Dutchman Henk Vink. Typical of drag-racing's engineer-racers, Hobbs has been successful with his double Weslake-engined (2 × 850 cc) *Hobbit*, while Henk Vink, Amsterdam importer of Kawasaki machines, gained recognition with his *Big Spender 4*, developed in 1975. When he gave *Big Spender* its first outing a year before in Holland, Vink made four runs under 10 seconds and at 172 mph (277 km/h) set perhaps the highest quarter-mile terminal speed in Europe at the time – though his supercharged Kawasaki special had only a 900 cc engine.

There is an heroic, almost gladiatorial atmosphere about drag racing with, at the glamour end of the sport, both machines and riders presenting a larger-than-life public image. It is an extremely expensive sport with the most exotic and largest machines being built only with the help of considerable sponsorship. This situation is in stark contrast with the origins of the sport, when riders raced each other on reasonably standard roadgoing machines. Links with the past are not entirely lost, however, because the high costs of drag racing at the higher levels developed the need for segregation and in the 1980s drag racing is organised into a number of classes, including one for ordinary roadster motorcycles, where modifications are rigidly controlled, and riders do whatever adjustments necessary when they arrive at a meeting – and ride the same bike home again.

In Britain, drag racing's first major boost came in 1964 when American stars visited the country for the first Drag Festival. Two years later the opening of the purpose-built Santa Pod Raceway in Bedfordshire was another vital stage in the development and popularising of the sport. The official bodies in Britain are the National Drag Racing Club and the British Drag Racing and Hot Rod Association.

Among machines and riders worthy of note are the British David Lecoq and his *Drag-Waye*, the American Elwood Speer and the 'Michigan Madman', E. J. Potter. Lecoq's *Drag-Waye* used a tuned, four-cylinder 1300 cc Volkswagen engine, Speer combined two 1200 cc engines to claim 300 hp, and Potter's monster was propelled by a 5359 cc V8 Chevrolet engine. Some of the extreme dragsters are show-biz pieces and are outside any normal regulations. So while being ineligible for entry in recognised races, they are used to give impressive and exciting demonstration runs, adding colour and impact to any drag meeting. Another American demonstration rider, Larry Welsh, produced a rocket-powered dragster which reached a terminal speed of almost 200 mph (322 km/h) over the quarter mile.

Drag racing has established a devoted following in the United States and Britain, though in Europe, except for Holland and Sweden, it has achieved little importance.

Chapter 13

The Big Marathons

Endurance events used to be the 'also-rans', of road racing. The machines were basically production models — nothing very exotic or exciting about that — and the purpose of it all, steadfast reliability and plodding staying power, were not designed to set the racing world alight.

But times change. If endurance road-racing in the 1980s still cannot claim to be the ultimate experience for the majority of motorcycle enthusiasts, there are few who would deny that it has made gigantic strides in the past 15 years. Nowadays, endurance racing has its own special heroes, machines are more interesting and exciting, and the major events attract important manufacturer support and big-time sponsorship. While it still remains very largely a passion of the continentals, the major events like the Bol d'Or and the Barcelona 24-hour race are followed with increasing interest, even if at a distance, by a growing number of enthusiasts in many other parts of the world.

To qualify as an endurance race an event must last at least six hours or be 500 miles. Some last 12 hours and the premier events go round the clock. Endurance racing used to be neglected or ignored by the major factories and riders, and by the majority of motorcycle enthusiasts, but important technical advances in production machinery and the identification of endurance racing by manufacturers like Kawasaki and Honda as a positive platform for the sale of their showroom superbikes, is what made all the difference. They brought a big-time atmosphere to the sport and so jacked up its prestige that the FIM, never given to act impulsively, were moved to grant world championship status to their Coupe d'Endurance series for 1980.

The key endurance race is the remarkable Bol d'Or. First run in 1922 on an improvised track near Paris, it has become an institution among French racing fans. Firmly established in recent years at the Paul Ricard circuit and Le Mans, it can draw crowds well in excess of 100 000 to witness specially prepared endurance machines hurtled round at speeds approaching 150 mph (240 km/h) for hour after hour. It's an enormous spectacle as darkness falls, lights are flashed on, and the bikes continue their relentless mission. Machines are subjected to excessive strain and the riders' powers of concentration and reserves of energy are stretched to breaking point. In 1979,

Darkness comes, but the racing goes on. Night riding during the Barcelona 24-hours race (*Mick Woollett*)

for instance, the victorious Chemarin/Leon partnership covered 620 laps of the Paul Ricard circuit in the 43rd Bol d'Or, a total race distance of 2251·3 miles (3624·6 km) with the fastest lap taken by Chemarin at 99·60 mph (160·29 km/h); of the 70 teams which started out, only 32 finished.

For some years the Bol d'Or was outlawed from the FIM's Coupe d'Endurance series because its regulations did not measure up to the official body's strict formula rules for marathon racing. It allowed modifications of various kinds, prototype machines and engines up to 1000 cc, whereas the FIM events were rigidly restricted to genuine production machines. The French organisers refused to budge so in the end the FIM modified their own rules in order to bring this most prestigious of all endurance races into the official racing calendar.

While endurance racing, by definition, can never be the spectacle or carry the impact of shorter Grand Prix racing, its special attractions have been exploited to the limit by the continental organisers. Both the Bol d'Or and the Barcelona race have been cleverly developed into special racing festivals incorporating a variety of other featured events and all kinds of special attractions to bring in the crowds. The racing itself has its own particular appeal and excitement. The sprinting Le Mans start at the Bol d'Or provides a spectacle in itself and as the race settles down there is a special brand of fascination and almost hypnotic attraction in seeing the gradual development of the event. Only when a commanding lead

A spanner for every job! Honda's pit set-up at the famous Bol d'Or, top event in the endurance series *(All Sport/Don Morley)*

is established in the early stages of the race can marathons become tame affairs. Even then there is often a lot of excitement and interest further down the field to maintain attention.

The team-work in the pits and indeed on the machines as the riders switch roles is another special feature of endurance racing. The riders and the pit crews share a common responsibility and the commitment to the team effort leaves little room for *prima donna* outbursts and rider tantrums. In a 24-hour endurance race, the drama builds up as the sky darkens and the lights are switched on. In the gloom the dangers are heightened and the leaderboard can change dramatically. In the 1979 Bol d'Or, for instance, Patrick Pons and Sadeo Asami were leading after six hours, but just before midnight, after having a new front tyre fitted, the Japanese rider crashed and the time lost while essential repairs were completed dropped the Yamaha pair completely off the leaderboard.

Exciting finishes may be rare, but are not unknown. Again in 1979 tension rose in the final stages as Pons and Asami, fighting back dramatically after their night-time mishap, were seen to be in with a chance of snatching the lead from the supreme French team of Christian Leon and Jean-Claude Chemarin; but the latter snatched victory as the huge crowd surged on to the start/finish straight and the organisers had to cut short the event to avoid a catastrophe.

Tactics are vital in marathon racing. Staying power and concentration come into the planning, for a couple of seconds lost in the early stages of the race can be sacrificed more readily than losing a much longer time in the final stages because of sheer fatigue. During a 24-hour race something like 16 000 gear changes will be made on each bike and a rider's hands and feet are almost constantly working to keep the machine on the fastest line. Strength, stamina and co-ordination are essential in long-distance racing. Night riding particularly can be a desperately exhausting business and Honda France at Barcelona in 1979 used oxygen to revive their riders.

In endurance racing's less professional days, private riders on semi-sponsored machines dominated. And at one time there used to be a lot of 250s racing. By the mid-1970s, however, the age of the superbike had arrived with the big 900 cc Kawasakis, mostly fitted with 1000 cc kits, 850 cc Ducatis, Honda-powered 1000 cc Japautos, 850 cc Nortons, 900 cc BMWs and 1000 cc Laverdas prominent. The way ahead to professionalism was forged by veteran long-distance pioneer Georges Godier. A Frenchman living in Switzerland, Godier had earlier specialised in hill tests on a

750 cc Norton. His interest in motorcycles was shared by Alain Genoud of Switzerland and the two came together to form the most formidable long-distance racing partnership of the time.

Because of the particular demands of marathon racing, the use of specially-designed frames was soon accepted. Fritz Egli, a former Swiss national hill-climb champion, was an expert frame builder and had at first concentrated on the conversion of mainly Honda roadsters, Honda machines at that time being dominant in endurance racing. When Egli began working on a Kawasaki machine, concentrating his work on the steering head and the pivoted fork mounting, the two most highly stressed parts, endurance racing was moving into a new era. For it was Godier/Genoud's victory in the Bol d'Or of 1974 on the Egli-Kawasaki machine which began to illuminate the possibilities inherent in this kind of racing.

Godier, in fact, was the key figure. It was his enthusiasm for the work of designer Pierre Doncque and engineer Michel Lambert in the building of a special cantilever frame for the racing Kawasaki-four, that persuaded Xavier Maugendre, the head of Sidemm, distributors of Kawasaki machines in France, to back the project. So successful was the partnership that in 1975 Godier and Genoud won the Bol d'Or for the second year running, and so strong was Kawasaki's influence in long-distance racing at this point that their machines occupied the top three places. At this stage in his illustrious career the legendary Pops Yoshimura had worked on the Kawasaki engine. Previously known for his expert tuning of Honda power units, he had produced a Kawasaki kit which converted the standard production engine into a racing version. Yoshimura's kit incorporated a racing chain and gearbox, 69 mm bore pistons, camshafts, valve springs and valves, though the remainder of the engine was pure Kawasaki, though work was done on balancing and lightening. With little remodelling the Kawasaki engine fitted easily into the special Egli frame.

Kawasaki had first taken seriously to long-distance racing in 1969 when a 500 cc model came second in the Bol d'Or, completing 435 laps. At this time endurance racing was dominated by works-prepared 750 cc Honda fours. By 1973 Hondas entered by their French importers, Japauto, and Kawasaki were battling for honours in the prestigious Bol d'Or, but the future success of the Kawasaki-Godier-Sidemm team flashed a warning to Honda, who weren't prepared to risk any possible detrimental effect Kawasaki's success might have on Honda's domestic sales in France.

Honda-France retaliated and BMW made a bid, but by 1975 there was no doubt that Kawasaki

Above : These custom-designed and constructed machines were introduced in 1976 to take over from Honda's converted roadsters which the factory had previously used for FIM long-distance road races. They had an output of 120 bhp and a top speed of 160 mph (258 km/h) (*John Nutting*)

Below : Le Mans-type start. Endurance race at Brands Hatch, 1979 (*All Sport*)

was the top factory in long-distance racing. The sport had moved out of the amateur ranks to be dominated by importer-sponsored entries, and now, with Kawasaki so strong, Honda took marathon racing into the next stage by fielding a full works team. They found it the only way to recapture the ascendency in a branch of motorcycle racing which was so influential in France and other parts of Europe. Keen to boost their sales on the Continent, particularly of their 750-fours, Honda turned to success in long-distance European events as an effective form of advertising, and although their machines were by no means revolutionary, effort was not wanting for Honda backed their scheme with a team of 40 or so specialists.

The Honda endurance race team arrived in Europe led by Michihiko Aika, with Japanese and European mechanics as basic crews and European mechanics attached to different riders. There were four racing machines, described as intelligently developed versions of standard production models, but with that special Honda pedigree of racing success. The entire effort was reckoned to have cost Honda at least £150 000 for 1976, but the investment brought success, for the famous Japanese factory won six out of seven races during the season and totally dominated endurance racing.

Their riders, Jean-Claude Chemarin and Christian Leon rode to victory at Mugello in Italy, the Liege 24-hour Race in Belgium, and the Bol d'Or to take the FIM Coupe d'Endurance title for Honda. In 1976, with new 1000 cc machines, Honda again stormed to victory in the endurance series, winning every round with a variety of riders, with Jean-Claude Chemarin and Christian Leon again jointly topping the riders points table, ahead of Britain's Stan Woods and Charlie Williams.

The story was the same in 1978 and yet again in 1979. Honda had proved that finance and resources count as much in endurance racing as in Grand Prix events, though Yamaha and Suzuki, the two factories who could make Honda fight harder for their endurance titles, had so far turned away from a showdown with their famous contemporary. The 1980s, of course, could change all that. With the promotion of the FIM Coupe d'Endurance to world status there is greater incentive for all the major factories to take a more positive interest in marathon racing than ever before and battles reminiscent of the Grand Prix series of the 1960s may well be the result.

As a world championship series, the FIM endurance events are not restricted, an earlier move to limit them to Formula 1 machines being defeated at the FIM Congress in 1979. The rules for the European championship were retained allowing Formula 750 machines to take part. Indeed, any machine up to 1000 cc can be raced in the series.

Until 1955 one rider only was permitted in the Bol d'Or. But machines weren't as fast then and with increased speed came increased dangers. That is why two riders now work as a team in endurance racing, crewing one machine, though each rider scores individual points. This is necessary in case some partnerships break up during the season, because of injury perhaps or for some other reason.

Because of the mechanical demands required in endurance racing, it's not entirely surprising that the four-stroke machines have dominated, in recent years particularly the remarkable RCB Honda. It was this machine on which Leon and Chemarin gained much of their success, though the two-stroke Yamaha OW31 must have made Honda think seriously, perhaps for the first time, about a two-stroke challenge. Two of these virtually standard machines finished second and fourth at Barcelona in 1979 showing that the two-stroke was capable of being run competitively for 24 hours.

Endurance racing has always been valuable to manufacturers as an effective testing ground for new ideas and this obviously brings spin-off benefits for the ordinary motorcyclist. Progress has resulted from the careful development of hybrid machines specially developed for endurance racing, both in the frame and the engine unit. The successful RCB Hondas formed the basis of the over-the-counter CB900 FZ and the fuel-injection Hondas raced as prototypes in 1979 will undoubtedly point the way to fuel injection on standard production bikes. Endurance racing has also played an important part in bringing improved performance and reliability to domestic bikes.

The greatest enthusiasm for endurance racing is in France and they have produced the most successful long-distance racers. In the final European championship in 1979, for instance, before the series received upgrading to world status, Frenchmen finished in the top five places, with Chemarin and Leon tying for the premier position with 49 points each.

All the major long-distance races were retained for the first World Endurance Championship in 1980, plus an additional round in Japan. The nine-round series comprised: Assen, Holland (six hours); Nürburgring, West Germany (eight hours); Osterreichring, Austria (1000 km); Barcelona, Spain (24 hours); Suzuka, Japan (8 hours); Misano, Italy (1000 km); Spa, Belgium (24 hours); Paul Ricard, France (Bol d'Or, 24 hours); and Brands Hatch, England (1000 km).

Chapter 14

Motorcycling in the USA

The impressive sweep of America's famous Daytona speed bowl in Florida, home of the historic Daytona 200 *(All Sport)*

Motorcycling in the United States owes a great deal to Sylvester Howard Roper of Roxbury, Massachusetts. This inventive American is generally reckoned to have brought out a workable steam motorcycle in the 1860s and was active in the promotion of his product at fairground demonstrations and circuses. By 1894 petroleum bicycles were being perfected, and the following year the first motor race in the United States attracted an entry of about 100 'motorcycles' (a loose term for all motorised vehicles at the time), though only six actually competed.

Although America's conversion to the motorcycle was sluggish, by the turn of the century what amounted to the country's first production motorcycle appeared, and in 1901 a 1¾ hp single-cylinder engine built by a Swedish immigrant, Carl

Hedstrom, was installed in an Indian bicycle frame belonging to the manufacturer George Hendee. That same year William Harley and Arthur Davidson came together to begin work on their first motorcycle as the American motorcycle industry gained ground rapidly.

In 1901 only three Indian machines were sold. Almost 150 were sold the very next year and the company couldn't keep pace with the demand. As many as a dozen different makes entered the market in the next few years, the first Harley-Davidson appearing in 1903. Working from a small wooden shed, eight Harley-Davidsons were

The wide open spaces of the famous Daytona race circuit in Florida, USA. First lap of the famous 200-mile race as the pack sweeps past the grandstand (*J.R.W. Associates*)

produced in 1904, almost six times that number in 1908. Harley-Davidson and Indian were the survivors until Indian, too, ceased production after the Second World War, leaving Harley-Davidson, the only major American manufacturer.

The American Indians triumphed sensationally in the Isle of Man TTs in 1911 and by 1912 the American motorcycle industry was reaching a

peak. Their models had developed along the lines of large size and impressive power and the big twin-cylinder models found a natural home in the sweeping expanse of the American terrain. Indian and Harley-Davidson machines led the world, admired and eagerly sought in Europe. Indians gained a reputation for performance, Harleys for more plodding power and reliability. Both employed the 45° V-twin engine with pushrod-operated overhead inlet valve and side exhausts, at around 750 to 1000 cc. Braking was excellent and

American Cal Rayborn, killed racing in 1973, was skilled on the dirt tracks which makes up so much of American championship racing (*Harley Davidson*)

An early Harley-Davidson dealership at San Jose, California, with co-founder of the famous firm, Arthur Davidson, seen third from left (*AMF Incorporated*)

power exceptional. There must have been about two dozen different American makes at this time.

In features like lighting American models were well advanced on European bikes and the Hendee Special Indian twin incorporated an electric starter operated through a chain-driven motor-generator and two six-volt batteries. When America entered the war in 1917 racing had taken a firm hold with racing versions of Harley-Davidson, Indian and Excelsior twins contesting an action-packed and crowded programme on mainly short tracks.

After the war, while the European industry struggled to revive itself, in America the battle had already been lost. Cars had become so cheap, due to the introduction of Henry Ford's famous Model T, that the motorcycle industry took a body-blow, with virtually only Harley-Davidson, Henderson and Indian remaining.

The Depression struck another serious blow to the American motorcycle industry which was left to depend largely on export trade for its survival. As the financial chaos on Wall Street brought hunger marches and lengthening dole queues to Europe, even this lifeline for the industry collapsed – less than one-third of the number of American motorcycles exported in 1920 being sent abroad in 1930. A year later Henderson disappeared as the Excelsior factory discontinued the manufacture of motorcycles and although the Hendee manufacturing company weathered the depression, their best days were over. In its latter years few designs of note emerged and the last true Indian machine appeared in 1953, leaving Harley-Davidson the sole American motorcycle company.

The Second World War was timely, for between 1942 and 1946 some 90 000 Harley-Davidson machines were built for American army use, a production boost for the flagging fortunes of the American industry. But an in-bred reluctance to change forced Harley-Davidson into a defensive role. In racing an amendment to AMA rules gave them the advantage for a few more years, then came an amalgamation with the Italian Aermacchi concern, Aeronautica Macchi, enabling them to benefit from a move into lighter machinery, but in the end survival came only after the company, held all this time by the original families 'went public' and was taken over in 1969 by AFM, the American Machine and Foundry Group.

The new boom in motorcycles in America in the 1970s brought better times. Harley-Davidson continued to dominate most national sporting events and their bulky and in some ways incongruous (by modern European and Japanese standards) big twins enjoyed a steady demand among American motorcyclists.

Until the 1970s motorcycle racing in the United States was totally separate from anything that went on in Europe. This split had occurred some 50 years before when the American motorcycling governing body fell out with the FIM on a basic approach to competition – the Americans standing firm on their belief in restricting machines used in competition to basically sports machines as opposed to racing 'specials'. In any event, until the 1960s there was hardly any road racing of a European kind in America, the sport there having developed along totally different lines. Their championship series tested all-round ability and riders were required to show their talent on the loose surfaced, mile and half-mile dirt tracks, in road racing, American style TT (somewhere between motocross and dirt-track racing) and events run on short-graded courses which included one motocross-type jump. The American approach also differed on financial grounds – championship points being decided in direct proportion to the prize money offered. This ensured good payments for riders, the attendance of the biggest stars at the most important events, and attendant prestige to the races which, in money terms, were the most important.

This was in contrast to the European approach through the FIM, the latter standing aside from finance to let organisers and riders argue between themselves over money. Another difference was in capacity classes. In Europe, races were split into a number of classes, but in the 1930s the Americans agreed that overhead valve and single overhead camshaft engines up to 500 cc should race alongside the 750 cc side-valve V-twins then the mainstay of the two American racing factories, Harley-Davidson and Indian. Thus only a single big machine class existed and not until the 1960s, when lightweights gained in popularity, was a 250 cc category added.

Despite a number of frail attempts to bring the two ruling bodies together and place racing on a more realistic world footing, nothing seriously was done until the late 1960s. The solution was the readmission of the AMA to the FIM and, coincidentally, the former's decision to lift the capacity limit for the American big bike class to 750 cc for all types of engines.

For the first time in 20 years European riders could ride in America without fear of losing their FIM licence and the moves paved the way for the American aces to ride in European events. It was to the advantage of everyone and at the famous Daytona race circuit in Florida, in 1970, European road racers met the Americans on level terms for the first time. With the vast American market open to them, Daytona became a virtual showcase

for the manufacturers, and the works teams, which had disappeared from Europe after the high-investment days of the mid-1960s, were back in force.

The momentous Daytona 200 prestige race of 1970 was supported by Yamaha, Honda, Harley-Davidson, Suzuki, Triumph and BSA. It was an exciting time as American topliners like Dave Aldana, Gene Romero, Gary Nixon and Dick Mann faced Britain's Mike Hailwood and Percy Tait. On the only Honda machine to last the race, the event was won by Dick Mann, though second place rider Gene Romero went on during 1970 to take the AMA championship for Triumph. Among European based riders who were the first to be attracted to race for American-based teams were the Australian Kel Carruthers, who was 250 cc world champion in 1969, and Paul Smart, after Triumph closed down their racing department. Carruthers, a former Australian champion, became the first rider to make his name on three continents and after he retired from racing became manager of Yamaha's international race team. Smart was offered rides on Kawasaki machinery as a member of the factory-backed Team Hansen. His most notable success in the United States was in 1972 when he won at Ontario, California, in what at the time was the richest two-wheel event in the world. Smart was the first British rider to hold an American racing contract.

The traffic was not all one way. Europe benefited too. When a common set of regulations drawn up by the A-CU and the AMA for the big machines was quickly adopted by the FIM, the door was open for American riders to try their skills on British and Continental circuits as Formula 750 cc racing gained ground.

Transatlantic racing received a further shot-in-the-arm in 1971 with the first of the Anglo-American Match Race series. A team of American riders came to Britain to contest a team of British riders in a three-day series of events held over the Easter weekend at popular Brands Hatch, Mallory Park and Oulton Park. The first year the series was sponsored by BSA–Triumph and restricted to their works riders, five from each country. In 1971 these restrictions were lifted and Cal Rayborn, less than two years later to die while racing in New Zealand, caused a sensation by winning three of the six races on his Harley-Davidson, though Britain won the series for the second year running.

Left: Motocross has made a big impact in the United States (*All Sport/Don Morley*)

These transatlantic team events were soon to attract enormous interest, being held annually in Britain.

Dick Mann, Gary Nixon, Gene Romero, Kenny Roberts, Yvon Duhamel, Art Baumann, Dave Aldana, Pat Hennen, Steve Baker, Randy Cleek and Ron Pierce were among the North American stars to race in Europe.

While the Americans seemed to relish road racing, European style, back home the key to racing success continued to be their Grand National Championship in which riders race in a punishing programme of more than 20 varied events on different types of machines. It is a severe test of a rider's ability and all round skill. In the late 1940s and throughout the 1950s, Harley-Davidson machines dominated the championship, but in 1962 Dick Mann made a breakthrough by becoming Grand National Champion on a BSA machine. He repeated his success, again on BSA, in 1971, in the meantime Gary Nixon bringing similar honours to Triumph, in 1967 and 1968. Kenny Roberts won for Yamaha in 1973, the first time the championship had been taken on a Japanese machine, and repeated his success in 1974. From 1950 to 1970 inclusive, Harley-Davidson machines triumphed 14 times. Carroll Resweber (Harley-Davidson) is the only rider to become Grand National Champion four times in succession (1958 to 1961). In 1976 Jay Springsteen was only nineteen when he won the championship,

Highway cops? They look the part but these riders are simply enthusiastic members of an American motorcycle club! (*Mick Woollett*)

A typical American scene with the inevitable parked Harleys by the kerbside (*Mick Woollett*)

to become the youngest winner ever. He won it again in 1977 and 1978, to bring Harley-Davidson right back in the picture.

In America Junior riders graduate to Expert status and thus ranked a rider qualifies to ride in the national races. First, one-lap times and, then, heats and semi-final events are used to decide the race line-up. A sliding scale of points similar to the FIM world championships gives winners 20 points, runners up 16, 13 for a third place, and so on down to one point for the fourteenth position. The series is generally monopolised by Harley-Davidson, though racing is generally exciting and close.

Motorcycles have enormous following in the United States. There is plenty of space for them,

the weather is right in many parts of such a vast country, and the business potential and exploitation has not been lost on the major manufacturers, who now tailor-make many new models largely to the North American market.

Cross-country riding, enduro racing, hill climbs, road riding and racing, trials, customised bikes, drag racing, world record attempts, stunt riding – all forms of motorbike activity find a natural home in America including motocross which shot to popularity in the 1970s after the American Motorcycle Association sanctioned its first professional motocross event at the beginning of the decade. By 1975 the premier Trans-AM series was providing as much as £70 000 (161 000 dollars) in prize money.

The Americans enjoy large-capacity machines which fit in well with their emphasis on active fun and leisure and which are designed for trouble-free, comfortable cruising on their country's long straight freeways.

Chapter 15

The Glory Riders

Mike Hailwood

Of all the racers, from all the years of racing, Mike Hailwood rises from the inevitable controversies and criticisms of his times to take his place as arguably the most popular and respected motorcycle racer of all.

He was the golden boy of motorcycle racing. His natural talent blossomed to fulfilment during the 'Swinging Sixties' and he epitomised the age – jet-setting across Europe as a member of the glamorous, highly-paid continental circus.

His rich father made the early going easier. There were no worries about money. Hailwood senior looked after the organisation and the arrangements. Mike was left to concentrate on riding. That is just what he did. He was born in 1940, and at the age of seventeen made his racing debut, in the summer of 1957 on a 125 cc MV. Hailwood's instant success made the headlines. In 1958, in his first full season of riding in Britain, he won three out of the four newly instituted A-CU solo road-racing stars and crossed the line first in almost 60 races at circuits all over Britain. He created 38 new race or lap records.

In 1959 he did even better! He won all four solo A-CU road-racing stars and was first in more than 60 per cent of the races in which he competed, though he was still only nineteen years old!

At 20 he became the youngest-ever works rider and in the 125 cc Ulster Grand Prix secured his first classic victory. Only mechanical failure robbed him of the 250 cc TT.

He entered the world championship charts in 1959 with a third position on a Ducati in the 125 cc class. In 1961, now Honda mounted, he became 250 cc world champion. He was second in the 500 cc class. In 1962, 1963 and 1964 he won the 500 cc world championship with maximum points for MV. It was a phenomenal achievement. In 1962 and 1963 he was also runner-up in the 350 cc category.

Hailwood's glittering career is so crammed full of wins, records and distinctions of one sort or another that a listing becomes tedious and does nothing to justify his domination of international motorcycle racing during probably its most vibrant, star-studded age. He was a superstar – and shone the brightest of them all.

Not that, at the time, he was everyone's favourite. In his early career especially, his position

Mike Hailwood (Mick Woollett)

attracted resentment from less fortunate riders. His father's bank balance set Mike up as an obvious target. Hadn't his father bought him the best bikes? Hadn't he been packed off to South Africa to gain priceless racing experience? Hadn't old man Hailwood formed Ecurie Sportive, a slick, administrative support and tactical organisation, to back his boy?

It's true that Hailwood set out with a head start, but all the money in the world won't win you a world championship. At the peak of his career, 'Mike the Bike' did it six times in four years; and that takes extraordinary talent even if you have a millionaire father and the best bikes in the business. Soon he was the most successful rider in the history of motorcycle racing.

He competed in his first TTs in 1958: 3rd (Lightweight 250) on an NSU; 7th in the Lightweight (125) on a Paton; 12th in the Junior and 13th in the Senior. Hailwood's TT breakthrough came in 1961. His brilliant riding dominated the

Above: Mike the Bike – as irrepressible as ever during his come-back rides of 1978 *(All Sport/Don Morley)*

Above: Britain's world sidecar champion in 1949, 1950, 1951 and 1953 Eric Oliver and his passenger Stanley Dibben, in 1953, with the famous Norton/Watsonian combination *(All Sport/Don Morley)*

Above: Old rivals Mike Hailwood (12) and Phil Read in close contention *(All Sport/Don Morley)*

Above: West German sidecar ace Werner Schwarzel and passenger Andreas Huber give a graphic demonstration of sidecar racing technique *(All Sport/Don Morley)*

Below: One-time world champions John Surtees (2) and Phil Read, both on the famous MVs, on the start grid at a special meeting *(All Sport/Don Morley)*

Island and he came home with three TT victories – Senior, Lightweight 250 and Lightweight 125. Between then and the end of 1968, when he retired to go racing cars, he won a TT race nine times to give him a career record of twelve TT victories – more than any other rider.

His first 100 mph TT lap was in 1960, on a single-cylinder Norton, shortly after Derek Minter had claimed the honour of the first 100 mph TT lap on a single-cylinder machine. In 1967 Mike set a new record lap for the TT on a 500 cc Honda-4 at 108·77 mph (175·05 km/h). It wasn't bettered for seven years . . . and then it had to be the powerful 750 cc Kawasaki-3, ridden by Mick Grant, which improved on Hailwood's record.

When the 1975 TTs came round Mike still held three lap records and two race records on the Island, although he had been retired for seven years!

Mike's early interest in motorcycles was not unanticipated by his father, Stan, who relished the idea of a new-generation Hailwood taking up racing. Stan, millionaire former boss of an important motorcycle dealership in Oxford, England, had been active in the 1930s on a 500 cc Cotton-powered sidecar, riding at grass-track events in the South of England.

He later raced cars, including an MG at Brooklands, with distinction. Mike was 14 and attending Pangbourne Naval College, but lived for weekends when he could get home to an old trials James which Stan had bought for him. His enthusiasm for motorbikes was exceptional; his dedication extraordinary.

At 16 Mike left Pangbourne prematurely. He objected to the discipline there and talked his father into believing it was time he began to make his way in the world. There had been a tacit understanding that when the time came Mike should join his father in the motorcycle business and Hailwood junior was set to work, running errands and doing all the odd jobs which nobody else wanted.

Within a year he moved on to Triumph, spending his weekends at scramble and trial meetings. His performances were noticed and at 17 he took part in the Scottish Six-Days Trial on a 200 Triumph supplied by the firm. He was the youngest competitor and was showing up well until ignition problems forced him to retire.

But already he had an eye cocked towards road racing, and soon after he borrowed a 125 cc single overhead camshaft MV from family friend Bill Webster for a race at Oulton Park.

Left on the line, Mike eventually got the machine mobile and worked steadily up the field.

He didn't win, but his style impressed Bill Webster so much that he took Stan Hailwood on one side afterwards and told him: 'He's a future champion'.

On the strength of the assessment, Hailwood senior bought his son a 196 cc MV, which he had bored out to 240 cc, and a 50 cc Itom. Hungry for racing, the young Mike got as many rides as possible, gaining experience and improving his technique, and was rewarded with a number of wins and places. This was 1957, an important year for Mike, for in Northern Ireland for the Cookstown race, he won the 250 cc event and cracked the record wide open.

Later there came an important tie-up with expert tuner Bill Lacey.

Mike's first visits to the Isle of Man in the three years 1958-60 produced little success, but in 1961 he became the first rider in the history of the TT to win three races in one week.

Honda had promised him 125 and 250 machines, but only after final practice was the 125 made available, and then it was a practice machine used by Luigi Taveri. Mike took it easy on the one lap obligatory practice, but was impressed with its performance. The race tactics were to ride it as hard as possible and run whatever risk there might be of it breaking down. Hailwood did just that – and on that first lap smashed the lap record from a standing start. The next lap was even more astonishing. He again set up a new lap record!

In the 250 TT later that day Bob McIntyre, so commanding on the Island circuit, was firm favourite, and the remarkable Scot registered the fastest lap at 99·58 mph (160·23 km/h). Bob, like Hailwood, was riding a Honda-4, but the overheating problems experienced by the machines that year forced McIntyre's retirement, his engine seizing on the final lap to leave Hailwood a clear winner.

So far the Hailwood entourage could be well pleased: two TT wins out of two entered. In the Junior TT of that year, Mike rode an AJS and a hat-trick looked certain as he rode into the final lap two minutes in the lead. Fifteen miles (24 km) from home the AJS broke down and Mike was robbed of his third TT victory in one week.

Hailwood had set his mind on four TT's. That prospect was now dead . . . but if he could win the Senior he would still have done what no other rider had recorded in the history of TT racing: three TT wins in the space of one week.

The opposition was daunting. Gary Hocking, on the powerful MV and in straight competition would be faster than Hailwood on the Norton. McIntyre, on a Norton, was also certain to provide tough competition. Luck was with Hailwood this time. Hocking had trouble with the mighty MV almost from the start so Mike was able to keep well in touch. When the MV finally died, Mike took the lead and was first across the line.

It was a popular win for patriotic folk particularly for it was just ten years since an English rider on an English machine had won the Senior TT, that during the halcyon days of British valour when Geoff Duke rode home first in 1951 to give Norton's their fifth consecutive post-war win.

By now Mike was growing out of the 125 class, both mentally and physically. The natural process of development for many riders is to move up the classes; and anyway Mike, at 5 ft 10 in (1·8 m) and weighing around 11 stone (70 kg), was finding it not at all easy to stay compact on a 125.

In 1961 Hailwood had Honda machines on loan from the Japanese factory, but he did so well with them in Grand Prix events that his victory in Sweden at the end of the season, when Jim Redman came a cropper, brought him his first world title and put Honda's name in the credits in the 250 cc class for the first time.

Mike's success must have embarrassed the official works riders, Tom Phillis and Jim Redman, but his style and winning ways were already being noted in influential circles. Bill Webster, MV's distributor in England, had reported enthusiastically on Mike's ability to MV boss Count Domenico Agusta, who had watched Mike in action. As a result Hailwood joined MV and had his first outings on full works 350 and 500 cc MVs at Monza towards the end of the Grand Prix season. He won the 500 cc event and was second to MV-mounted Gary Hocking in the 350 cc race.

At the end of 1961 Stanley Michael Bailey Hailwood, 21-year-old motorcycle racer, had, in just one season, won three TTs, secured a contract with one of the best racing factories in the world, and won the first of his nine world titles.

Mike celebrated the close season by renting a flat and living up to what he felt his new-found glamour image demanded. There were plenty of parties and the high life was good in the early days of London's 'Swinging Sixties'. Britain was the place to be, particularly if you were a racing star.

The new season brought Hailwood abruptly back to reality. He found the complicated four-cylinder MVs more difficult and temperamental than the straightforward singles he had previously ridden, and it was hard for him to find his form. But in the Isle of Man he managed to win the Junior after a breathtaking duel with MV teammate Gary Hocking.

It was Hailwood's race by seconds, snatched in dramatic style in one of the most sensational dices seen on the Island. Mike was to start ten seconds in front of Hocking and, going flat-out all the time in a race as demanding as the TT, would certainly run the risk of a breakdown. Tactics are important on the Isle of Man, and Hailwood was to let Hocking catch him on the first lap, then sit tight behind him, not attempting to overtake. This would avoid blasting the revs out of the MV. The plan was for Hailwood to make his effort on the fifth lap, coming down the Mountain, where his greater experience on short circuits should enable him to overtake Hocking so that he would be in front for the last lap which he would take flat-out.

If he could make five seconds down to the start line and a further seven seconds on the final lap he would be home and dry on corrected times by two seconds.

The margin was close, but the scheme worked well until Mike's MV developed trouble going up the Mountain. His eight-second lead was cut back to five. Then Gary's MV began misfiring and both riders were struggling with ailing machines. There was only 5·6 seconds in it at the end (on corrected times) but how Mike had travelled: he set up a new lap record of 101·58 mph (163·48 km/h) and a winning race speed of 99·59 mph (160·27 km/h), incredible for a 350 and well in excess of anything before witnessed in the Junior TT.

Hailwood spent three more years with MV and totally dominated the 500 cc championship. The partnership had its turbulent times. Even so, Mike's stature increased enormously during his years with MV. He became a legend long before he retired. All over Europe he won countless races and was by far the biggest name in the business at all the Grand Prix circuits.

In 1965 Hailwood's performance in the Senior TT was so outstanding that it is still considered by many to be his most outstanding ride. Above all his other races, it showed the champion's extraordinary will to win, even in the most extreme circumstances.

On lap three he led the race quite comfortably, accelerating up the hill forming the exit to the bend at Sarah's Cottage at 80 mph (129 km/h) when the machine slid away from him. Recovering instantly from the impact of hitting the road, Mike looked around for the MV and saw it, battered, some yards away. Waving aside the marshals, he hoisted the bike upright, turned it round so that it faced downhill, and pushed it hard until it fired. He U-turned in the road and set off.

It was a brave effort, but when Hailwood steered the machine into the pits the crowd didn't believe he could continue. The MV was badly

Heroes from outer space? The start of the 1977 500 cc Belgian Grand Prix at Francorchamps, the fastest Grand Prix circuit (*All Sport/Don Morley*)

battered: megaphones flattened; gear-lever buckled; on one side there was only part of a footrest; windscreen flapping. It looked a dismal sight, but Mike stayed in the saddle and after ripping away what remained of the windscreen, pushed off again into the race. Travelling at 160 mph (258 km/h), with face exposed, the rain felt like knife points, but he raced on. On lap five the engine faltered and Hailwood rode into the pits with a broken throttle cable. During the remainder of the race the throttle continually stuck and he had to control the bike on corners by the use of the brake only.

It was the slowest Senior TT victory in seven years, but the splendour and magnificence of Hailwood's win was obvious to all who saw it.

In 1965 Count Domenico Agusta wanted Hailwood to remain with MV, but for the new 1966 season Honda were anxious to sign him to give even greater strength to their already formidable team of Jim Redman, Luigi Taveri and Ralph Bryans.

In November, before leaving Tokyo for South Africa with his old rival Jim Redman, Mike signed a Honda contract. The invincible days of Hailwood and MV in the 500 cc class had ended and in 1966 he rode against the famous Italian factory, becoming double world champion for the first time, taking the 250 and 350 cc titles. In the 500 cc class, however, he was beaten into second place by Agostini, riding a three-cylinder MV developed from their 350 cc model. Hailwood found the big capacity Honda disappointing, yet his riding of it was exceptional. He might have won, but team politics got in the way. Redman, team captain and with the end of his racing days in sight, had still to win a 500 cc title and planned to go all out for it himself, happy, in return, to concede the 250 cc and 350 cc world championships to Hailwood.

The early rounds fell into place well, with Redman winning in West Germany and Holland, but in Belgium he crashed in the rain and never raced for Honda again. So Hailwood was left to take up the challenge without a point to his name at that stage and already half the rounds raced. It was too much – even for Hailwood.

After a disappointing start to 1967, on the Isle of Man Hailwood showed his most devastating form. He won the Senior, Junior and Lightweight 250 cc events, and distinguished these Diamond Jubilee TTs with some of his most scintillating riding, shattering race and lap records three times in a week.

In the six-lap Senior, Hailwood wrestled with a roaring, bucking Honda in one of the toughest classic events he had ever raced, his final victory

giving him his twelfth TT win. In the Lightweight TT earlier in the week he equalled the immortal Stanley Woods' record of ten TT victories. His Junior win took him beyond that and his Senior victory showed what a commanding rider he was.

Agostini on the MV was Hailwood's constant worry in the Senior. The talented Italian, on his 25th birthday, started 30 seconds behind Hailwood and for almost five laps celebrated by keeping ahead on time. On lap 3 Mike hoisted the lap record to a staggering 108·77 mph (175·05 km/h) and was only a second behind at the end of the third lap. But at the end of the fourth lap Agostini was still ahead. On lap 5 Hailwood's pit signals showed him 11 seconds down on Agostini. Mike blasted the Honda hard and at Ballacraine had slashed Ago's lead to 9 seconds. Soon it was down to seven and at Ballaugh Agostini was only 2 seconds ahead. At Ramsey Hailwood held the lead . . . by just one second.

What a battle. At the Bungalow, Agostini had powered his MV into the lead once more and it was still very much an open race. The tension in the Grandstand as Hailwood blasted through to start his sixth and final lap was heightened by the surprise non-arrival of Agostini. As the seconds ticked away the anxiety mounted. Then the news came through that Agostini's machine had broken down at Windy Corner and he was coasting home.

In the Belgian Grand Prix, on the fastest circuit in the world championship calendar, the Honda's poor handling forced Hailwood to lose ground round the ultra-fast curves at Francorchamps and he was defeated. But in Czechoslovakia Mike powered his way back into the reckoning. Around the tricky 8·66 mile (13·94 km) Brno circuit, he set a new lap record of 103·77 mph (167·00 km/h), and led Agostini home by almost 20 seconds to bring him within six points of Agostini in the world championship race, with four races to go. It was a good meeting for Mike, who made sure of the 1967 350 cc world championship for the second time running.

In the 250 cc world championship, a season-long battle with Yamaha saw Hailwood and Phil Read at the end tied with 50 points each. Hailwood took the title by virtue of his five wins to Read's four and so, for the second year running, made sure of the 250 cc/350 cc double world championship.

Mike's challenge in the 500 cc title race received a body-blow in a race which many believe should not have taken place. A cloudburst just before the start of the Finnish Grand Prix in August saturated the track and Mike moved off to a slow start half-way down the field. Agostini was soon well placed with a 22-second lead. Mike took up the challenge and on lap 4 had overtaken John Hartle to move into second place behind Agostini.

During a torrential downpour, with Hailwood touching 70 mph (113 km/h) and well banked over to take a corner, the front wheel of the big Honda-four hit a puddle, aquaplaned, and hurtled out of control off the famous Imatra circuit. The engine was wrecked and Hailwood miraculously escaped unhurt, though he missed several trees only by inches.

At the end of the season, with all Grands Prix run, Hailwood and Agostini each had 46 points. Moreover, each had five wins to his credit. The championship had to be decided on the number of second places scored by each rider and as Agostini had been runner-up on three occasions and Hailwood twice, the Italian retained the 500 cc world title. It was the slimmest of margins and in spite of an unruly Honda machine, Hailwood had battled magnificently in his determination to give Honda the 500 cc championship.

Soon after Honda retired from racing Hailwood quit in favour of cars, and the greatest career in motorcycle racing ended.

Although Mike Hailwood will always be securely linked with the golden age of Grand Prix riding in the 1960s, he was active in other forms of racing and his capture of the one-hour record at Daytona in 1964 is still talked about whenever racing enthusiasts forgather.

Bob McIntyre had travelled at 141 mph (227 km/h) at Monza in 1957 to secure the record and Hailwood, who had much respect for the resolute Scot, would have been content to let the record stand for all time as a permanent tribute to such a fine rider, who was killed while riding an experimental Norton at Oulton Park in 1962.

But as Stan Hailwood remarked at the time: 'We knew that one day it would be broken and had already heard rumours of an attempt by someone else'.

Mike was at Daytona anyway, preparing for the United States Grand Prix, and the 'ifs-and-buts' about whether he should go for the one-hour record centred mainly on the need to attempt the record on the same day.

As it happened, Hailwood accepted the challenge with his customary ease. He captured the record before breakfast, and went on to win the Grand Prix in the afternoon!

Before the Hailwood entourage left England, Dunlop competition manager Dickie Davies had expressed doubts about the wisdom of such an attempt, emphasising the need for special track tyres (which would take weeks to make) and advising strongly against the use of ordinary road tyres for such an arduous task under the Florida sun.

Yet the opportunity seemed too good to miss. Mike knew he was well within reach of the record, having a year before lapped a Norton at Daytona at 139.6 mph (224.8 km/h).

When Count Agusta refused permission that seemed to be the end of the idea, but the Daytona authorities – as keen as Hailwood to see the record set on their circuit because of the prestige – sent a cable to Italy asking the MV boss to reconsider. Whether permission was ever received seems open to doubt.

But as dawn broke, old-man Hailwood made up his mind. 'I decided to take the chance and let Mike make the attempt', he said later. He had already convinced himself that it would be idiotic for Mike to use the race machine. The attempt would have to be made with the practice bike, whose tyres had already clocked 100 miles (161 km).

As Mike slept on, Hailwood senior roused the MV mechanic, then went to enlist the help of sprint expert and British racing journalist Charlie Rous. With enthusiasm, the tyres were changed, the fairing refitted and generally, and with great haste, the MV was prepared. At 9.00 a.m. Charlie Rous informed the FIM officials and timekeepers. Only then was Mike telephoned and told the record attempt was on and to get down to the track right away.

Within an incredibly short time all was set. It was to be a standing start, but with the engine running. Mike was ready. With press, radio and television present, Major David Goode of the FIM lowered the Union Jack and Hailwood was away.

On the first lap, from a standing start, Mike could only make 136.5 mph (219.8 km/h) and it was clear that he would have to do some real travelling to bring the record in sight. The aim was 145 mph (233 km/h). After fifteen minutes Mike had pulled up the average to 141 mph (227 km/h), lapping consistently at 146.5 mph (235.9 km/h). But with half the time gone, the average was still falling short at 142.9 mph (230.1 km/h).

Frantic signals from the pit urged Hailwood to do even better and with fifteen minutes only to go, he had taken the average to 145.2 mph (233.8 km/h), enough to give him the record.

The object now was simply to maintain that speed, but it was obvious that he was beginning to drop a second or two on each lap. But then the hour was up, the attempt was over and Mike claimed a new record at 144.8 mph (233.1 km/h).

That same afternoon, Hailwood was in the saddle again racing in the United States Grand

The cornering technique of a modern road racer. The Dutchman Wil
Hartog in action (All Sport/Don Morley)

Prix and won the 500 cc event with new lap and
race records.

There is no denying that Mike Hailwood was a
champion of champions. It may be argued that
racing had seen riders of greater courage, more
instinctive skill, greater flamboyance and some
who would be prepared to ride nearer to the limits.
But while a rider might well have had one or even
two of these characteristics in greater abundance,
it would have been hard to find a rider capable of
producing a more all-round performance than
Hailwood.

This quality, combined with consistency, good
machinery and the right circumstances, made him
perhaps the greatest rider of all time.

In the last three years of his motorcycle racing
career – the third year as a private rider after
Honda had largely lost interest – Hailwood added

five TT wins and four world championships to his
already formidable total, an incredible performance in view of the Honda 500 cc-four's atrocious
handling.

Hailwood's quiet sense of humour is one aspect
of his character which many people seem to
overlook. Though tagged at one time with the
playboy image, he rode seriously and diligently,
but his off-track antics added colour and life to a
sport which, before Hailwood, was badly in need
of both. His flower-powered moustache, his
Indian-brave head-dress, and the post-race party
pranks which became part of the folklore of the
continental circus during the 1960s, epitomised the
times and were natural antidotes to the misery and
discomforts of riding in the wet, the crippling
fatigue of racing under a sweltering sun, the
tensions of riding for the major factories who

In the saddle, but only just, is South African Kork Ballington, in Kawasaki green. Kork was 250/350 cc double world champion in 1978/79 (All Sport/Don Morley)

demanded results, and the obvious risks as you raced into every corner.

When Mike the Bike called it a day at the end of 1968 his impressive list of achievements included nine world championships. There were countless other victories and race and lap records on practically every major motorcycle circuit in the world; and all in less than ten years of racing.

Mike Hailwood was the first of a completely new type of racing record breaker. Earlier champions had been known almost as much for their ability as mechanics as for their skill in the saddle and when not winning races could often be found in the paddock, in overalls, tinkering with an engine or poking about in a pool of oil.

Hailwood changed all that. Even before he joined a factory team and was not required to look after his own machines, he showed scarce inclina-

tion to get close to the grimy, greasy workings of his machines. He preferred to concentrate on riding, leaving technical labours to those who knew more about them.

This was strange and alien to the character of the sport at the time and many enthusiasts found it hard to accept. They didn't much like the way he refused to become too closely involved; quietly objected to the way he would arrive, not too long before a race, in his gleaming expensive sports car.

Yet it was largely Hailwood's attitude which showed how the sport could climb out of its 'cloth-cap' image on to a higher, more sophisticated plane: and for this too, motorcycle racing owes much to Mike Hailwood.

Those who never saw Hailwood ride Honda machinery cannot begin to appreciate the strength, skill and courage behind his successes. Many of his earlier victories were against faster Yamahas and in the 500 cc class he fought a perpetual battle, not only against Agostini on the fast and comparatively docile MV, but against the often appalling handling of the big Honda.

His results were impressive, but they don't begin to tell the whole story.

Hailwood never achieved a similar measure of success racing cars. 'When Honda pulled out I'd done just about all there was to do. But my bike career was happier and more remunerative', he once told a reporter.

And when he came out of retirement for his token and emotion-packed 'comeback' rides on the Isle of Man in 1978 and 1979, he proved the Hailwood magic was as strong as ever. He drew huge crowds and his smooth riding brought him success in the Formula 1 race in 1978 on an 860 cc Ducati and, also appropriately, in the Senior TT of 1979 on a 500 cc Suzuki. He underwrote his premier position as a TT rider in that victory in 1979 – it was his fourteenth win on the Isle of Man.

Giacomo Agostini

The most successful Grand Prix road racer of all time reached the peak of his career in the late 1960s and early 1970s. It takes a lot to win a world championship just once. The remarkable Italian, Giacomo Agostini, achieved that distinction 15 times, and in ten years of incredibly successful racing secured both 350 cc and 500 cc world titles five years running, 1968-72.

In the 'swinging sixties', when top-flight road racing was dominated by British and British Commonwealth riders, Agostini alone kept the Italian flag flying. He was their national hero and an international celebrity. His wholesome good looks, flashing smile and attractive Latin temperament, combined with his circuit brilliance to make him big box-office. He was drawn into films, paid to endorse products and welcomed into the world of modelling. Along with contemporaries Mike Hailwood, Bill Ivy and Phil Read – and later, Barry Sheene and Kenny Roberts – he was one of only a few riders ever to make an impact on the world outside motorcycling.

He won additional acclaim in Italy because almost all his success came while riding the home-produced MV Agusta machines, developed and tuned in the famous race shop in Verghera, just outside Milan. The exception was in 1975 when, after rejecting the plainly ageing and uncompetitive four-stroke MVs, he switched to two-stroke machinery for the first time in his professional career to prove his versatility and machine mastery by gaining the 500 cc world title on the ultra-fast Yamaha.

Agostini was born in Lovere, near Bergamo, Northern Italy, in 1943 and gained his early experience in hill-climb events and in Italian road races on a 175 cc Morini. In 1963, on a borrowed Morini, he showed so much promise that he became the Italian factory's number one rider for the following season. He beat the established Tarquinio Provini to take the Italian Championship that year and for 1965 was signed by MV Agusta, despite his lack of experience on anything more than a 250 cc bike, to ride the factory's famous 350 cc and 500 cc thoroughbred machinery. Riding as a junior team mate to Mike Hailwood, Agostini won his first Grand Prix race at the Nürburgring in 1965 in the 350 cc event and that same year scored an impressive double victory in Finland and the 350 cc class of the Italian Grand Prix.

His big chance came when he was promoted to senior rider with MV after Hailwood had left to join Honda. Epic battles between the two former team-mates during 1966 and 1967 ended in cliff-hanger situations with Agostini taking his first world title in 1966 (350 cc class) and the 500 cc world championship in 1967. His inspired record of success had begun and Agostini took the 350 cc title for the next seven years and the 500 cc title six more times in the following eight years. It was Agostini and MV who denied Honda their last ambition in road racing. Having won all other solo classes they signed Hailwood specifically to capture the most prestigious world title of all, the 500 cc class, but even the exceptional talent of the famous British rider was insufficient to make up for the unstableness at speed and the mechanical undependability of the big Honda.

During his years of stardom, Ago, as he affectionately became known, remained a bachelor. His family wealth was substantial and he could easily have followed his parents' wishes and worked in the family transport and road-building business. Instead he chose a career racing motorcycles, his interest in the sport developing after his father had bought him a Vespa scooter. This gave way two years later to a Bianchi moped and at fifteen he was the owner of two machines, a 175 cc Guzzi roadster, and a Parilla, which he used for trials.

Agostini's competence on a racing motorcycle has never been in doubt and in those glorious days of the late 1960s, he was an impressive sight on the flying MV. But was his ability flattered by those 15 world championship wins? It would be a point unworthy of debate had not much of his success unquestionably been gained when factory opposition was minimal. Certainly, for much of his career, because of the superiority of the MVs, he was left to occupy a rather lonely role while others scrapped for second and third places. On the other hand, it cannot be denied that he fought off a formidable challenge from Hailwood and Honda in 1966 and 1967, and again kept MV in front when the sensational Finnish rider, Jarno Saarinen, was creating all kinds of problems for all sorts of machines in the 350 cc class in 1971 and 1972.

After many years of comparative harmony, when he was seldom outspoken and hardly ever controversial, Ago more latterly ran into heavier weather. He fell out with MV once Phil Read started riding for the factory and his repeated public criticism of the Isle of Man Mountain Circuit got him into hot water with the many thousands of supporters who looked upon TT week as the highlight of the road-racing calendar. His pride took a battering when Phil Read, after Agostini had left to go to Yamaha, robbed him of the 500 cc title, ironically on the MV, though he retained the 350 cc title. He failed to win it back the following year, but in 1975 responded strongly to take the title from Read and MV, though the Venezualan sensation Johnny Cecotto beat him to the 350 cc crown.

However, his earlier enchantment with the Isle of Man was never recaptured. He refused to ride there after 1972 when he was visibly distressed after his close friend, Gilberto Parlotti, was killed while racing there. His active campaign against the Mountain Circuit thereafter contributed to the TT Races' ultimate downfall as a Grand Prix venue. He first competed on the Isle of Man in 1965, finishing third in the Junior event and retiring in the Senior. In the next seven years he won ten TTs. In his swan-song in 1972 he was brilliant, winning in both the Senior and Junior events. His record on the Isle of Man includes four Senior/Junior double victories.

Agostini's riding style was conventional and although he won so often he was a relatively safe rider. In his peak years the MV Agusta machines he rode so superbly were far enough ahead of the opposition that Agostini spent most of his time on his own, at the head of the race. But his consistent form was another feature of his career and whether you have the best bike or not, it takes much more than average skill to do as he did in 1968 and 1969 when he won every world championship race in the 350 cc and 500 cc classes he competed in – a total number of 35 consecutive Grand Prix races without defeat. He won the fastest world championship race, the Belgian Grand Prix, eight times in succession and for four years running scored 350 cc and 500 cc doubles in East Germany.

Though little more than 5 ft 5 in tall (1·6 m), he could handle the big MV with disarming ease and in the saddle was consistently conscientious and determined. He was paid handsomely by MV

Giacomo Agostini *(Mick Woollett)*

and most times was content for them to call the tune when it came to sorting out his race programme. In the astringent days of the 1960s and 1970s it was refreshingly different for a top rider to be content with his lot, as was Agostini. But for a bad fall in Italy which gave Phil Read his chance with MV, and an unusual spell when Ago went off song, he might well have ended his racing days with the factory with which he shared all his success.

His switch to Yamaha was a sensation, for never before had he ridden two-stroke machinery in his professional career. Moreover, his victories had, for years, come with comparative ease so that those who were too young to remember his earlier, dashing rides, and others who chose to forget them, gave him few marks for courage, determination and fighting spirit. On the sweeping, banked Daytona circuit in the United States he was to cut that uncharitable image to ribbons.

It was 1974 and by now Agostini was 31. His career had slumped. He had lost the 500 cc world title after being undisputed champion for seven continuous years. He had crashed heavily while testing an MV in Italy but six months before and was still in pain. Opposition at Daytona was formidable and Agostini had to confront it on a two-stroke Yamaha acknowledged to be far less amiable than the familiar four-stroke MV on which he had gained all his success.

The race was critical to Ago's reputation,

though few ticked him off as a favourite. Kenny Roberts, Barry Sheene, Gary Nixon and even the fearless hard-riding French-Canadian superstar, Yvon Duhamel, had all, unlike Agostini, raced at Daytona before. The Italian would also start the race under the pressure of knowing that Yamaha had for the previous two years won at Daytona in this most prestigious and important race, and from a factory point of view he would be under close scrutiny.

In a race cut to only 47 laps in the interests of fuel economy, Agostini gained a new stature, both as a man and a rider. He rose above the self-doubts and pre-race problems and answered those who claimed he was past his peak by thrusting the screaming Yamaha into the lead from the start. He was still there, pursued closely by Yamaha-mounted Hideo Kanaya, at the end of the first 3.84 mile (6.18 km) lap. The rival Suzuki factory were desperately keen to make an impact in this race to enhance and consolidate their standing in big bike motorcycling, but in the early laps they weren't in touch with Agostini. The Italian's worry came from Kanaya, but Agostini kept the lead. On lap 5, in a courageous bid to outride Agostini at the fast infield left-hander, Kanaya crashed and although he was not seriously injured, his machine cartwheeled across the infield in spectacular style.

For a while Agostini was in command, but pushing hard from behind, and closing the gap noticeably, were a group of riders led by Barry Sheene. When Sheene went ahead and both Roberts and Nixon were seen to be outriding Agostini, the race seemed to be falling into a more predictable fashion. Fortunately for the Italian, Sheene's Suzuki developed mechanical problems and, later, a menacing Duhamel had to retire with gearbox trouble. Roberts and Nixon were still ahead of Agostini with less than half the race still to run. Roberts looked a certain winner as he opened the gap between himself and Nixon in second place, but then a broken expansion chamber slowed him down and as Nixon took over the lead Agostini was hanging to him grimly.

Though Agostini technically took the lead later in the race, he rode with the discomforting thought that Nixon had already been into the pits for his second refuel while he had still to make his second pit stop. Nixon looked to have the race secure until his machine began to misfire. There was great excitement as Gary Nixon raced onto the banking in an effort to lap a rider. He lost control of the Suzuki and in the crash the machine was too damaged for the American to continue racing. Agostini now had a clear field and he raced on to win the £6500 prize and the day's glory.

It had been a gruelling race and temperatures had been well into the nineties. So exhausted was Agostini after crossing the finishing line that it was fully 20 minutes before he was sufficiently recovered from the exhaustion to take his place in Victory Lane to receive the Daytona trophy.

For a while Agostini was a hero again. He had shown once more that he could be a winner. But his Italian fans, passionately nationalistic, never really forgave him for leaving the Italian MV Agusta factory for a new contract with Yamaha, even though he won the 350 cc world title in the year of his Daytona success, and recaptured the 500 cc world championship the following year.

In 1976 there was hope of something of the glorious past re-emerging as Giacomo Agostini returned to MV, but sadly the Italian machines had seen little development in recent years and were uncompetitive against the formidable 500 cc Suzukis and the 350 cc Yamahas. After some disappointing rides which, nonetheless, showed snatches of vintage Agostini-MV magic, Agostini switched once again to Yamaha though in the end made little impact in either class, finishing in seventh place with his 500 cc machines and six-teenth on the 350 cc MV. But in a year when many people seemed eager to write him off, Ago showed that occasionally he could still produce the old fire and sparkle. At Assen, in the Dutch TT of 1976, he took the 350 cc MV to its first Grand Prix victory for three years, riding in convincing style, and in the final world championship race of that season, at the Nürburgring, gambled every-thing on the 500 cc MV, disregarding a Suzuki ride, and scored a dramatic win in an inspired display which not only included a new class record for the famous circuit, but was effectively the last international success for both Agostini and MV.

Like other motorcycle racers, Agostini later left bikes for cars, but he wasn't successful.

Carlo Ubbiali

Another Italian eminently successful in motorcycle road racing was Carlo Ubbiali. Had this gifted rider competed in the more glamorous, headline-making 500 cc class, he might easily have become as prominent outside motorcycling as Hailwood or Agostini. But he insisted on riding exclusively 125 cc and 250 cc machinery and did it so well that he became one of the best and most successful racers of lightweights of all time.

At the height of his career no other rider had won more world championships. He was a mag-nificent tactician, with the ability to get that extra performance out of an engine without blowing it up, and gained widespread admiration for his untemperamental approach to racing.

Ubbiali was born in Bergamo, Italy, in 1929 and took up motorcycle racing when he was

Carlo Ubbiali *(Mick Woollett)*

twenty. He was signed as a works rider by Mondial and in 1951 won his first world championship, in the 125 cc class. He joined MV Agusta in 1953, finished third in the 125 cc class that year, second the following year and gained the 125 cc world title on the MV in 1955. For the next five years he was by far the most impressive rider in the lighter classes. In ten years of competition up to 1960 he was 125 cc world champion six times, runner up on three occasions, and secured the 250 cc world title three times. In 1956, 1959 and 1960 he won both 125 cc and 250 cc world championships. He was also a TT winner on seven occasions. Until Mike Hailwood shattered the record, no other rider had won more world championships.

In his early days with MV he had to battle against the superior NSU machines, but with the German factory's retirement from racing, there was nothing to touch the combination of Ubbiali and MV and he won more than 30 classic races at a time when the world championship calendar was less extensive than now.

A small, slight man, handsome with dark wavy hair, Carlo Ubbiali fitted ideally onto the smaller capacity machines. He had a sensitive feel for a race and his guile and craft would often contribute as much as outright speed to his success. Until Agostini came along several years later, Carlo Ubbiali was by far the best post-war road racer to come from Italy. In 1956 when he won his first double world championship, Ubbiali won five of the six events he contested in the 125 cc class and in the 250 cc class that same year, where he again won five of the six world championship rounds, he was, on the 250 cc MV Agusta, the fifth fastest rider of the day in all classes. Three years later, in 1959, Ubbiali scored another impressive world title double, by which time he had won 39 Grand Prix events and secured 15 Italian national championships.

In the late 1950s the MVs ridden by Carlo Ubbiali and his team-mate Tarquinio Provini

were under increasing pressure from the fast and successful East German MZ two-strokes and would soon face a further threat from Honda. Ubbiali rejected attractive offers from the Japanese and in 1960 remained faithful to MV Agusta. Again he achieved the world championship 'double', winning four out of the five rounds in the 125 cc class and four out of the six on the 250 cc machine. After 14 years of highly-successful racing, he retired at the end of 1960 to concentrate on his motorcycle business. John Surtees, who had done for MV in the heavier classes what Ubbiali had accomplished for them on 125 cc and 250 cc machinery, retired at the same time. It was probably not altogether coincidental that MV, facing the prospect of no Surtees or Ubbiali in 1961, withdrew from the world championships at the end of 1960.

Geoffrey Duke

In the early days of the formalised world championships, from 1949 onwards, the ultimate success was to secure that coveted world title. Geoffrey Duke was the greatest racing motorcyclist of his time, becoming the first ever double world champion (in the 350 cc and 500 cc class) in 1951. He went on to collect the 350 cc title the following year and the 500 cc title three more times, in 1953, 1954 and 1955.

In just five seasons of racing in the two most important machine classes, he won 30 Grand Prix events and in the 500 cc world championships in 1954, riding the multi-cylinder Italian Gilera, he ended the season a commanding 20 points ahead of his nearest rival, the Rhodesian Ray Amm, on a Norton.

Between 1950 and 1955 he won the Senior TT three times and the Junior event twice, setting up fastest lap times on six occasions. He was the two-wheel hero of his time and his fast racing and immaculately stylish riding won him acclaim on race circuits all over Europe. His riding was superbly controlled. He was also compact on a machine and was one of racing's great stylists.

Duke's motorcycle career began at 13 when he and a friend had equal shares in a modest machine. Three years later he had an ancient Dot of his own. At eighteen he entered the British army, and later became a despatch rider. The Second World War over, he was demobilised in 1947 and having bought a 350 cc BSA made his debut as a competition rider as a trials expert in the BSA works team, at the same time working for the firm as a tuner of their trials machinery.

Duke's interest focused on road racing and it was to further his ambitions that he moved to the famous Norton factory after the prominent Irish rider of the day, Artie Bell, noticed his potential.

Geoffrey Duke (Associated Press)

But for the war Geoffrey Duke would almost certainly have embarked on his racing career earlier. As it was, he was already 26 in 1948 when he made his road-racing debut. It was on a 350 cc Norton in the Manx Grand Prix, a race he was leading until he retired with a split oil tank. He won the Senior Manx the following year.

Nine months later he made a dramatic debut in the TTs, gaining second place in the Junior race behind Norton team-mate Artie Bell and ahead of Norton-mounted Harold Daniell. In the Senior he beat Bell to take the race at an average of 92·27 mph (148·49 km/h), clocking the fastest lap at 93·33 mph (150·20 km/h).

By this time, Duke had found a regular place in the famous Norton team and went on to contest a full round of Grands Prix. In the 350 cc class, he was second in Belgium and Holland and third in Switzerland. On the 500 cc Norton he finished fourth in Switzerland, won in Ulster and brought the Grand Prix season to a dramatic end by winning both the 500 cc and 350 cc events at Monza in the Italian Grand Prix. In his first year in international competition he secured second place in both world championship classes.

Geoffrey Duke always had a great affection for the Isle of Man and after retiring from racing he settled in Douglas. He was a world champion in an era of motorcycle racing which was far less sophisticated than now. His approach to racing, which in those days was shared by many of his most famous contemporaries, is perhaps best encapsulated in his views about later riders' criticism of the Isle of Man TT Course. He once said: 'What I can't understand about riders these days is that they don't seem to want to know about a challenge any more. To me, the TT course was a challenge; so was the Nürburgring. I got far more satisfaction winning a race on either of those circuits.'

It was on the Isle of Man that Duke enjoyed some of his greatest successes; and some of his most bitter disappointments. In 1952, for example, he looked set to achieve the 350/500 cc 'double' for the second year in succession until he was unable to restart the 500 cc Norton after refuelling. Two years later in 1953, particularly keen to show how well he could do on his debut on the multi-cylinder Gilera, Duke was ill at ease in practice as he struggled to tame the road-holding problems of the four-cylinder Italian machine. Duke admitted afterwards that the first lap of the race was the most hectic 37¾ miles (61 km) he had ever ridden. Two hair-raising moments were the unforgettable slide at the exit from Greeba Castle and the remarkable journey across the road into the left-hand gutter at Alpine House. He caught up with Ray Amm and even moved in front, but lost the lead again as he missed a gear change. With an easy time lead on Amm, Duke was not unduly troubled and as Amm pulled in to refuel, Duke raced on and seemed to have the race comfortably in control. But further on throttle control problems ended his race.

In 1953 it was Duke's experience and expertise which enabled Gilera to break strongly into big-time international racing. After leaving Norton for the famous Italian factory, he worked effectively and closely with development engineer Piero Taruffi, the pair giving the powerful Gilera additional race qualities like superior handling and general ease of riding; and the Duke-Gilera combination was supreme for three years.

The ascendency of Geoffrey Duke coincided with the revitalised world championship structure. In the years leading up to the war a system of European titles was introduced, but this didn't really carry much impact and achieved little public recognition. Nor was it vastly popular with race fans.

But in the years following the war, the personality cult was in its infancy and the new comprehensive arrangement of world championships introduced by the then FICM (now the *FIM – Fédération Internationale Motorcycliste*) captured the imagination.

Motorcycle racing entered a new era, and Geoffrey Duke became its first post-war hero.

British machines, with Norton still supreme, found the spotlight, the famous featherbed model at this time in an advanced stage of development. Duke's artistry and speed soon enabled him to dominate British circuits and Norton signed him in 1950.

In a disappointing first season when the combination was plagued by tyre problems, which robbed Duke of a Norton victory in Belgium and Holland, he nonetheless finished in second place to Umberto Masetti on the Italian Gilera in the 500 cc championship, just one point dividing the two riders. Duke was also second in his bid for the 350 cc world title, the Velocette of Bob Foster winning three Grands Prix to Geoffrey Duke's one, the Italian at Monza.

But in 1951 Duke and Norton were an unbeatable combination in both classes. In the 350 cc class he rode to impressive victories on the Isle of Man, and in Belgium, France, Ulster and Italy, ending the Grand Prix season with 40 points against the second place winner's 19. It was closer in the 500 cc class. He won races on the Isle of Man, in Belgium, Holland and Belfast, but was strongly challenged by Afredo Milani on the Gilera, only four points separating the two riders at the end of the season.

In 1952 Duke continued his brilliant form and again won the 350 cc world title with ease. Victories in the first four Grands Prix in Switzerland, Isle of Man, Holland and Belgium made the remaining rounds of only academic interest and he took the championship by a margin of ten points. In the 500 cc class, he found life tougher as he strove to compete with the fast four-cylinder Gilera of Masetti and the MV of Les Graham, both machines basically much faster than Duke's Norton.

He managed second place in Holland and Belgium, but in July, contesting a minor meeting at Schotten in West Germany, he crashed and was out of action for a year.

It marked the end of an era, for when Geoffrey Duke was ready for action once again, the days of British big bike supremacy were over.

For a while, he tried car racing with an Aston Martin, but a tempting offer from the Gilera factory brought him back into motorcycling in 1953 to begin the second part of his remarkable career. With the handling of the Gilera much improved, not insignificantly through Duke's help, the incredibly fast Italian machine was in a class all of its own in the major 500 cc category, Duke winning in Holland, France, Switzerland and Italy to take his fourth world title by a margin of 14 points.

He secured the title once more in 1954 and yet again in 1955. On the Isle of Man he completely dominated the 1955 event and came very close to establishing that first 100 mph (161 km/h) lap. It was even announced over the loudspeaker system that he had achieved the long-hoped for milestone, but almost immediately came the correction: his time was 99.97 mph (160.89 km/h). It was two more years before the record was broken, but by this time we had seen the best of this outstanding rider. Although he continued to ride for another four seasons, a succession of unfortunate events meant that 1955 was to be the last great season for Geoffrey Duke.

At the Dutch TT of 1955 there was a serious dispute by a number of private riders over start money in the 350 cc event. They boycotted the race, doing only one lap at slow speed before returning to the pits. Duke's support of these private riders, although he was not personally involved, cost him dearly and he was suspended by the FIM until July 1956.

It was then too late for him to go for the championship and although he did win the final Italian Grand Prix at Monza, a talented young man named John Surtees, having shown outstanding promise on Norton machines, had by this time moved to the ultra-fast Italian MV factory and had already won three of the five rounds to become world champion, though an injury at the West German Grand Prix kept him out of the last two rounds.

Undeterred, Duke intended competing again in a full round of world championship events in 1957, but his career was effectively ended when he crashed the Gilera at Imola in an early meeting, injuring a shoulder, and he competed in only two of the six classic events. Later that same year came the shock retirement from racing of Gilera, along with Guzzi and Mondial, and the number of available works contracts shrank dramatically.

Duke maintained his interest in racing, however, riding a BMW in 1958 and was Norton mounted again in 1959. In 1960 he tried car racing again, crashed in Sweden the following year, and retired from racing altogether.

His isolated moments of glory during the twilight years were his double 350 cc and 500 cc victories riding Norton at the Swedish Grand Prix in 1958, his third place in the same class at Monza that same year, and the flurry of third places he secured, again on Norton machinery: in Belgium in the 500 cc class; Ulster in both the 350 cc and 500 cc classes; and in the 500 cc at the Italian Grand Prix.

Geoffrey Duke, born 29 March 1923 was 36 when he retired and had dominated Grand Prix glamour races for some five years. He is still generally acknowledged as one of the greatest road racers of all time. Many of his finest triumphs were achieved on the Norton machine against considerable odds, winning with an easy grace and supreme style perhaps unmatched by any other rider. He had an instinctive and rare talent for racing machinery and while with Norton made a significant contribution to the introduction of important modifications and developments generally. Later, with Gilera, his views on the big machine's handling problems were readily acknowledged by the famous factory in their notable successes in 1953, 1954 and 1955.

In fact, such was the esteem and respect Gilera held for Geoffrey Duke (and their other works rider at the time, Reg Armstrong) that they refused to contest the 1955 TT, when both star riders were still under suspension because of their support for the private riders' cause at the Dutch TT.

Duke also had the reputation of being a great sportsman and his passion for motorcycle racing was insatiable. Since retiring he has kept closely in touch with the sport and in 1963 made an exciting move to inject more interest and combat into the top classes of Grand Prix racing, and stop the succession of runaway, monotonous wins by MV against little opposition. He formed his own racing team, called Scuderia Duke, with riders Derek Minter and John Hartle, and later, Phil Read, and although the challenge was unsuccessful, his move for a time brought a special brand of excitement and relevance to the 500 cc class.

John Surtees

In the second half of the 1950s the biggest name in motorcycling was Britain's John Surtees. Son of a racing father, Surtees dominated the prestigious 500 cc class for six years and from 1958, for three years running, captured world titles in both 350 cc and 500 cc classes. His career coincided with the Italian dominance of Grand Prix racing and when he retired at the end of 1960, the Japanese insurgence had already begun.

Surtees holds another important distinction. While many motorcycle racers, both before and after, have tried to carry forward their triumphs into motorcar racing, John Surtees is the only man to become a world champion in both motorcycling and in cars. It was an enormous achievement.

His motorcycle racing career followed a pattern dictated by the changing times in the 1950s, as the British industry declined and the Italian factories emerged as the powerhouses of the day. Thus, Surtees' early rides were spent on Norton machinery and he joined the famous factory team in 1956. His earlier experience had been in grass-track racing, but a win on a 500 cc Vincent Grey Flash gave him enough money to invest in a 500 cc Manx Norton and it was his wins in national events in Britain as a private rider that captured the attention of Norton. On his Norton, and on an NSU machine, he won an astonishing 65 races out of 72 in which he was entered and on Britain's short circuits he became practically unbeatable. The crowds at the famous Brands Hatch circuit adopted him as their uncrowned 'king'.

But in 1955, Norton had little to offer a rider of such outstanding merit. As a factory force in racing, their distinguished reign was sadly almost at an end and when Surtees was offered works rides with the famous MV Agusta factory in Italy he saw it as a great opportunity to further his ambitions. He was always a serious character with a profound dedication to his sport and it is typical of him that he had to visit the MV factory to convince himself that he would be happy riding the Italian machines before he put his signature to the contract. He also 'went foreign' only after confirming with Norton that their racing days were virtually at an end.

John Surtees was an ambitious rider and was determined to become world champion. To achieve that object he had to move to one of the Italian factories and Gilera were also interested in signing him. As it turned out, his move to MV was right for, whereas Gilera and contemporaries Guzzi and Mondial all retired from racing within a couple of years, MV Agusta, inspired by the remarkable Count Domenico Agusta, continued racing. Fatal accidents to Les Graham and Ray Amm, the latter on his debut for the factory, had robbed MV of their main force. Surtees turned out to be an ideal successor.

He was an outstanding engineer and his technical knowledge combined with his racing experience to help MV sort out some of the frame and mechanical problems they were experiencing with their machine. In that first year with MV, John Surtees took full advantage of Geoffrey Duke's suspension because of his support for private riders at the previous year's Dutch TT, and with no Gilera presence to impede him, won the 500 cc class on the Isle of Man and also in Holland and Belgium. He had done enough to win the title before a fall at Solitude in Germany in the fourth round resulted in a fractured arm. In 1957 strong opposition in the form of Guzzi and Gilera in the 350 cc class and Gilera in the 500 cc class was sufficient to keep Surtees, still suffering the effects of his injured arm, and MV, with repeated mechanical failures, out of the running for the championship. But their turn came in 1958. With the departure of Gilera and Guzzi, MV had an almost clear field and the great talent of Surtees was directed into beating previous records, not merely in the winning of races.

He was a superb rider to watch – so immaculate, so measured in performance. In 1958, when his race-winning performance at Monza in the Italian Grand Prix was timed, there was only two tenths of a second between his first and twentieth laps. His shattering performance two years later in winning the 500 cc world championship with victory in all seven rounds was accompanied by new world records at every Grand Prix circuit.

His successes on the Isle of Man were similarly impressive, and it was perhaps only the possibility of a unique distinction there which kept him in motorcycle racing in 1960. His programme of races on first joining MV had been prolific and he had competed in some 70 events during that first season. But Count Agusta's developing interest in only the world championships and Italian national events had reduced Surtees' programme of racing so that in 1959 he competed in only about 20 races. Surtees had won the Senior TT in 1958 and 1959, and if he could win it again in 1960 he would have done what no other rider in history had done – a Senior TT victory three times in succession. There was also the possibility that he might achieve a Senior/Junior 'double' for the third year running.

The 'double' eluded him. He set a new class record at 98·26 mph (158·13 km/h) on the opening lap of the Junior race and looked set for victory with a second lap at 99·20 mph (159·65 km/h), but then mechanical problems on the MV gave the initiative to MV team-mate John Hartle who eventually beat Surtees by 1 min 55·4 sec. In the Senior event Surtees roared round the Mountain Course, his opening lap of 103·03 mph (165·81 km/h) being almost two miles per hour faster than the lap record; and he pushed that new record out of focus with a second lap of 104·08 mph (167·50 km/h). He won the race at a new average of 102·44 mph (164·86 km/h) and became the first rider to win the coveted Isle of Man title three times in a row.

John Surtees left the bike world at the end of 1960 and in 1964 became Formula 1 car racing champion in a Ferrari. In 1969 he formed his own racing team and in the 1970s became a manufacturer of Formula 1 racing cars.

On two wheels he won a total of seven world championships and had nothing really left to prove when he moved to car racing. He was certainly one of the all-time greats of motor cycling. His immaculate style and his serious dedication to his sport won him admirers all over the world and his motorcycle racing days are remembered with respect and a great deal of pleasure. He was not of

John Surtees *(Mick Woollett)*

a temperament to develop a close, informal rapport with the crowd in the way that, for instance, Hailwood did a few years later, but among fellow riders and racing supporters alike, there was no rider who commanded greater respect.

He was one of the youngest champions and had amassed five world titles and six TT wins by the time he was 25. His mechanical skill was well known and one of his major disappointments was that the main opposition disappeared after 1957 with the withdrawal of Gilera and Guzzi. Many of the improvements he had been working on for MV were incorporated in the 1958 MV racers, when he was left to compete largely against the clock.

Two epic rides continue to be remembered from his outstanding career. In 1955 on a Norton, he would almost certainly have snatched victory from the works Guzzis in the Ulster Grand Prix, but for mechanical failure; and at Ulster again, in 1960, his battle with John Hartle was memorable. After losing considerable time with a troublesome MV, he finally got things sorted out and set off in pursuit of Hartle. No one gave him a chance, he was so far behind, but he smashed the lap record time and again in a glorious ride and only just failed to win.

Stanley Woods

Out of half-a-dozen or so riders who dominated racing between the two world wars, the name of Stanley Woods perhaps conjures up most magic. He was an outstanding all-rounder and excelled at speedway, scrambles, trials, grass track and even long-distance record attempts. But it was as a road racer that Stanley Woods captured most public acclaim, becoming a hero in racing's dashing and comparatively uncomplicated days of the 1930s.

Woods was born in Dublin in 1905 and raced in the TTs for the first time in 1922 as a works rider for Cotton in the Junior event. He simply wrote to them explaining how good he was and asked them for a ride. His audacity won the day and Cotton gave him a bike to ride. He was only

seventeen, but was quickly into the news: his engine caught fire! Yet he still managed to finish fifth and went on the following year to win the Junior TT for the Cotton factory.

His racing career spanned almost 20 years and in the nine years from 1930, when he was at his peak, he won approaching 40 international races in Britain and Europe, an impressive record in those days when the racing calendar was far less crowded than it is today. Douglas, Ariel, Royal Enfield, Scott, New Imperial – he rode them all, but it was only after he signed for Norton in 1926 that his career really flourished. His potential had been brought to Norton's attention by a Dublin motorcycle dealer, but the famous factory were by no means anxious to sign him up. They did, however, invite him to join their team on the Isle of Man that year and he repaid them by winning the Senior event with a new record race speed of 67·54 mph (108·70 km/h).

Woods stayed with Norton for eight years and was especially successful for them on the Isle of Man in 1932 and 1933. He scored Senior and Junior TT 'doubles' in both years with fastest laps in the Junior of 1932 and in the Junior and Senior of 1933.

His split with Norton came after the Ulster Grand Prix that year. For some time the famous factory's supremacy meant that their works riders were competing more against one another than against rival factories, and Norton, as other factories have done in similar situations, began dictating which of their riders should win. Woods objected to this policy and had virtually made up his mind to move on as he travelled to Northern Ireland to compete in the Ulster Grand Prix. Norton made it clear they didn't require him to win the 500 cc event there.

He might have defied team orders, but in the event it wasn't necessary. Other Norton works entries retired and the Irish champion went on to win.

But the incident decided Woods on his break with Norton and he signed for the Italian Moto Guzzi factory. In 1935 he brought them particularly sweet success on the Isle of Man. A Guzzi machine had first been raced in the TTs as early as 1926 and what a sensation! Pietro Ghersi finished second in the 250 cc event, but was excluded for using a sparking plug of a different make from that declared at the weigh-in. In 1935 Woods brought the Italian factory the revenge they sought by scoring a remarkable Senior/ Lightweight 'double', setting fastest laps in both races. His outstanding record at this time was three TT doubles in four years and five out of a possible six fastest laps.

Stanley Woods *(Mick Woollett)*

Before his 1935 successes on Guzzi machinery, Woods had ridden a Husqvarna in the Senior of 1934 and after leaving the Italian factory to ride British machinery again in 1936, when he signed for Velocette, he also rode a DKW in the Lightweight race of 1936, but these 'foreign' rides were unsuccessful and he retired on both occasions. By 1936 Velocette had realised their loss of prestige by not keeping pace with 'works' support in classic races and had improved their basically ten-year-old engine by bringing in double overhead camshafts for the first time. It was Stanley Woods who was directly responsible for getting something done about the frame, with his recommendation to reintroduce the rear-sprung design. It was the first ever example of swinging arm rear suspension and although it didn't bring immediate success, Woods' considerable influence and outstanding riding ability paid off in 1938 when he took the Velocette to victory in the Junior event and to second place in the Senior race. Woods established a new Junior TT race record of 84·08 mph (135·31 km/h) and a new race record at 85·30 mph (137·28 km/h). In the Senior event, he missed victory by 15 seconds after an epic battle with Harold Daniell on a Norton.

The career of Stanley Woods ended effectively with the outbreak of war, but he again won the Junior TT for Velocette in 1939 and that year came fourth in the Senior, also on a Velocette.

Mike Hailwood alone has beaten Stanley Woods' record of ten TT wins, which has been equalled by only one other rider, Giacomo Agostini. The chirpy Irishman's jaunty personality and natural ability on a bike made him one of racing's greatest personalities. In 1957 he made a special racing return to the Isle of Man to commemorate the TT Races Golden Jubilee, lapping in practice on a 350 cc Guzzi at more than 82 mph (132 km/h) on his first TT gallop for 18 years. In 1968, when he was 64 years old, he was voted the greatest TT rider of all time by a panel of judges in a special competition.

Kenny Roberts

The road-racing world championships are very much European based and it is only really since about the mid-1970s, and following the settling of differences between the American Motorcycle Association and the FIM, that American riders have been able to interest themselves actively in European competition. The British Transatlantic Trophy Races, a series of team events held over Easter on three British circuits, showed the way in 1971. Pat Hennen advanced the American influence in 1976 when he became the first American to win a world championship round, beating all

Kenny Roberts (B.R. Nicholls)

opposition on his Suzuki 4 to take the 500 cc Finnish Grand Prix

Consolidating American interest in top-flight Grand Prix racing was the success of Californian Kenny Roberts in winning the 500 cc world championship from Barry Sheene in 1978. At home the Americans have to prove themselves in different kinds of events, not just road racing. The country's racing demands exceptional versatility on the part of the riders, making Roberts' world championship successes all that much more outstanding.

In 1978 Kenny Roberts became the first American ever to win a world championship. To prove his triumph was no fluke, he repeated his success in 1979, winning five of the twelve Grands Prix rounds to put a defiant end-of-season 24 points between himself and 500 cc runner up Virginio Ferrari of Italy. Roberts takes a serious view of racing and portrays that kind of cool, almost robot-like detachment characteristic of most American topliners. He is strong, positive, and soon stamped his personality on the European race scene. Yet behind the bold exterior is, to those who know him, a personable young man with a sense of humour. He is articulate and certainly proved he could ride a motorcycle with greater meaning than his contemporaries in 1978 and 1979.

Born in 1951, Kenny Roberts rose sensationally in the United States, becoming American National Champion only four years after entering his first professional race. In 1970 he was AMA Novice champion and a year later collected the Junior championship. His first Grand National Championship was secured in 1973 with a record 2014 points. At 22 he was the youngest rider ever to gain the American championship. Out of 25 starts he finished in the top three 13 times and scored points in all but four of the 25 races. But for mechanical failure it is likely that Roberts would have won his first American national senior title a year earlier, for he led the table for the first half of 1972 and was unfortunate to end the season in fourth position.

He won the American title again in 1974. In a phenomenal series, his victories included the San José mile, the Hinsdale race, the Peoria TT and road races at Atlanta, Monterey and Talladega. In taking the title he became only the second rider in history to win in all forms of American racing – road, mile, half-mile TT and short track.

Roberts raced in Europe for the first time in 1974, getting close to winning the famous Imola meeting at his first attempt. On his 700 cc Yamaha he was a sensation in the Transatlantic Race Series that same year by winning four of his six races. He was included in the team which brought America its first victory in the series in 1975 and led the winning American team in 1977.

On his factory supplied Yamahas Kenny Roberts has made greater impact on European racing than any other American. His off-track comments and campaigns have also made him one of the most controversial and dramatic personalities in motorcycle racing. His European baptism was in F750 racing (he was second to world champion Johnny Cecotto in 1978) and his simple philosophy about the financial side of racing is succinctly crystalised in his comment: 'I came over because the offers I had were too good to turn down'. But almost since the beginning of his Grand Prix racing in 1978 he has been highly critical of the way the FIM organise things and the start money that is paid to riders in Europe.

His forceful campaign to improve the rewards for star riders resulted in something of a showdown with the FIM towards the end of 1979 with the announcement of plans for big-money World Series Racing in 1980. He was also a central figure in the riders' walk-out at the Belgian Grand Prix of 1979 after most of the top riders, Roberts included, had judged the new section of the re-organised Francorchamps circuit unsafe for solo machines.

In the short space of two years, Kenny Roberts moved into European racing and in addition to providing its biggest shake-up in years, calmly overhauled Europe's established stars to take the coveted 500 cc world title two years running – pushing even Barry Sheene into the shadows.

As a rider, Kenny Roberts' approach is as tough and unyielding as are his off-circuit comments. 'Anyone who isn't prepared to scrape his knee on the ground and hang his butt out isn't going to win. It's as simple as that,' he told Chris Carter in an interview for *Motor Cycle Weekly*.

It summarises the kind of typically blunt approach to life and to racing which won Kenny Roberts many friends, some foes, and brought him success at the highest level of international road racing.

Yvon Duhamel

One of the fastest and most exciting of all road racers was the spectacular French Canadian Yvon Duhamel. His abandoned, fearless style earned him the reputation as the wild man of American road racing. He had boundless courage, was brave in the extreme, and often rode too close to the limits for comfort. A colourful and outstanding character, he gained his fame appropriately on the 'performance' motorcycles made by Kawasaki. He crashed often, but his battered body exercised no influence on his mental attitude to riding, and his all-action uncompromising style was a feature of his racing right until his retirement from top-class competition.

Born in Quebec, Canada, in 1941, he was only 18 when he started racing round the half-mile dirt tracks of North America. He appeared at Daytona for the first time in 1966 on a 500 cc BSA and two years later finished eighth in the famous 200-miler and won the 250 cc event. That year he also won the world snowmobile championships.

Duhamel rode for Kawasaki for the first time in 1971 when the factory was desperately trying to get their machines competitive. His fearless racing made those early Kawasakis look better than they were and his instinctive bravery and tenacious attitude captured a lot of attention and created much impact for the 'green meanie' factory during these important early years.

Yvon Duhamel was only 5 ft 1in (1·6 m) tall, but he had the stature of a giant. His 'wild riding' image tended unfairly to obscure his finer talent on a motorcycle, and his sense of balance when he was on top form, and especially through corners, was exceptional. Astutely, he combined motorcycle racing with snowmobile competition to become one

Yvon Duhamel *(Mick Woollett)*

of the highest earning road racers in the business at the peak of his career. From Kawasaki in America his contract was said to be worth around 90 000 dollars even back in the 1960s and at one time it was widely accepted that he was the biggest earner in the business.

It was on North American circuits like Ontario and Talladega that Duhamel established his reputation, rocketing Kawasaki into the forefront of American road racing. He brought them their first victory in an AMA National Championship race and at Talladega bettered more highly-rated teams from BSA and Triumph to win the famous 200-mile race by 78 seconds at a new record average speed of 108·46 mph (174·62 km/h). In numerous other races Duhamel roared to the front of the pack, only to find his machine surrender to the relentless pressure he imposed or to slide from under him as he spurned compromise.

In Britain he appeared at Mallory Park in the Race of the Year and was joint highest scorer, along with Britain's Peter Williams, in the 1973 Transatlantic Road Race Series.

His lucrative contract with Kawasaki's American subsidiary ran out at the end of 1976, by which time the factory had cut back severely on their race programme. The tough road racer, now 37 and battle-scarred, decided to retire. But at 38

he caused a minor sensation with a surprise ride on a Kawasaki in the F 750 world championship round at Mosport Park, Canada. He came third in the first leg, was runner up in the second, and at the same meeting won the 250 cc event.

Angel Nieto

A 50 cc class wasn't introduced into the world championships until 1962 and for the first seven years the Japanese dominated. In 1969 Angel Nieto, riding a Spanish Derbi machine, took the title for the first time and in the next decade the Spanish rider became the key figure in lightweight racing. Born in Madrid in 1947, Nieto first raced when only 13 on a secondhand Derbi and a year later was working in the racing department of the famous Bultaco factory in Barcelona, determined to make motorcycle racing his career. But Bultaco had as many riders as they could handle and with that particular door blocked, Nieto moved to the race department of Derbi, was loaned machines for 1962, and in 1963, when only sixteen, became a works rider. He finished fifth in the 1964 Spanish Grand Prix, was fifth again in the German Grand Prix at the Nürburgring the following year, fifth yet again, this time in France in 1967, and after racing second in Holland and fourth in Belgium that same year, scored his first world championship victory in East Germany at Sachsenring in 1969.

By this time the Japanese had withdrawn from the 50 cc class and Nieto was sufficiently experienced to push through his challenge. A further win in Northern Ireland and second places in Spain, France and Yugoslavia were enough to give him the 50 cc world title for the first time by just one point. In 1970 his five Grand Prix wins from ten races gave him absolute supremacy over his nearest rival, Toersen of Holland on a Jamathi, while good performaces in the 125 cc class, also on a Derbi machine, took him into second place behind world champion Dieter Braun. In a highly competitive and entertaining year for 50 cc racing, the Dutchman Jan de Vries proved just too good in 1971 for Nieto, who finished second, though the Spaniard took the world title in the 125 cc class. But Nieto became double world champion in 1972, capturing the 50 cc and 125 cc world titles.

After that Derbi retired from Grand Prix racing and Nieto was left without a Grand Prix ride, though he continued to race for the factory in Spanish national events, in which Derbi retained an interest. He then moved to Morbidelli, but after two disappointing years when he failed to win a single Grand Prix race, he bought a Van Veen Kreidler used with success by Henk van Kessel and Jan de Vries in 1973 and 1974, and on

Angel Nieto *(Mick Woollett)*

this competitive machine recaptured the 50 cc world title in 1975 by the slimmest of margins.

Nieto had returned to two wheels in 1974, after a largely unsuccessful liaison with motor racing, gaining two Grand Prix wins on a Derbi in the 125 cc class that year. On the Kreidler machine in 1975, Nieto became a convincing 50 cc world champion again after winning six of the eight Grand Prix races. For 1976 and 1977 the Spaniard rode Bultaco machinery, thus resuming a relationship started some 15 years before when he was an apprentice with the famous factory. He was successful both years, adding two more 50 cc world titles to his impressive record.

The firebrand determination of Angel Nieto's character combined with exceptional racing talent on the 'tiddler' machines to make him a supreme world champion in 50 cc racing, but for some time the talented Spaniard's ambition to move up into 125 and even 250 cc racing had been well known. In 1977 he had shown Ricardo Tormo, taken on by Bultaco to understudy the world champion, the way round the Grand Prix circuits, giving him the benefit of his experience. In 1978 Nieto displayed a notable indifference to the retention of his 50 cc title, preferring to concentrate on the 125 cc class. Tormo took the title with ease, while Nieto finished down in eleventh place though in the 125 cc championship he ended the year as runner up to Eugenio Lazzarini.

In 1979 Nieto moved strongly into 125 cc racing to gain his third world title in this class and his ninth world championship overall. Now Minarelli mounted, he showed his total command by winning the first seven rounds, before injury eliminated him from a number of races. He returned with a firm win at Silverstone in the British Grand Prix to take the title with a commanding 120 points, against the 53 scored by his nearest rival, Mauizio Massimiani, of Italy, on a Morbidelli.

There is no doubt that Angel Nieto, without further accomplishments, has done enough to be listed as one of the best-ever riders of 50 cc machinery. He proved that in gaining three world championships in the 125 cc class, he could handle these somewhat more powerful machines too, but the biggest disappointment in a distinguished career has been his failure to become a champion in the heavier machine classes, an ambition almost certainly now to remain unfulfilled. Impetuous in the early part of his career – he has come off as many as five times in a day! – high spirited and perhaps temperamental, he refined his style over the years but never failed to stake everything on winning. Although never receiving the worldwide recognition reserved for champions of the more prestigious heavier machine classes, Angel Nieto was one of the most outstanding riders of the 1970s and in his native Spain became a national hero, being his country's first and most consistent motorcycle world champion.

Klaus Enders

In sidecar competition West German riders have dominated the class for all except a few of the 30-plus years of the world championships. Their reign began in 1954 with their superior, low-torque BMW outfits and West German riders were successful 21 times in the next 23 years.

Most successful of all was Klaus Enders. With his passenger Rolf Engelhardt, this talented driver benefited from the fatal crash of previous world champion Fritz Scheidegger and the retirement of Max Deubel, and with this formidable opposition removed, took the title for the first time in 1967, winning five of the eight sidecar events making up that year's championship. A lean 1968 was fol-

Klaus Enders *(Mick Woollett)*

lowed by further success in 1969 for Enders and Engelhardt, who took the title for a second time with four Grand Prix wins out of a possible seven. After securing the title yet again in 1970, this time with passenger Wolfgang Kallaugh, Klaus Enders decided to retire in favour of four-wheel racing. His car-racing career was short and undistinguished and at 35 he returned to sidecar racing to gain the title for a fourth time in 1972 with Rolf Engelhardt.

Despite strong opposition provided by new four-cylinder Königs, Klaus Enders became the most successful of all sidecar drivers by taking the title once more in 1973, winning all seven races in which he took part. With Rolf Engelhardt once again as passenger, Enders secured the title for the sixth time in 1974. He effectively retired from racing then and left the sport completely two years later.

Eric Oliver

Two other sidecar specialists have taken the world title four times (up to the end of the 1970s) – Britain's Eric Oliver and Germany's Max Deubel. Oliver raced solo machines with success before switching to and specialising in sidecars after the Second World War. Born in Sussex, England, in 1911, Oliver began his competitive career in grass-track events in the early 1930s and after moving into road racing developed a special interest in sidecars in 1936. With passenger Denis Jenkinson, Oliver won the first sidecar world championship in 1949 with wins in Switzerland and Belgium and in 1950, this time with the Italian Lorenzo Dobelli as passenger, he took the title once more, winning all three events and registering 16 victories during the season. Success for the same combi-

nation came again in 1951 and Eric Oliver went on to win one more world title, his fourth in five years, in 1953. By 1954 the BMW outfits were superior to Oliver's previously victorious Norton/Watsonian combination and after fighting valiantly that year he retired from active competition in 1955. The battle in 1954 was not all Germany's way, however. Oliver won the first three rounds, but a broken arm he sustained in a non-championship event gave the BMW combination of Wilhelm Noll and Fritz Cron the opening they were looking for and they made no mistake, the German pair gaining the title by just four points on their superior placings, though the British and German combinations ended the season with three wins each.

Apart from being the first ever world sidecar champion, Eric Oliver is also credited with being the first to race a fully-faired, integrated-chassis three-wheeler with a kneeling riding position. He died in 1980.

Max Deubel

The German sidecar specialist, Deubal holds two particular distinctions in sidecar road-racing. He became only the second rider to win the world championship four times and the only one, up to the early 1980s, to have won his four titles in consecutive years. It was after the crashes in 1961 of Florian Camathias and Helmut Fath at Modena

Max Deubel *(Motor Cycle Weekly)*

Eric Oliver *(Motor Cycle Weekly)*

and Nürburgring respectively, that Max Deubel took up the running. He and passenger Emil Horner formed a talented partnership to win in Germany, the Isle of Man and Holland to take the title for the first time with their sponsored BMW outfit. For the next three years Deubel and Horner dominated the sidecar scene. In 1962 they proved that they could win the championship on merit alone and overhauled their major challengers, Camathias and Burckardt and Scheidegger and Robinson, to win in Spain, France and Germany.

Impressive success was theirs in 1963 and 1964, but in 1965 the Swiss sidecar ace Fritz Scheidegger and his English passenger John Robinson, finally dethroned Deubel and again in 1966 brushed aside the West German's efforts to regain the title and beat Eric Oliver's record of four world titles. At the end of 1966 Max Deubel retired from road racing to concentrate on his career as hotel owner. In a distinguished career Max Deubel rode in the Sidecar TT on the Isle of Man seven times from 1960. He won in 1961, 1964 and 1965, was second on his last appearance in 1966, retired in 1960 and 1962 and finished eighth in 1963.

Patrick Pons

With France active in motorcycle racing from the earliest times it is surprising that the country had to wait until 1979 before producing her first world champion. Patrick Pons, born in 1952 in Paris, son of a wealthy French businessman, brought his country that particular credit by winning the world Formula 750 championship – but he was only just in time. The FIM, having granted the series world status only in 1977, took it away again after 1979.

Pons began motorcycle racing in 1971, his first international appearance being at the French Grand Prix of 1973 at the Paul Ricard circuit when he finished ninth in the 250 cc race. From about the mid-1970s he emerged as a first-class competitor after a disturbing early tendency to fall off – over 50 times in just two seasons! Riding Yamaha machinery, Pons competed in 350 cc, 250 cc and F750 racing in 1976, being placed well down the tables, but in 1977 he rose to equal twelfth with America's Skip Aksland in the first F750 world championship, a fifth at Hockenheim probably being his best performance. Consistent riding the following year with a fourth place in Austria, fifth at Hockenheim and Paul Ricard, and sixth positions at Imola and Assen, bolstered his fine third place behind Kenny Roberts and Johnny Cecotto at Brands Hatch to give him a creditable fifth overall placing at the end of the year.

So his consistent improvement had made him a worthy candidate for top honours in 1979. Less prone to fall off and riding steadily during the year, Pons deserved his triumph. The opening round at Mugello gave no real hint to the season's form, for Pons, hampered like some other riders in choosing tyres unsuitable to conditions in which the second leg was run, finished only fourth, with the Italian Virginio Ferrari overall winner, reigning world F750 champion Cecotto second, and Pons' compatriot Christian Sarron third. In the British round Cecotto advanced his chances of retaining the title by winning both legs and adding a handsome 30 points maximum to put him well into the lead at this early stage. In France for round three, Cecotto was absent because of an injury sustained at the Austrian Grand Prix and Pons' toughest opposition was the blond Australian Kawasaki rider, Gregg Hansford. Pons won the first leg and finished second in the following race to bring him jointly into second place in the championship table with Hansford, though Cecotto still led by a considerable margin.

In the Swiss round, held at Paul Ricard, Pons fell in the first race and was third in the second, but a second place performance overall in Austria enabled him to close the gap on Cecotto and pull himself clear of Hansford. Cecotto, it should be said, had lost the initiative by, first, his injury and then, by a clashing of dates, the Austrian F750 round being held at the time of the Swedish Grand Prix, to which the talented Venezuelan rider was committed.

Patrick Pons *(Motor Cycle Weekly)*

After the Dutch round at Assen, Patrick Pons was sharing the lead with Michel Frutschi. The German round at Hockenheim virtually settled the issue. While both Cecotto and Frutschi faltered badly, substantially by their choice of experimental tyres, Pons romped home first in both legs, his 30 points overall tally now placing him well in the lead. It only required one point from the final round in Yugoslavia to put the issue beyond all doubt, and that the new French champion more than secured by finishing third in each leg, giving him 20 points from the round and a finishing total of 154 against the 132 of runner-up Michel Frutschi.

It was a particularly meritorious performance by Patrick Pons because he had won the championship as a private rider on a Yamaha in the face of hard competition from the official Yamaha riders.

Derek Minter

Short-circuit racing in Britain was particularly competitive in the 1960s and a natural stage in the accepted progression from an undistinguished privateer to what many promising racers hoped would be a lucrative works contract with one of the leading Japanese factories. Hailwood took this route to fame. So did Phil Read, Bill Ivy and others. A rider who rejected this course and preferred to remain substantially a short-circuit specialist throughout his career was Derek Minter. Outspoken, independent, and often too critical for his own good, Minter was undoubtedly the best short-circuit rider of his day and arguably one of the best of all time.

His record in 1962 was outstanding. At his peak then, he rode in five races at Brands Hatch in one day, won five times and created five records.

In 1962 he became British champion for the third time (and was later to win the championship twice more to create a record); won Mallory Park's 1000 guineas race, the richest in Britain; and was voted *Man of the Year*.

It was also in 1962, in the Isle of Man, that he created a sensation by winning the 250 cc TT on a year-old Honda provided by the then British concessionaires, scooping the power of the Honda works team led by Jim Redman.

To his exceptional skill and technique he added an immaculate style which made him a joy to watch. Notoriously a bad starter, he would weave and thread his way through the field, his outstanding ability on the corners more than enough to gain him yards, even against talented opposition. He was a safe rider, intelligently refusing to go beyond the limits, neat and compact. He ridiculed the knee-out technique, which was then gaining

Derek Minter *(B.R. Nicholls)*

ground among the younger riders, as an unnecessary display and a frivolous sop to the crowds.

There was no silver spoon for Derek. Born in 1932, the son of a pit worker in Kent, his first bike was a 350 cc BSA, bought from what he could save from his £1 a week earnings as an electrician's mate, and a supplementary £2 which he could make from evening and weekend apple picking in the lush orchards near his home village, five miles from Canterbury in Kent.

After promising rides in Britain and on the Continent, Minter decided to turn full-time professional. It was an audacious step, for as he left that year to prove himself on the Isle of Man, the only money he possessed was £100 in his post office savings account. He finished fourth in the Senior and ninth in the Junior TTs.

Several years later Minter was one of the most forthright critics of the rewards offered to TT winners and competitors. He claimed it just wasn't worth his while competing and in the years leading to his retirement in 1967, doggedly refused to race there.

On mainland circuits like Brands Hatch, Mallory, Oulton Park, Snetterton and Castle Combe, Derek Minter quickly became supreme. His form at the famous Kent track was devastating and he was the automatic choice as the circuit's uncrowned 'king' after the former hero John Surtees had forsaken bikes in order to race cars.

Minter was a dedicated professional. He would go to endless trouble to learn a circuit, walking round it several times, studying corners, making notes, working out his strategy.

As a motorcycle racer Derek Minter was admired and respected. He attracted a large, dedicated following; but as an individual he was not always the most popular rider in the race. His outspoken comments, individuality, difficulty in submitting to discipline and often uncompromising attitudes, though born largely out of the constant battle for self-survival he was disposed to wage as a freelance fighting for his own opportunities, nonetheless cost him some of the full works contracts which might otherwise have come his way.

But he did have a number of works rides and received factory support for the first time in 1959 when he rode a 125 cc MZ and a 250 cc Morini. In the Dutch TT he led for seven laps on the Morini, gave workmanlike performances in the Belgian and came fourth in both classes at Monza.

It was an appropriate warm-up to a sensational start to 1960 for Minter. Over Easter he entered nine races, won eight and was second once. This was the measure of his mastery of the short circuits and although the remainder of the season was disappointing, he added considerably to his status by becoming the first man to lap the TT course at over 100 mph (161 km/h) on a single-cylinder machine.

Two years later, on a comparatively shabby privately-entered Honda, he outrode the powerful official Honda factory team to take the 250 cc TT title.

It was an outstanding performance for the King of Brands – 'The Mint' as he was now popularly known in racing circles. In a dramatic battle, Minter and Redman exchanged places five times. Bob McIntyre raced into the lead in the early stages, putting himself thirty seconds up on the first lap. When he retired because of mechanical problems Jim Redman, racing as the 250 cc world championship leader at that stage, moved into the lead, though by lap 3 Minter had overtaken him. On the last lap and well in the lead, Derek heard noises from the area of the rear chain; but the machine kept going. When the mechanics stripped it down after the race they found the crankshaft broken in three places.

It was a supreme moment for the Brands Hatch hero, and a popular victory. For Derek, despite being a full-time professional racer, could still be seen most weekends galloping round the home circuits. In contrast many of his contemporaries, having secured lucrative works contracts, now spent most of their time contesting the Grands Prix all over Europe and were seldom seen by the fans who had cheered them to victory earlier.

But Derek, for all his success, was still around to thrill the fans who had made him famous; and for that they loved him.

Back from the glory of his TT victory, the remainder of 1962 was vintage Minter, almost all the way. A double at Castle Combe, in which he broke his own 500 cc class record at 89.99 mph (144.88 km/h), was followed by a remarkable demonstration of riding power at Brands Hatch with five wins in five races and five records broken. In the 250 cc race he smashed Mike Hailwood's lap record by more than 2½ mph (4 km/h) and in the 125 cc event, after struggling to get the Honda to fire, bettered his own race and lap records at 77.71 mph (125.11 km/h) and 80.84 mph (130.15 km/h).

At Oulton Park Minter kept the fans yelling. He took three British road race titles, winning the 250, 350 and 500 cc races.

Most riders are a bit superstitious, Minter no exception. He always rode with a St. Christopher hung round his neck and another one sewn into his leathers.

The great thing about Minter was that throughout his long career he was always master of his machine. Seldom did cc's and precocious handling beat him, even on the Gilera. He rode a variety of machines from the big Norton and Gilera to EMC, AJS, REG, MV, Benelli, Honda, Matchless, Morini, MZ, BSA, Bianchi, Ducati and Cotton. Never did he look out of his element.

Shunned by Honda – he was never forgiven for beating the official entry on the Isle of Man – and with little hope of other factory contracts, Derek pinned his hopes and his ambitions on a Gilera comeback which never came. With Gilera he saw the means of realising his potential as a Grand Prix racer on the European circuits, fighting it out on equal terms against the likes of Hailwood, Redman and Read. It was not to be. After the failure of a spirited Gilera comeback through the enterprise of Geoffrey Duke in 1963, Minter returned to racing Nortons in a successful partnership with ace tuner Ray Petty.

In 1965 the authorities at Brands Hatch, realising the potential in an official 'King of Brands' race, put Minter's official title into the open arena and arranged a race for the official title. The atmosphere was tense as the riders lined up. Minter's reputation was at stake. Phil Read was on the extremely fast 254 cc Yamaha. Dave Degens had Dunstall's 650 cc Norton twin. Derek was riding his 499 cc Norton.

Uncharacteristically, he was in the lead by the end of the first lap. Bill Ivy's challenge ended on the second lap when he came off at Druids, but by the end of lap three Phil Read was closing dramatically on Degens in second place. But Minter was moving too and as Read raced ahead of Degens, Derek was four seconds in the lead and had no intention of being caught. On that day he was the greatest, a worthy 'King', and he held the title for a year.

That Good Friday in 1965 was one of Minter's greatest moments. It wasn't a Grand Prix event. It did not count towards the world championship, but it was a psychological victory of immense proportions and Minter displayed his stature as a racing champion in a way which delighted his thousands of fans. They'd put him to the test, called his bluff; but he had proved himself more than equal to it.

But time was running out. Minter had lived through, and with, the oriental domination of European road racing and, with Japanese investment in racing dramatically slashed as Honda departed and cut-back programmes were announced by Yamaha and Suzuki, the really big-time had gone out of the game. At the end of 1967 Minter retired – and it was also the end of an era in British short-circuit racing.

Jarno Saarinen

The number of world titles attained is not always the true measure of a Grand Prix road racer. Jarno Saarinen and Bill Ivy each won only one world championship, yet in their time there were no more exciting racers and few who created as much impact. Saarinen, from Finland, was an instinctive champion with an abundance of natural flair and a swashbuckling style which made him a crowd hero within months. He was Finland's first road-racing champion and in the early 1970s created a sensation almost everywhere he raced.

Born in the port of Turku in 1945, Saarinen raced on dirt and ice in Finland and became Finnish ice-racing champion in 1965. His career in motorcycle racing developed after riding a 125 cc Puch in 1967 and his own Yamaha in 1968. As a private rider he won the 350 cc Czechoslovakian Grand Prix in 1971, leading to works rides the following year. In 1972, in a series of brilliant wins, he became 250 cc world champion. Earlier that year Saarinen had staggered the critics by beating Agostini on the MV-3 – the first time the Italian combination had been bettered on equal terms in five years.

At the time, road racing was in the market for a new hero. After the scintillating years of Hailwood and Honda, the early 1970s were anti-climatic. When Saarinen came along with his devastating, dashing style, he instantly claimed the spotlight, rousing crowds with one racing drama after another.

Jarno Saarinen *(Mick Woollett)*

Saarinen gained his world title with only the support of the Yamaha importer in Finland. His success brought him a full works contract for 1973. He began the season in giant-killing style, becoming the first European to win the highly prestigious Daytona 200 in the United States. A month later, Saarinen took to his 500 cc Yamaha and at the Paul Ricard circuit, before a record 65 000 crowd, humiliated the previously all-conquering Agostini/MV combination, lapping in 2 min 14.8 sec to set a new absolute lap record for the 3.6 mile circuit. That same month, in the Imola 200, he led the field on all except the first lap of the two 32-lap races, winning both legs at average speeds in excess of 100 mph (161 km/h). In May, he shattered all opposition to win the 250 cc West German Grand Prix at Hockenheim with a new lap record at 102.7 mph (165.3 km/h).

At this point in 1973 there was no more successful or exciting road racer in the world. His sensitive balance, derived from his ice-racing experience, was a joy to watch, though his heart-pounding drifts and slides took him repeatedly too close to the limits. As the Grand Prix circus travelled to Monza for the Italian Grand Prix Saarinen was in an exceptional position. In France, and then in Austria, his devastating riding had taken him to victory in both the 250 cc and 500 cc classes, and he had also won the 250 cc race in Germany. He led in the race for the world championship in both classes. But then, in one of the worst racing tragedies in the history of the sport, Jarno Saarinen was killed instantly in an appalling 50-machine first-lap pile-up in the 250 cc event, which also took the life of Harley-Davidson racer Renzo Pasolini.

Bill Ivy

Four years earlier a racing tragedy ended prematurely the career of the brilliant Bill Ivy, pocket-sized but with a giant's heart for racing. Ivy's fame flourished in the 'swinging sixties' and he caused a sensation with his Beatle-type long hair, candid accounts of off-circuit frolics and his pop-style image. His lucrative Yamaha contract brought him a rich life style and he committed himself completely to his racing. Ivy, from Kent, was born in 1942 and first started racing in 1958 as a grass-track rider. One of his early sponsors was Frank Sheene, father of Barry. He also rode for Geoff Monty and Tom Kirby. Though only 5 ft 3 in (1·6 m) tall he could handle big bikes with ease. Wins on AJS and Matchless machinery led to his first factory outings for Yamaha in the 125 cc and 250 cc TTs of 1965. He gained a full-blown works contract for 1966.

By this time he had won the British championship. He scored his first TT win in 1966 in the 125 cc race. Two years later he became the first man to lap the Isle of Man course at over 100 mph (161km/h) on a 125 cc machine – a feat he accomplished during practice, and then during the racing itself lapped at an astonishing 100·32 mph (161·52 km/h). In the Lightweight 250 cc TT he shattered Mike Hailwood's Honda lap record – from a standing start!

His first win for Yamaha was in the Spanish

Bill Ivy *(B.R. Nicholls)*

Grand Prix of 1966 and from then he became a towering figure in Grand Prix racing, for all his diminutive size. He was brave and flamboyant. Times and racing were never dull when Bill Ivy was around. He won the 125 cc world title in 1967 and in 1968 his feud with his Yamaha team mate Phil Read was headlined all over the racing world. Team orders came into the reckoning. A bitter situation developed between the two riders. Finally Read ended the season with two world titles while Ivy finished with none.

Ivy felt cheated and announced his retirement. A contract to ride Jawa machinery for 1969 tempted him back and he soon showed he had lost none of the old Bill Ivy magic. In the Dutch TT at Assen he fought a tremendous battle with Agostini in an outstanding ride, but sadly time was running out for Ivy. It was while practising for the East German Grand Prix at Sachsenring less than a month later that he crashed and was killed, on 12 July, 1969.

Bill Ivy rode a number of memorable races in his short career. The single world championship which he won, and the sole world title won by Jarno Saarinen, don't even begin to justify their dynamic talent as motorcycle road racers or the enormous impact they made on the sport.

Kent Andersson

At the peak of their careers at different times, Grand Prix racers Kent Andersson, Keith Campbell and Werner Haas nonetheless share similar distinctions in being the first riders from their countries to win a world title. Kent Andersson was born in 1945 and began his racing career in 1963 after breaking his back in a motorcycle road accident, and after some wild rides in the early part of his career he soon settled down to become one of Europe's top racers. His first international appearance was at Britain's Oulton Park in 1965 and a year later he scored his first international win in Belgium. His form at the Japanese Grand Prix that year, when he finished sixth in the 250 cc race, captured the attention of Yamaha, who provided support for 1967.

By 1969 he was a regular member of the Grand Prix circus, doing well on Yamaha in the 250 cc class and also claiming attention with some good rides on Maico-provided machinery in the 125 cc class. That year on the Yamaha he won in Germany and Finland and gained good second places in the lower capacity class in Spain and Holland. He had a number of Yamaha rides in the 350 cc class during 1970, but made more impact in the 250 cc class that year, winning in Spain and gaining second places in Yugoslavia, Czechoslovakia and Finland. Back in 125 cc racing

Kent Andersson (Mick Woollett)

Keith Campbell (Motor Cycle Weekly)

for 1971 he seemed unable to make much impression on the acknowledged experts like Angel Nieto and Barry Sheene, battled similarly in the 250 cc class, and didn't win his next Grand Prix until 1972, in the mid-season battle at Yugoslavia. Two further wins that year in Finland and Spain gave him the runner-up position to Nieto in the 125 cc class at the end of the season, to add to the third place he claimed in the 125 cc class in 1970.

Andersson gained the first of his two world titles in 1973. He stormed to victory in the early rounds winning the first five continental events, but a fall at Assen in Holland forced him to miss the Belgian and Czechoslovakian races. He rejoined the contest in Sweden and with his leg still in plaster finished a creditable second there, and again in Finland, to take the title. He gained the 125 cc title again in 1974, but with less ease, his main opposition coming from Yamaha team mate Bruno Kneubuhler and the now Derbi-mounted Angel Nieto. A versatile rider, Andersson also won the 250 cc Belgian Grand Prix that same year. In an attempt to gain the 125 cc world title for the third successive year, Kent Andersson could do no better than third and he retired from racing in 1976.

Andersson had won national titles in 1966 and 1967 and his 125 cc world title in 1973 was the first to be won by a Swedish rider in road racing.

Keith Campbell

Keith Campbell did for Australia what Kent Andersson had done for Sweden by becoming his country's first road-racing world champion when he took the 350 cc title in 1957. Wins in Holland, Belgium and Northern Ireland gave him the title from Bob McIntyre on a Gilera. Before travelling to Europe in 1951, Campbell had been a scrambles

rider and then a road racer in Australia, but his first attempts in Europe were unsuccessful. After returning home, he tried Europe again in 1955 and did enough in ensuing months to capture the attention of Guzzi, for whom he signed in late 1956. A determined character, Campbell is also remembered for his 500 cc lap record at the Belgian Grand Prix on the powerful eight-cylinder Guzzi. When Guzzi, along with Gilera and Mondial, retired from racing at the end of 1957, works rides became scarce and Keith Campbell was forced to become a private entrant again and in 1958 he was killed while racing at Cadours. By no means a great stylist, Keith Campbell was a great character and a rider of limitless enthusiasm. He raced with remarkable dash and courage and always with every bit of effort.

Werner Haas

While it took Campbell a long time to gain his world title, Werner Haas, on the other hand, had a meteoric rise, gaining three world titles in just two years. He was also the first German to win a road-racing world championship. Born in 1927, Werner Haas died in 1956 in an air crash, but only four years before he was on the brink of a brilliant, but all too short, racing career. After a few rides on Puch machinery, Haas was taken on by NSU to race their new single-cylinder 125 cc and twin-cylinder 250 cc machines. He created a sensation by beating the machines then dominating the class, MV Agusta and Mondial, to win the 125 cc German Grand Prix at Solitude; and at Monza in the 250 cc race he ran second to Guzzi, then supreme among 250s.

Haas quickly made an outstanding impression as a rider, his form reaching a peak in 1953 when he took the NSU to three Grand Prix victories to gain the title in the 125 cc class by ten points. Despite fierce opposition, he became only the second rider in world championship history to gain a double championship. Fergus Anderson and NSU team mate Reg Armstrong were formidable opponents in the 250 cc class that year, but Haas secured the title by just five points with wins in

141

Werner Haas (Motor Cycle Weekly)

Holland and Germany. The very next year Werner Haas rode magnificently in the 250 cc class, winning five Grands Prix in a row and establishing new record race averages at Solitude in the German Grand Prix and on the Isle of Man to take the Lightweight 250 cc TT, hoisting the average speed for the class to over 90 mph (145 km/h) for the first time.

At the end of 1955 the Neckarsulm factory decided to quit racing and because his personal successes had been so closely related to NSU activity, Haas, too, decided to call it a day. During the spring of the very next year, 1956, came the fateful air crash.

Walter Villa

An Italian from Modena, Walter Villa is noted not only for his brilliant riding, but for being the only racer to gain world championships on American Harley-Davidson machines. Villa was born in 1944 and began racing in 1962. After achieving notable success at home, winning five Italian championships, he first attracted notice on the Grand Prix circuit riding a Yamaha in 1973, finishing second in the Austrian Grand Prix on a 350 cc machine. That year saw the merger between Harley-Davidson and the Italian make, Aermacchi, and this indirectly helped Villa's ambitions in the world championships. The very

next year he secured the 250 cc world title for Harley-Davidson and in spite of strong opposition from a variety of riders on Yamahas, won four of the ten rounds to finish the season with 77 points.

Serious illness during the close season cast doubts on Villa's ability to retain his world title, but in the face of a strong challenge from new racing sensation Johnny Cecotto and equally formidable opposition in the form of Harley-Davidson team mate Michel Rougerie, Villa won in Germany, Spain, Italy, Holland and Sweden to gain a second and most impressive world championship in 1975.

Villa was in even more scintillating form in 1976. He held on to his 250 cc title to record three championships in a row and underlined his class as a foremost rider of middle-power machinery by collecting the 350 cc title as well. Both series were highly competitive and his double success was a fitting peak to a number of years of outstanding riding.

The Villa family were also widely known for their manufacture of mini bikes and road racers, and Walter's elder brother, Francesco, was also a road racer. Walter, quiet and unassuming, has nevertheless overcome more than his fair measure of controversy and mental pressure. Although the immediate enquiry into the crash which killed Saarinen and Pasolini at Monza in 1973 put the blame for the pile-up on the seizure of Pasolini's Harley-Davidson, there was a measure of opinion which implicated Walter Villa because of the oil which his Benelli-4 had leaked onto the track in an earlier race. In the multiple crash Villa himself was badly injured and it says a lot for his maturity as a man that he was able so commandingly to overcome the physical and psychological hazards which faced him following the crash.

Villa has also raced impressively his own Yamahas and Kawasaki machines, as well as factory Benellis, but nobody has remotely approached his success in Europe with Harley-Davidson machin-

Walter Villa (Mick Woollett)

ery. Right through until certainly the 1980s, he is the only rider to bring Harley-Davidson world road-racing championships and the only racer during the same period to gain a hat trick in the 250 cc category.

Jim Redman

In the big-money days of the 1960s when the Japanese formed full-scale factory teams in their quest for Grand Prix road-racing honours, the managing and skilful organisation of a team and its tactics could be an important contribution to racing success. No team captain was shrewder or cleverer than the naturalised Rhodesian Jim Redman. His astuteness repeatedly gave his Honda team the advantage, though when it came to a choice between a team mate's success against his own, he was not averse to giving himself the advantage. Hailwood claimed he suffered in this way when he first joined the Honda team. Redman, nearing the end of his racing career, was determined to add the prestige of the 500 cc world championship to the six world titles he had already won riding Honda's lighter machinery, and took the best bike for himself, even though Hailwood had been taken on specifically to bring Honda the 500 cc title, their one remaining unfulfilled ambition. When Redman made good progress in the early rounds Honda didn't object and when his challenge ended when he was injured, it was too late for Hailwood to catch up.

Though born in Britain in 1931, Redman emigrated to Rhodesia when he was eighteen and after winning the South African 350 cc championship in 1957 travelled to Britain the following year, making his debut at Brands Hatch. He could make little headway in Europe, however, and returned home disillusioned in 1959. He came back to Britain in 1960 to try his hand just once more and got his break by filling in for Tom Phillis after the latter had been injured at Assen during practice for the Dutch TT. He showed good promise in both the 125 cc and 250 cc races, was taken on by Honda and was soon a cornerstone of one of the most powerful works teams in racing history.

In 1962 Redman became world champion in both the 250 cc and 350 cc categories riding Hondas and impressively repeated this title 'double' the very next year. During these years Yamaha had been developing some very fast 250 cc models and by 1964 were ready to throw down the gauntlet to Honda and Redman. With Phil Read signed to spearhead their challenge the epic races which developed between Redman on Honda and Read on Yamaha made for a brilliant season of racing. The Yamaha machines were by this time faster,

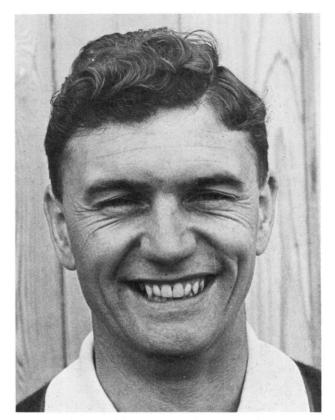

Jim Redman *(B.R. Nicholls)*

but Redman's skilful and intelligent riding forced Yamaha to fight hard for their world title.

Meantime, in the 350 cc class, Redman continued to be the undisputed king for two more years. In an outstanding career, he won the 350 cc world title four years in succession, 1962-65, and in 1962 and 1963 also took the 250 cc world championship. After crashing in Belgium and breaking a forearm, Redman tried desperately to take up his Honda bid for the 500 cc title again in Northern Ireland, but after a 6000 mile dash from his home, his arm stiffened so badly in practice that he was unable to race. It was virtually the end of Redman's competitive career and when Honda pulled out of racing at the end of that season, he too, called it a day.

Jim Redman as a champion was a little distant and uncommunicative, but there was nobody tougher or shrewder when it came to negotiating a contract and his quarrels with race organisers for terms he thought were just were well known within the racing business. He was a true professional, a stylish rider who never wittingly travelled faster than was necessary in order to win. He was always sensibly cautious, never taking unnecessary risks. He was Honda team leader during their most successful and brilliant days and personally contributed very much to their phenomenal success.

143

Until 1971, when Agostini stripped him of the distinction, Redman was the only rider to take the 350 cc world championship four years without interruption. His best year in this class was 1964 when he won all eight rounds making up the championship and in the four years of Jim Redman's domination of this category, he won 22 of the 31 rounds, a remarkable record. In the two years he dominated the 250 cc class, he won ten out of 20 rounds. On the Isle of Man he won the Junior TT and Lightweight 250 cc TT in 1963, 1964 and 1965 – a unique record.

Phil Read

In an unusually long racing career which began at Mallory Park, England in 1956 when he was only seventeen and ended at the ultra-fast Francorchamps circuit in Belgium twenty years later, Phil Read was seldom for long out of the headlines. His feud with Yamaha team mate Bill Ivy in the mid-sixties is now part of racing folklore. Later he antagonised Giacomo Agostini as he took over from the Italian to gain the 500 cc world championship on the MV Agusta machine which had taken Ago to 12 previous 500 cc and 350 cc world titles. He was one of the first superstars to live like one, with a luxury home, flourishing business and fast cars. He criticised the TTs, yet when the opportunity was right, he returned to the Isle of Man to win a world title. And at Francorchamps, in a sensational move, he walked out on the eve of the Belgian Grand Prix, for personal and domestic reasons, and calmly announced his retirement from Grand Prix racing.

Without Read, racing lost some of its colour and controversy. It also lost a lot of talent. For Phil was good enough among the world's best to win seven world titles, excluding the 'special' he secured on the Isle of Man. He was forthright, frank and positive, in his racing and his off-track comments, and had a sharp eye for the main chance.

Born in Luton in 1939, Read became one of Britain's most successful road racers. His appetite for the sport developed after he had been taken to the Silverstone race circuit by his father and he owned his first machine, a 250 cc side-valve Matchless, when he was only thirteen. He entered his first race in 1956 on a 350 cc BSA Gold Star and in 1958 won his first important event on a 350 Norton. Inspired by boyhood heroes like Jimmy Guthrie, Freddy Frith, Stanley Woods and, later, Ray Amm and John Surtees, Read took part in the professional TT Races for the first time in 1961. His retirements in the Senior and Lightweight 125 cc events were forgotten against his victory in the Junior race at an average of 95·10 mph (153·05 km/h) on a Bill Lacey Norton. That year he went racing to the Continent for the first time, but had to wait until 1964 before winning his first Classic, the French Grand Prix with new lap and race records. By this time Read had switched to Yamaha and was on the brink of a brilliant spell with the Japanese factory which was to bring him 250 cc world titles in 1964, 1965, 1968 and 1971. In 1968 he also secured the 125 cc world title for Yamaha in a year in which his personal clash with team mate Bill Ivy claimed as many headlines as the races themselves. How much was inspired publicity and how much genuine friction between the two riders was difficult to assess at the beginning, but certainly when Read won his double world championship and Ivy was left with no honours at all, the latter rider seemed genuinely upset and left racing in a flurry of recriminations.

After Yamaha reduced their racing effort, Read was sufficiently well established to become a private rider on the Japanese machines. After a short spell in the John Player Norton team he saw an opportunity to make his mark with MV Agusta, who gave him a two-year contract to team with Agostini in 1973. The partnership was stormy with the Italian complaining about Read's tactics, but the British rider went on to win his first 500 cc world title on the MV in his first year with the factory. And once Agostini had left the Italian factory in a huff, Read beat his old opponent to the title again the following year.

There was never any doubt about Phil Read's talent on a racing motorcycle. He was skilful, quick and had the shrewd capacity to identify and create his own opportunities. After competing on the Isle of Man for ten years out of eleven from 1961, he refused to go back there until an offer from Honda came in 1977 to compete in the new Formula 1 race. Through a curious technicality, the winner would win a world title and Read was not only drawn back to the Island racing he had so bitterly criticised, but won the race impressively, boosting his personal tally of world titles to eight.

Read's success has been exceptionally durable. Some rate his best times as being in the mid-sixties while with Yamaha, when racing was fiercely competitive and he had to ride against, among others, the formidable Jim Redman on the Honda to take his 1964 and 1965 world titles. On the more difficult to handle four-cylinder Yamaha in 1966 and 1967, he faced the might of Hailwood on the Honda and lost the championship only by the narrowest of margins, gaining as many points as Hailwood, but losing the title because of Hailwood's five wins to his four.

Phil Read *(Mick Woollett)*

He showed his versatility and basic skill as a racer by successfully switching from the two-stroke Yamahas to the 500 cc MV-four and his impressive winning of the 500 cc world title which ended a seven-year domination by his MV team mate Agostini.

Phil Read has an impressive Grand Prix history. By 1971 he had become the world's most successful 250 cc Grand Prix racer, having won 25 races in the class, and had amassed a total of 36 GP victories. In 1974, at the Czechoslovakian Grand Prix, he recorded his 50th Grand Prix win and that same year, after more than 18 years, was so impressive and popular that he was declared 'Man of the Year' in the annual poll organised by the British weekly, *Motor Cycle News*.

Johnny Cecotto

In 1974 respective champions in the five solo classes were Phil Read, Giacomo Agostini, Walter Villa, Kent Andersson and Henk van Kessel. No one knew much about a curly-haired fun-loving 18-year-old from far away Venezuela called Alberto 'Johnny' Cecotto. The very next year he was an international racing sensation, grabbing the headlines and monopolising the circuit-side talk from France to Finland, Imola to Hockenheim. Riding against established racers like Agostini, Dieter Braun, Hideo Kanaya and emerging stars like Ekerold, Pons, Korhonen, Chevallier and Buscherini, Cecotto captured the 350 cc world title from, of all people, Agostini, at his first attempt to become, at 19, the youngest-ever world champion in the history of road racing.

He also finished fourth in the 250 cc class in a sensational season which began dramatically when he won both the 250 cc and 350 cc races at the Paul Ricard circuit in France in the opening round and on his Grand Prix debut. Virtually unheard of outside Venezuela, Johnny Cecotto was not intimidated by the big names of racing, and with his dashing style and friendly personality he was soon challenging Agostini and even Sheene for the devotion of the crowd.

Cecotto was born in the Venezuelan capital of Caracus in January 1956. His parents were Italian but his father, who owned a garage and was a past racing champion on a Manx Norton, bought son Johnny a 750 cc Honda 4 on which he had his first races. The story goes that his first competitive rides were illegal, since he gained acceptance only after changing his date of birth. He was only sixteen and officially too young to ride. The Honda was discarded following the offer of an ex-works 750 cc Kawasaki, and he showed such promise that the Venezuelan Yamaha importer, Andres Ippolito, became his sponsor and manager.

A student of mechanical engineering, Cecotto was his country's 1000 cc champion in 1973 and 1974, and he branched out in 1974 by going to Daytona for the first time. On a 350 cc Yamaha he finished 35th, but his success in Europe in 1975 led to official factory support. He packed in his studies and became a full-time professional racer. In the year he won his first world championship he went to Daytona and qualified on the front row of the grid, and in 1976 was at 20 the youngest-ever winner of the Daytona 200, at a record speed of 108·77 mph (175·05 km/h) and lapping all his rivals.

The racing world buzzed with the name and deeds of young Johnny Cecotto and early in 1976 he was probably the most exciting rider on the

Johnny Cecotto *(Mick Woollett)*

Grand Prix circuit. Yamaha signed him to race their 350 cc, 500 cc and 750 cc machines, but the year ended disappointingly. There were no further world titles, although Cecotto ran Walter Villa close for the 350 cc crown. The young Venezuelan had already hinted at an interest in car racing and his regular falls during 1976 seemed to show that his heart was not completely with the bike scene, though machine problems didn't add to his chances. In 1977 he collected a fourth place in the 500 cc race and won the 350 cc event at his home circuit at San Carlos in the opening round, but in Austria for the second round, he was badly injured in a multiple pile-up in the 350 cc race and didn't return until the season was two-thirds over. With 500 cc wins in Finland and Czechoslovakia and a second place in Sweden he raced with more relish than for some time and ended the season in an impressive fourth place behind Barry Sheene, Steve Baker and Pat Hennen.

Cecotto had proved how well he could race a motorcycle, but the root of his problem was inconsistency. His superb rides in Austria, Holland and Germany would have brought him the 500 cc world title had he maintained form, but his natural flair which made him such an exciting racer seemed too often to yield to a temperament not ideal for season-long racing. On the bigger Yamaha in 1978, however, Johnny Cecotto was supreme and after a hard tussle with Kenny Roberts, he took the FIM 750 cc championship in its first year of world status. With three wins and three second places, he was ahead of Roberts at the end of the season by just five points.

While Cecotto failed to retain his title in 1979, finishing third behind Patrick Pons and Michel Frutschi, there was no doubt that on his day he was liable to outrace the best.

Kork Ballington

The instant success which is so instinctively acclaimed by the crowds, and which so rarely

happens, wasn't the way to international recognition for Hugh Neville 'Kork' Ballington. Certainly, when fame and success came, they came quickly. But the apprenticeship was long and often hard. It was only when he was taken on by Kawasaki in the UK to ride their exciting 250 cc and 350 cc racers for 1978 that he really made his mark. That first year, dedicated, consistent and stylish, he became double world champion, winning ten Grand Prix races and finishing in second place five times in the two classes. He beat Takazumi Katayama to the 350 cc title 134 points to 77, and pushed team mate Gregg Hansford of Australia into second place in the 250 cc table, 124 points to 118.

Kork Ballington was born in 1952 in Salisbury, Southern Rhodesia and began racing there when he was sixteen. After winning a number of national championships, he travelled to Europe, but the acclamation which he might have hoped for wasn't immediately forthcoming. He struggled to get into the big league, helped on his way by Aldridges and later, Sid Griffiths, who set him up for a positive crack at the Grands Prix.

Ballington had ridden Kawasaki machines successfully in South Africa and in 1974, after winning a number of British national races and finishing fourth in the Superbike championship, he attracted the attention of Stan Shenton, which led to a successful Kawasaki long-distance ride with Barry Ditchburn at Thruxton. While Ditchburn was soon claimed by Kawasaki as a works rider, Ballington's opportunity was longer in coming. Mick Grant was then the mainstay of the Kawasaki twosome in the UK and Ditchburn's

Kork Ballington

signing left no room for Ballington. Ironically, it was a shake-up of the Kawasaki team, with both Grant and Ditchburn departing, that resulted in Ballington's recall by Kawasaki and he repaid their confidence handsomely.

Kork Ballington brought Kawasaki their first world championships for nine years, for not since Dave Simmonds success in the 125 cc category in 1969, had the Japanese factory won a world road-racing title. Little wonder Ballington's place in the Kawasaki line-up for 1979 was assured.

He left the Kawasaki hierarchy in little doubt that they had made the correct decision, and stormed ahead in the 250 cc class, winning three of the first four rounds and taking a second place in the other. He was slower off the mark in the 350 cc races, though wins in Austria, Spain, Yugoslavia, Sweden and Great Britain gave him a total of 99 points against his nearest challenger Patrick Fermandcz's total of 90. His form in the 250 cc championship was more commanding and he amassed 141 points against the 81 of Gregg Hansford, who finished in second place.

Four world titles in just two years wasn't bad for someone who had been racing for twelve years and as motorcycling moved into the 1980s Kork Ballington was one of the leading figures, totally professional and able to combine fast riding with discipline, style and safety. In the space of two years there are few who have equalled Kork Ballington's remarkable consistency of performance and only two riders, Jim Redman and Mike Hailwood, who have been double world champion in the 350 cc and 250 cc classes for two years running.

Barry Sheene

A horror crash at the Daytona circuit in the United States which took Barry Sheene to the brink of death in 1975 ironically catapulted him into the public gaze with an intensity and brilliance not experienced by any other rider. What made the difference was that Barry's appalling high-speed crash was captured on film for the world to witness. After such exposure Barry Sheene's name became a household word and in a grim kind of way, motorcycle racing benefited, being thrust into the headlines to be noticed by thousands of people who previously hadn't given the time of day to motorcycle sport.

Barry survived, magnificently, and went on to become one of the sport's greatest and most effective ambassadors. He typified the age in which he lived, dressing casually, living spectacularly, facing both friend and foe with a disarming frankness and honesty, and presenting an image of ease and composure as much in television chat shows and press interviews as in Grand Prix paddock conversations and aboard the super-fast Suzuki which took him to the world championship.

Sheene was born in London in 1950 and grew up into a family which was motorcycle orientated, his father Frank being a former racer. His sister Maggie was also to marry the British racer Paul Smart. Barry was riding his father's Bultacos at seventeen and made his racing debut a year later. In 1970 he captured the 125 cc British championship and the very next year, in a dramatic season of racing, almost won the world championship in the class, finishing second to Angel Nieto in his first season of Classic racing. His first Grand Prix win was in Belgium that year and later in the season he won in Sweden and Finland. His talent was spotted by Yamaha and he joined their factory team for 1972 already, it seemed, well on the way to a brilliant future. His Yamaha rides, however, were disappointing and it was only after he joined the Suzuki GB team in 1973 that he was able to make further progress.

One success followed another – the British Superbike championship, the Shellsport 500 cc title, FIM Formula 750 cc championship – with impressively fluent rides at circuits all over Europe. Already he was being tipped as the new Hailwood. He steadily consolidated his growing reputation in 1974, but then came that fateful day at Daytona early in 1975 when, during practice for the big race, the Suzuki threw him off at a speed approaching 180 mph (290 km/h). The film cameraman, already recording Barry in practice, kept the film moving as the rider lay inert on the desolate track, chronicling the tenderness as helpers eased him onto a stretcher. His injuries, including five fractures, were serious, but Sheene pulled through with an impish kind of Cockney indestructibility, and with an 18in (45cm) pin keeping his leg in place, raced again at Britain's Cadwell Park circuit after only a month. It was an exceptional recovery and Barry was soon riding his heart out again, his cheery courage greatly admired: but later that very season, he broke his leg once more at Cadwell, irrepressibly practising 'wheelies'!

Friendly, approachable, always with time for a word, Barry Sheene nevertheless is a rider of serious intent. He knows his worth in the modern world, sticks out for the right price, is solidly patriotic, and at the beginning of 1976 was determined to hoist Britain back on top of world championship racing. Only twice in the last ten years (Phil Read in 1973 and 1974) had a British rider won the prestigious 500 cc world crown. With wins in France, Austria and Italy at the start of the season, and further success at Assen in

Barry Sheene (B.R Nicholls)

Holland, his win in Sweden clinched the championship title with a net total of 72 points against the 48 points of his nearest challenger, Tepi Lansivuori.

He then threatened not to ride in the remaining three rounds unless he considered the start money acceptable. He claimed it wasn't and kept his word, ignoring the Grands Prix in Finland, Czechoslovakia and Germany. Sheene has since been a vigorous and voluble campaigner for what he believed to be the rights of riders. After an unsuccessful excursion to the Isle of Man in 1971 he wasn't interested in returning, and he has stood firm and refused to race when he considered circuits were too dangerous. For the traditionalists and purists who remember previous generations of road racers, his finely developed business sense and acute respect for the monetary side of racing cuts across fading standards, but the fans of the seventies and eighties have different values and follow him manfully.

With one impressive 500 cc world championship under his belt, Barry set out on the Grand Prix trail again in 1977 beating Steve Baker and Pat Hennen to win the opening round in Venezuela. In Austria, in the second round, Sheene was among the majority of riders who confronted the organisers and refused to race after a multiple pile-up in the 350 cc event, but in a mangnificent run of success he dropped only three points in the next six rounds to win his second 500 cc world championship in two years by the magnificent margin of 107 points to Steve Baker's 80.

By this time Sheene was firmly at the top of Grand Prix roadracing and for one reason or another was seldom out of the news. Some claimed he was in danger of suffering from over exposure by the mass news media, though Barry himself couldn't have harboured many misgivings for the attention certainly wasn't doing his bank balance any harm. There looked to be no serious challenge to Sheene superiority on the Suzuki in the 500 cc class and barring accidents you could have put your money on his winning the championship yet again in 1978, perhaps 1979 and even 1980.

When American superstar Kenny Roberts came over to Europe at the beginning of 1978 to compete in the Grands Prix for the first time he had already won the United States' Grand National Championship twice. The versatility required to win such honours in America, however, needn't necessarily be of much advantage in the specialised techniques required to win all-out road-racing championships and while Roberts' skill and ability was never in doubt, how he would make out on the circuits of Europe was anybody's guess.

Until now Steve Baker had been America's best performer in Europe, but Sheene quickly knew that Roberts meant business. In the opening round in South America, Roberts' Yamaha surrendered and he was back in the pits after only two laps, but his practice times had been good and he showed his form by winning the 250 cc race. In Spain he came second to Pat Hennen, Sheene adding a seventh place to the winner's points he scored in Venezuela. Barry was again bettered in Spain, taking the third spot as Roberts won his first 500 cc race. Barry's only other class win during the season was in Sweden and he finally surrendered the title to Kenny Roberts, ten points separating the two riders at the end of the season.

To set the reckoning straight, it is true that Sheene had not been fully well physically during the early part of the season, and there was little doubt that his Suzuki didn't have as much edge on the Yamahas of Roberts and others as against Yamaha opposition in previous seasons. He rode some magnificent rides during the year, however, employing race tactics skilfully and rounding corners superbly on line, but his best form was all too frequently lacking in world championship races and Roberts deserved his title.

Despite their keen rivalry, a firm friendship developed between Barry Sheene and Roberts. They both voiced their strong advocacy for a better deal for riders, Roberts' frankness more than a match for Sheene's when it came to condemning the conduct and general attitude of the FIM and of many race organisers.

Sheene's image had taken a knock in 1978 and he was out to regain his title in 1979, but Roberts again barred his way. With three outright wins during the twelve-round season – in Venezuela, Sweden and France – Barry had to be content with third position at the end of the season. Roberts again won the championship with the Italian Virginio Ferrari in second place.

By this time Kenny Roberts had announced his plans for a breakaway World Series and Sheene, along with other top riders, lined up in support in a direct threat to the FIM's authority.

Barry Sheene had done the cause of motorcycle racing enormous good and it is true to say that not even Hailwood had as much impact on the world outside racing. While much of his early glory was gained through his horrific Daytona crash, his recognition later came from his pure ability to race a motorcycle at speed. He alone of the British riders was able to maintain UK prestige against the continental riders particularly, and the Americans, who dominated the 500 cc class during the late 1970s.

Chapter 16

Famous Factories round the World

Honda, the biggest name in motorcycling. This 100 cc two-stroke has reduced oil consumption through careful pump design, so exhaust emission is reduced (*Honda UK Ltd*)

The greatest influence on modern motorcycling has been the Japanese factories and, in particular, **HONDA**. The biking revolution which began in the 1960s, and was continued and developed in the '70s and into the '80s, began insignificantly enough in war-torn Japan at the end of the Second World War. Soichiro Honda was 40 years old, an impassioned inventor with a sharp eye for an opportunity, and not alone in having to abandon his car because of the fuel shortage. There was little public transport and incredible crowding on buses and trains. This was the scene of social disorder as Mr. Honda came upon a consignment of 500 war surplus small two-stroke engines which had been used by the Japanese army to power communications equipment. He bought them cheaply and after adapting one to power a bicycle for his own use, began the work of conversion commercially.

It was 1946 and from a tiny shack built on a roughly-levelled bomb-site in the small Japanese city of Hamamatsu, where he lived, Mr. Honda set up business. Capital resources amounted to little more than a dilapidated machine tool, an old belt-driven lathe and a few salvaged desks and chairs. There were just 12 workers. When all the original engines had been sold, Mr. Honda set about making his own.

The remarkable business enterprise which was to become a household name across the world within such a short time and which totally changed the entire character of motorcycling, was established, and in September 1948 the Honda Motor Company Limited, with a capital of £900 (2777 dollars in those days), was registered.

Less than a year later Honda broke new ground by becoming the first motorcycle manufacturer in Japan to manufacture both the engine and the frame. Though Honda's first complete bike – the two-stroke, single-cylinder D-type Dream – was a success, it broke into the market at a bad time. The post-war depression blew bitterly across Japan, but the young company survived the crisis to build up to a production rate of 100 units a month. The firm ran into cash-flow problems but with the help of new executive director, Takeo Fujisawa, again survived so that in March 1950 Honda opened a Tokyo office. An important loan from the government enabled production of the Dream to go up to 300 a month, an impressive figure when compared with the 1608 machines which the remaining nine Japanese manufacturers in total produced *per year*.

After the introduction of the first Honda four-strokes in 1951, Honda saw the vast potential of the small, efficient clip-on unit to power the thousands of bicycles which were then standard transport in Japan, and in May 1952 introduced the Honda Cub. With a sparkling white fuel tank and a bright red cover, the Cub was quickly snapped up. Any bicycle mechanic could fit it to the rear wheel within just a few minutes. More than 6500 Cubs were being manufactured monthly by October 1953 and in less than 18 months from the introduction, Honda had captured 70 per cent of the total Japanese market for clip-on units.

Established as the major manufacturer in Japan, Honda looked to export markets for major expansion. They ran themselves close to bankruptcy in financing a massive investment programme, in preparation for their expansion. Automatic lathes and other sophisticated machine tools were bought from America, Germany and Switzerland. The staggering bill: over one million dollars. The firm ran close to disaster as Japan found itself in deep recession in 1953 and 1954. Motorcycle manufacturers had mushroomed, yet the market had virtually collapsed. To help save the company Honda workers did their part by going without holidays and getting the new machinery working as soon as possible so that money could once again start flowing into the company.

When the economic situation improved, Honda were ideally placed to exploit it. Mr. Honda now looked to the vast opportunities overseas for Honda machines and recognised the need for publicity to get his products known. He turned to racing and visited the Isle of Man in 1954. Unnoticed among the large attendance of overseas visitors, he was astounded at the performance of European racing machinery, which was turning out three times the power of Honda bikes of the same size. It was five more years before he felt sufficiently confident to expose the Honda name on the Isle of Man. In the meantime factories had been established in Saitama and Hamamatsu, and in 1957 the first Hondas were shipped abroad – just two machines to nearby Okinawa. In 1958 the Honda 50 cc Super Cub (C100) was launched with massive promotion and this remarkable runabout bike was a phenomenal success, 24 000 being sold during the first year. In 1958, too, the first Hondas arrived in the United States (just two machines!) and in Holland and Britain.

In the late 1950s and '60s Honda's progress was gigantic. In 1959 they entered the TT Races for the first time, sold a staggering 167 443 Super Cubs, set up an American subsidiary, became the first Japanese manufacturer to exhibit in Europe, showing the Dream at the Amsterdam Show, and significantly and in contrast to British and European outlook at the time, set up a completely separate company to concentrate on research and development.

Until 1967 Honda invested prodigious sums of money to gain racing success, establishing highly-paid teams of factory riders and applying enormous effort into the development and production of highly-sophisticated racing specials. They were eventually to gain 16 road-racing world championships and almost 140 Grand Prix wins during this exhilarating period. Their racing success with riders like Mike Hailwood, Jim Redman, Tom Phillis, Bob Brown, Bob McIntyre, Luigi Taveri, Ralph Bryans and others was reflected commercially. By 1961 Honda's total monthly sales reached 100 000 for the first time, total exports were more than 49 000 and a subsidiary company was established in West Germany. In 1963 total annual exports had risen to 338 000 with 114 000 Hondas sold in the United States alone. With an annual production running at 1¼ million, Honda was by now by far the largest motorcycle company in the world. Their United Kingdom subsidiary was set up in 1964 and in 1967, when Honda officially retired from Grand Prix racing, after winning almost all the major awards, their total production of Super Cubs reached five million.

A year later total production of Honda machines exceeded ten million and the firm celebrated its one-millionth sale to the United States.

Honda has no match in the entire history of motorcycling. In the production of machines, in their emphasis on research and development, their impact on racing, in their innovative approach to the marketing of motorcycles and the racing of them, they set totally new standards. Honda, with their gleaming, handsome and sophisticated machinery, and their trouble-free, easy-to-ride commuter models, hauled motorcycling out of its backyard image for ever, giving it a new respectability and popularity when it seemed that nothing could save it from permanent social dereliction. Honda created an entirely new motorcycling conception and a vast, totally new market.

Honda continued to maintain the initiative by bringing out a stream of new models and for years they were so technically advanced that competitors were left well behind. They gave motorcycling a civilised appeal by incorporating such refinements, even as early as 1959, as electric starters, overhead-camshaft multi-cylinder engines, improved silencing systems and machines which could be easily cleaned. Their 'step-through' commutor bikes were vastly superior to the crude runabouts offered by competitors. In terms of research and development, Honda were the first to set entirely new horizons, when, in 1959, these essential activities were formed into a separate organisation and 2½ per cent of Honda's annual turnover was automatically directed back into research and development. There was a modern business outlook about what they did and they were anxious to invest in the future as well as the present. Their factories were show-places with machines doing most of the work and operatives smartly attired in white overalls and peak caps. Automated units gave them prodigious production figures, perhaps twice that of their major rivals.

Having used racing intelligently to gain commercial recognition and worldwide sales, Honda kept ahead of the times and in 1969, when they produced more than 1½ million machines, they introduced the CB750, heralding the era of the superbike and once again extending the frontiers of motorcycling. With a specially prepared Honda 750 the factory won the world's most prestigious race, the Daytona 200 in America, and then moved into endurance racing through subsidiary companies and importers. They won the most important race of this kind, the Bol d'Or in France, and when they later applied full-scale factory backing, dominated marathon racing for a number of years.

There were repeated rumours of a Honda return to Grand Prix racing, but instead Honda's effort was directed towards the vastly-developing off-road market, particularly in the United States. By the mid-1970s they had secured national trials and motorcross championships in America. In 1973 the man whose inspiration, energy and vision had started it all, Mr. Soichiro Honda, retired from the active day-to-day running of the vast empire which by now had been created, and the very next year Honda introduced the remarkable GL 1000 cc Gold Wing. This majestic machine was the ultimate heavyweight, high-speed tourer and the extreme example of superb Japanese motorcycling engineering. Keenly sensitive to environmental issues, Honda had produced a whispering giant, for the Gold Wing was said to be the quietest running bike in the world, well in keeping with Honda's modern policy of developing machines which were not only mechanically advanced, but socially acceptable. The Gold Wing, remarkable as an example of unique motorcycle engineering, was nevertheless only the first of an entire series of technically adventurous machines which were to appear from Honda in the late 1970s.

Today, Honda not only make motorcycles, but generators, cultivators, industrial engines, and motor cars with increasing success.

Soon to follow Honda's example was the second Japanese company to make an impact in motorcycling, **SUZUKI**. Originally a textile engineering firm founded by Michio Suzuki in 1909, Suzuki turned to building motorcycles when post-war recession forced them to diversify. Though they had made a motorised bicycle two years before, the first Suzuki motorcycle appeared in 1954, when the Suzuki Motor Company Ltd was formed. Such was their progress that within 14 years they had become the world's biggest manufacturer of two-stroke machines.

Suzuki entered classic racing for the first time in 1960, but their 125 twins, with piston-controlled inlets, were largely outclassed. Suzuki were hardly more successful the following year when they took the MZ 125 cc and 250 cc racers as their example – and inherited some of their faults, the East Germans in the meantime having corrected them on their racers. When a 50 cc class was added to the world championships in 1962, however, Suzuki were immediately successful. Ernst Degner, MZ's skilful engineer-racer, was largely responsible. After defecting from East Germany at the Swedish Grand Prix of 1961, he took his knowledge and experience to Suzuki and, riding 50 cc racers derived from the 125 cc machines, brought the Japanese factory their first Grand Prix victories and their first world title in 1962. This success, achieved with comparative ease, was won with an

Britain's golden boy of racing, Barry Sheene, on the 500 cc Suzuki *(Motor Cycle Weekly)*

air-cooled 50 cc single with one rotary valve, and although it had been given only moderate development it was much too good for the current challenge from Kreidler and Honda.

After signing Hugh Anderson to succeed Degner, Suzuki triumphed in both the 50 cc and 125 cc world championships the following year, and the New Zealand rider went on to bring them two more world titles – the 50 cc class in 1964 and the 125 cc class in 1965. It was in 1964 that Suzuki developed an extremely powerful 250 cc four-cylinder two-stroke to challenge Honda, which was little more than the 125 with a pair of cylinders added to the front, and it was not successful. The four cylinders were placed in a square, each requiring a feed by rotary valve. The cylinder block was water-cooled and it had a six-speed gearbox. The 250 was beset with mechanical problems, though with the smaller models Suzuki continued to do well. Before the factory officially withdrew from racing at the end of 1967, the West German rider Hans-Georg Anscheidt brought them world titles in the 50 cc class twice more, in 1966 and 1967. By this time the single had been replaced by a twin and although a three-cylinder racer was said to be in preparation, it was never raced. On a Suzuki 50 cc twin which Anscheidt kept for his own use after the factory withdrew, he once again headed the championship table at the end of the season. For the remainder of the 1960s Suzuki racing activity was kept alive by private riders like Dieter Braun and Holland's van Dongen in the 125 cc class.

Suzuki came back into racing prominence in the 1970s, this time building big 500 cc and 750 cc racers derived from standard models to gain a bigger hold in the vast American market. A new four-cylinder 500 based on the earlier, unsuccessful 250, was introduced in 1974 and, as the RG500, was much more reliable and became outstandingly successful, being put into production. Barry Sheene, who had ridden a 125 cc Suzuki into second place in the world championships in 1971, was signed by Suzuki's concessionaire organisation in Britain and with a developed version of the RG500 brought Suzuki their first world championship in the 500 cc class in 1976, securing the title for a second time the following year. Both Sheene and Stan Woods made an impact in British superbike races and in 1973 Sheene brought Suzuki the European Formula 750 cc title.

Suzuki have also supported other branches of motorcycle sport. They were the first Japanese factory to take an interest in motocross, developing their first prototype machines in 1965. After signing Swedish rider Olle Petterson to develop the machines and Belgian superstar Joel Robert to ride them, they captured their first motocross world title in 1970.

Suzuki's progress has been impressive. In 1953 they produced 4400 lightweight machines in their first full year of production. By the mid-1970s they were producing 800 000 machines a year, a fifth of Japan's total production, with half going abroad. Since moving into motorcycles, Suzuki have also produced engines for cars, vans and boats and in 1979 introduced their first small car to Britain.

Suzuki are also known for their promotion of the Wankel engine, which they designed specially for their RE5, but in a world alarmed by rapidly diminishing oil supplies and more sensitively aware than at any time in the past about environmental issues, its heavy fuel consumption and emission pollution levels gave it no hope of commercial success in that form. Suzuki also moved into four-stroke production, introducing some nicely-engineered machines, and in 1979 claimed they had the fastest production motorcycle in the world with the GS1000. Like all the Japanese manufacturers, Suzuki now produce a wide range of machines of all capacities and styles.

If a move from textile engineering to motorcycle manufacture seems unusual, particularly perhaps in view of Suzuki's enormous success in the latter, then surely even more unlikely is that a company with a world reputation for producing fine musical instruments should start making motorcycles. Yet **YAMAHA** proved the astuteness of their action by reaching enormous levels of success, both on race tracks round the world and commercially through the vast sales of over-the-counter models. Where Suzuki were forced to find a new outlet because of the failure of their original industry, Yamaha, indeed, had no such self-survival motive. The company's diversification developed from the founder's personal interest in motorcycles and where Suzuki quickly abandoned their original production, Yamaha, founded in the late 1880s as a manufacturer of reed organs (later to add pianos), were to maintain their reputation in these spheres.

Yamaha made their first motorcycles in the 1950s, formed their motorcycle company in 1955 and by 1960 were making approaching 160 000 machines a year. By 1969 the figure had risen to 450 000, and they were certainly the most prolific manufacturer in the 1970s in international road-racing. Their first racing department was set up in 1960, their first racing machines said to have been produced in just one year. Competing with 125 and 250 cc air-cooled twins, Yamaha made their racing debut in the French Grand Prix of 1961, but not until the following year, after the 250 RD56 had been back to Japan and given more power, did they achieve success, the Japanese rider Fumio Ito winning the Belgian Grand Prix against competition from the Honda 4, with a new record lap of 117·82 mph (189·69 km/h).

Yamaha's first major racing impact came in 1964 after they had signed the British rider Phil Read. He brought them their first world championship that same year, in the 250 cc class. The winning combination succeeded again the following year, with Yamaha-mounted Canadian Mike Duff finishing in second place. Read went on to become Yamaha's most successful 250 cc racer, winning world championships for the factory again in 1968 and 1971. Despite strong opposition, Yamaha dominated 250 cc racing during this period and also performed well with 125 cc machines. Bill Ivy joined the factory team to take the world 125 cc title in 1967 and Read completed a double success by bringing Yamaha the 125 cc crown again in 1968. Yamaha captured the 250 cc world championship once more in 1970 through Rodney Gould and dominated 250 cc racing in the early 1970s through riders like Read, Gould, Braun and the Finnish sensation, Jarno Saarinen. At this stage the factory's 250 cc racer was perhaps faster than the 500 cc MV Agusta machine on which Agostini was taking his world championships. Had not Saarinen been killed it seemed certain that he would have brought Yamaha the 350 cc and 500 cc world titles in 1973, for he was heading both tables at the time of his death. Kent Andersson of Sweden kept Yamaha firmly on

course in the 125 cc class by taking two more world titles in 1973 and 1974.

In the 1970s and into the 1980s Yamaha machinery has dominated motorcycle road competition. In terms of sheer volume they have created more in-depth impact in road racing than any other manufacturer in the world. The reason for this has been Yamaha's policy of producing over-the-counter racing machines in far greater numbers and in more configurations than any other manufacturer, so that private riders can race competitively on racing machines freely available. This means that the ambitious privateer does not have to face the astronomical costs of producing a competitive machine out of his own pocket or through sponsorship. This policy has revolutionised racing and has given Yamaha a near monopoly in many events. Even in the upper echelons, Yamaha machinery dominates. Take the 250 cc world championship placings in 1979, for instance. Walter Villa and Franco Uncini (on Harley-Davidsons) and Mario Lega (Morbidelli) were the only three riders in the top 34 positions to be riding machines other than Yamaha. This was the measure of Yamaha's domination of race results.

Machine development, rather than profit, was the object behind Yamaha's racing policy and although the name became so synonymous with racing, there have been periods when they withdrew official support and in the late 1970s and early 1980s preferred to offer support through subsidiaries.

Yamaha began moving up the classes in 1973, as we have noted, with official entries in 500 cc races, and in May that year the first TZ750 was produced, at first fitted with a 700 cc unit. It was Giacomo Agostini, for so many years 500 cc world champion on MV Agusta, who brought Yamaha their first world title in this class, in 1975. Suzuki's domination of the class in 1976 left no room for Yamaha, but Steve Baker finished in second position in 1977 riding a factory four-cylinder Yamaha, and fellow American Kenny Roberts brought Yamaha the most prestigious world title again in 1978 and 1979.

In Formula 750 racing, Yamaha's stranglehold has been virtually complete. Victor Palomo, Steve Baker, Johnny Cecotto and Patrick Pons brought them top honours in four consecutive seasons in the late 1970s.

Giacomo Agostini on a 350 cc Yamaha in Austria, 1974 *(Mick Woollett)*

With three Japanese manufacturers dominating world markets, could there possibly be room for a fourth? **KAWASAKI** thought so and produced their first motorcycle under that name in 1962. They were already an industrial giant, involved in the high technological fields of trains, ships and aeroplanes. The business had originated when Mr Shozo Kawasaki founded a dockyard in Tokyo in 1878. Then came the manufacture of locomotives, railway coaches, freight cars, bridge trusses and steel, before the formation of the Kawasaki Aircraft Company in 1937.

Kawasaki were massive and successful, but they enjoyed little public recognition. To give them a platform publicly, they moved seriously into motorcycle production, following limited involvement in the industry through Japanese makes like Meihatsu, for whom they originally supplied engines, and Meguro, an old established motorcycle company they owned. Shrewdly, they decided to make their pitch on a 'performance' image and became one of the most dynamic and vigorously attacking factories of all. With the formation of Kawasaki Heavy Industries Ltd in 1969 greater attention was paid to motorcycle activities and the British rider, Dave Simmonds, with, it must be said, little support from Kawasaki, secured the 125 cc world championship riding a Kawasaki machine.

For a long time Kawasaki's racing policy was obscure and they shunned the world championships, but the raw power of those early 'Kwackers', and in particular the 500 cc Mach III H1, which led to the 750 cc H3 racer, contributed substantially to the development of the superbike era, to which Kawasaki were to make such an important contribution.

Brash and beefy in the early days, Kawasaki added sophistication with the years and displayed in their marketing policy an inventiveness and enterprise which drew worldwide attention. Like Honda, particularly, Kawasaki saw their future motorcycle prosperity in the lucrative American market and by 1966, with a Chicago office already established, they were offering a wide range of lightweights for sale in North America. They later set up directly owned subsidiaries to take over in many areas from local concessionaire arrangements and by the middle 1970s Kawasaki were exporting to some 90 different countries. They broke new ground in 1975 by becoming the first Japanese manufacturer to set up a full-scale production unit outside Japan; their Lincoln, Nebraska assembly plant complex representing an investment of about £7 million (15½m dollars) at 1975 values. By the early 1970s some 80 per cent of Kawasaki's total production was going abroad.

Kawasaki's line in commuter models – the KC100 Companion *(Kawasaki Information Service)*

After rather patchy excursions into racing, Kawasaki took a more serious look at competition after the introduction of the famous 500 cc H1 which, as the H1R, was raced by Yvon Duhamel. It was the first 500 cc racer to be offered for sale by a major motorcycle manufacturer for 10 years. Duhamel, along with Paul Smart and Gary Nixon, brought Kawasaki a number of successes in 1972 on the new 750 cc H2 Mach IV superbike. Kawasaki also involved themselves in motocross and trials. Their first off-road machines in 1970 led to the big 450 cc F12, a purpose-built motocrosser, and with this machine Brad Lackey captured the AMA motocross championship in 1972. Other off-road successes in America came Kawasaki's way through Jim Weinert.

Unashamedly, Kawasaki went into racing to gain 'brand awareness' and they have constantly displayed a commercial flair and an entrepreneurial approach with their exciting models and spirited marketing techniques.

In 1967 Kawasaki's 650W, their first four-cylinder machine, was the biggest capacity machine ever produced in Japan, but to launch themselves into the 1970s a new model was required. They started work on a new superbike, a powerful 750 cc tourer, but unknown to Kawasaki, Honda were working on a similar project and unveiled their CB 750 first, at the Tokyo Show of 1968. Kawasaki, in characteristic style, not only went ahead with their project but decided to up-stage Honda by developing the 750 into a 900 cc bike. This new machine, the Kawasaki Z1, was introduced in 1972 and became the famous flagship of the Kawasaki range. It won many awards and distinguished itself in long-distance endurance races like the prestigious Bol d'Or.

In British superbike racing, Mick Grant and Barry Ditchburn were popular Kawasaki entries in many events, but for a long time the factory held back from a full-blooded Grand Prix race programme. When they finally hoisted the green flag in the late 1970s, they were very successful. They gained 250 cc and 350 cc world championships through South African Kork Ballington in both 1978 and 1979, with the Australian superstar Gregg Hansford finishing in second and third positions in both years in the two classes.

Where now the Japanese manufacturers are the most influential in the motorcycle industry, 40 and 50 years ago it was the British makes which were looked upon with admiration by enthusiasts from all over the world. **NORTON** was the British factory supreme. Founded by James Lansdowne Norton, the Norton Manufacturing Company's original business was the production of fittings and parts for the two-wheel trade. That was in 1898, but in 1902 the first motorised bicycle to bear the Norton name appeared, powered by a French-made Clement engine. On a standard production machine bought direct from the factory, but incorporating a Peugeot engine, H. Rem Fowler won the twin-cylinder class of the first Tourist Trophy race on the Isle of Man in 1907. His success, remarkable against the factory 'specials' which faced him, helped to consolidate the Norton name, but after developing the first Norton engine, a 633 cc single-cylinder long-stroke known as the Big Four, in 1908, Jimmy Norton's business

suffered when the founder became ill and only reorganisation, following a takeover by an engineering company run by R. T. Shelley, saved it from collapse. The new company, Norton Motors Limited, had a wider outlook, developing the Big Four with the introduction of a couple of sports models offered in limited quantities. A 490 cc machine, developed from the original 633 cc model, was to endure for more than 40 years as the 16H, remarkably with comparatively few major modifications.

Government orders in the First World War helped Norton to prosper and 1916 witnessed the move to the firm's famous premises in Bracebridge Street, Birmingham. Norton's activity in motorcycle sport from earliest times was well reflected in the sale of their touring models for domestic use so that they were less affected by the recession of 1930, having by then built up a formidable reputation, and during the Second World War Norton's production was kept high with military orders for the 16H, now decidedly elderly. In the post-war world, however, and once the immediate advantage of their uninterrupted manufacture disappeared as the Italian and German factories came back into the picture, their models didn't alter radically enough or frequently enough and Norton, along with the few British makes still surviving, found themselves increasingly at odds with changing market requirements.

Confronted by the sales onslaught of the Japanese factories in Europe in the 1960s the British industry reeled and closed ranks. Norton was taken over by Amalgamated Motor Cycles Ltd (AMC) in 1952 and only four years later further reorganisation was necessary in a bid to stem increasing financial losses, Norton Villiers being formed under the banner of Manganese Bronze

For years Norton had the finest reputation of any motorcycle manufacturer in the world. This is the 'big four' of 1924

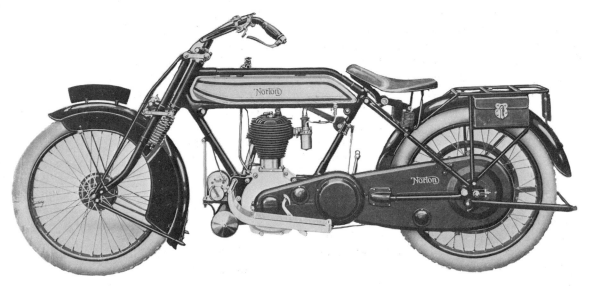

Holdings. By now, of course, Norton's most glorious days were over.

The fame of Norton had been gained largely through their active interest in motorcycle sport, in which their record is outstanding. Linked solidly with racing on the Isle of Man, the factory supported the Tourist Trophy races from the beginning, in 1907, right through continuously until the mid-1950s, except for the war years. Even today, Norton's record of continuous support of racing is a supreme example. Norton machines and riders, during the factory's halcyon days, secured 17 world championships, more than 30 TT wins, and an impressive number of victories in continental Grands Prix and other international events. In 1924 alone, they collected 123 first places. Norton machinery was also used successfully in sidecar events. The factory also entered record breaking with relish and even before the outbreak of the First World War the single-cylinder belt-driven Norton, aptly named 'Old Miracle' and which finished up as an exhibit at the British National Motor Museum, set numerous national and world records.

Norton based their race machines very much on their standard designs, relying on the development of comparatively simple single-cylinder machines. While this gave Norton riders the benefit of superior handling and steering for many years, they relied for too long on these virtues. Certainly, had it not been for the banning of supercharging and the enforced use of 'pool' petrol in the early post Second World War years, Norton machinery would have been eclipsed sooner. The famous 'Featherbed' frame was introduced in 1950 and this machine, brain child of the McCandless brothers of Belfast, gave even better road holding and handling qualities. The combination of the new frame and the riding skills of Geoffrey Duke kept Norton in the racing picture until the multi-cylinder machines from Italy overtook them. In 1955, with Norton officially out of racing, they failed to take the Senior TT for the first time in nine years.

In their heyday a Norton racing contract was the final accolade. All the most brilliant riders of the time rode for Norton including Jimmy Guthrie, Jimmy Simpson, Stanley Woods, Freddie Frith, Harold Daniell, Geoff Duke, Ray Amm, John Surtees and Bob McIntyre. Production of the famous Manx Norton was continued until 1962 and was ridden afterwards by many successful privateers, including Derek Minter, on machines brilliantly tuned by engineers like Ray Petty, Steve Lancefield and Francis Beart.

In the early days Norton supported racing at Brooklands, gaining many distinctions, and in happier times for the British industry, when British machines were popular in America, Norton in 1949 contested the Daytona 200, gaining an impressive one-two-three in the major race with their works machine. Norton dominated the race again in 1950, with first, second and fourth places and yet again in 1951, with Norton riders first and second home. The following year saw the merger with Associated Motor Cycles Ltd.

It is impossible to separate Norton's success from their brilliant development engineer and team manager for many years, Joe Craig. He developed the famous single-cylinder Nortons painstakingly over the years and was largely responsible, not only for maintaining Norton's technical superiority for so long, but for building up such an impressive list of team riders. The single-cylinder machine had been the basis of the British industry's business for years and Craig's skill enabled Norton to keep winning races, and keep sales going, even when the greater power potential of the multis was well known.

The factory's founder, James L. Norton, died in 1925 at 56 years of age after a long illness.

In the days of British motorcycle supremacy, no country produced more different makes than Britain, and of the 2000 or so manufacturers of motorcycles it is estimated there have been, more than 600 were British companies. Among the most prominent were **BSA, Triumph** and **AJS.**

BSA are significant because for almost 50 years they were among the biggest producer's of motorcycles, yet showed little real interest in road racing. They preferred to build up a reputation for reliability through large numbers of dependable models in everyday use. Adding to this image was their active support of, and outstanding success in, trials and scrambles. After an early disappointment with modified roadsters when BSA first entered the TTs in 1913, successive managements were not to be tempted into racing – particularly after a disastrous effort in 1921 when six racing machines specially prepared for the Isle of Man all retired with valve or piston failure. To attract publicity, however, BSA decided to try to win a race at the famous Brooklands circuit. Wal Handley was given a specially developed 500 cc Empire Star and on this machine he won a three-lap, all-comers race at an average speed of 102·27 mph (164·65km/h) with a fastest lap speed in excess of 107 mph (172km/h). Handley, a well known retired TT rider and motorcycle dealer, was awarded a Gold Star by the BMCRC for exceeding a 100 mph (161km/h) lap at Brooklands (a routine acknowledgement), and when BSA were considering names for the following year's model, the choice was obvious: Gold Star. In 1938 as the 500 cc Model M24, the Gold Star or 'Goldie' was launched and was to become one of the most famous models manufactured by any British factory.

Post-war 350 cc and 500 cc versions were superbly competitive and as a clubman's racer the Gold Star was outstanding. Bob McIntyre and Phil Read, along with Derek Minter, were to gain much of their early road-racing experience on Gold Stars, but a prototype racer produced by prominent engineer Doug Hele and tested by Geoffrey Duke – and considered to have outstanding potential – was not exploited because of the management's timidity towards racing. The BSA name was strongly promoted through the sidecar racing successes of Chris Vincent and, of course, by outstanding motocross performance by Jeff Smith.

In the 1970s, with the growing importance of production racing and Formula 750 events, BSA, now merged with Triumph, competed through their American subsidiary in a number of important American races and did extremely well, John Cooper's winning of California's Ontario Classic at his first attempt giving BSA an enormous boost. BSA also benefited through impressive performances in long-distance events and prominent British road-race meetings.

TRIUMPH, another well known British make, was manufactured by the Triumph Engineering Company Ltd at Meriden, near Coventry, and gained widespread public attention when Norton Villiers Triumph tried to close down the Meriden works in the 1970s. After Government intervention and support a workers co-operative was formed, but suffered financially. Although Triumph machines figured prominently in early TT events, their overall record in racing was undistinguished. In the early 1900s, however, Triumph laid the foundations for later machines which were to prove so successful. Their first motorcycle appeared in 1902 and had a 2 hp Minerva engine clipped to the frame. A year later they began to build lightweight models powered by JAP engines. Two years later they were producing simple, robust designs of an extremely progressive nature with a reliable 3½ hp engine and such advanced items as high-tension magneto, spray carburettor and a pivoted type of spring fork. Later, improved versions proved very reliable and were soon in demand for touring which was a strong platform for Triumph sales in succeeding years.

Triumph's early reputation was built on mechanical reliability and their quality of finish and

Triumph machines were manufactured for military use during the First World War (this picture c 1915) (National Motor Museum)

they succeeded impressively. At a time when motorcycle sales were falling, Triumph's business soared – 1000 sold in 1907 and three times that number in 1908. In 1914 Triumph produced an experimental vertical twin 650 cc machine, perhaps the most important to be produced during this period since it was the forerunner of several designs which were widely used after Triumph revived it for production in the mid-1930s.

Like BSA, Triumph made motorcycles for army use during the war years, the 550 cc single-cylinder model H being very popular with army despatch riders. In the 1920s co-operation with fuel technologist Harry Ricardo resulted in the highly-successful road-going Triumph Ricardo, and in the mid-1930s designer Edward Turner's 500 cc vertical 'speed-twin' was a major success for Triumph, setting new standards in quiet-running, acceleration and general specification and performance. In the 1950s Triumph were among a number of manufacturers to develop small four-stroke, single-cylinder engines with their 150 cc 'Terrier' and then the 199 cc Tiger Cub. In the late 1960s Triumph machines set high standards in 750 cc and Production events with their Bonneville and Trident models. The merger of Triumph with BSA was completed in 1951.

Another British factory with an impressive pedigree was **AJS**, the initials representing the name of the founder, Albert John Stevens. The business had been established as early as 1897 by Stevens and his four brothers, who fitted American Mitchell engines to ordinary pedal cycles. Later they produced their own air and water-cooled units and proudly introduced the first AJS machine to carry the name in 1909, a 292 cc single-cylinder model with two-speed countershaft gearbox and choice of belt or chain drive. A. J. Stevens used his ability as a rider to establish the name of the company in trials and in racing events.

First major racing success came in 1914 when newly-designed 350cc singles took first and second places in the Junior TT on the Isle of Man.

The war broke into the commercial production of the road-going version and the factory's ambitions in racing, but at the end of the war Cyril Williams caused a sensation on a new six-speed 350cc AJS, which incorporated unique push-rod operated ohvs and hemispherical cylinder head. Although he had to push home from Craig-ny-Baa, he won the Junior TT by ten minutes with a new class lap record of 51·36 mph (82·69 km/h). The following year another Williams, Eric, repeated AJS's Junior TT success, Howard Davies and T.M. Sheard completing AJS's fine one-two-three performance.

Considerable prestige followed when that meteoric rider Jimmy Simpson, who made a routine out of breaking records on the Isle of Man, used AJS machines to burst through the 60 and 70 mph TT barriers. His 64 mph (103 km/h) was set in 1924 and his 70 mph (113 km/h) in 1926, his first record coming in the Junior event and the latter in the Senior, on a 500 cc ohv model.

AJS benefited from their racing success with a growing reputation for the reliability of their road-going bikes, but the 1930 depression saw them taken over by the Matchless concern run by the famous Collier brothers. However, AJS machines were continued in production and sold under their own brand name. Matchless were themselves later to be absorbed by AMC Ltd. Against works Norton and Velocette machines AJS machines found racing difficult, but in 1938 they produced a 500 cc V-4, with two cylinders angled forward and two back, in an effort to counter 'foreign' opposition from, particularly, Guzzi and BMW. With this machine Walter Rusk set the first 100 mph (161 km/h) of the Ulster Grand Prix in 1939. Their famous racing twin, called the Porcupine because of its unusual cylinder head fins, was introduced in 1947, and AJS continued racing until 1954, a year which saw virtually the end of all British 'works' racing.

ARIEL, BROUGH, DOUGLAS, EXCELSIOR, MATCHLESS, RUDGE, SCOTT, SUNBEAM, VELOCETTE, VINCENT and **HRD** are among other once-distinguished British motorcycles which sadly no longer exist. As we have seen from the chapter on the United States, the once-flourishing and lively American industry was reduced until only Indian and Harley-Davidson remained, the latter becoming the sole survivor after 1953, when the last real Indian machines were made.

INDIAN machines were made by the Hendee Manufacturing Company, which began in business

The first Indian motorcycles were produced in 1901, as a development of cycle manufacture, a 'between-stage' motorised bicycle showing the potential of full-scale motorcycle production *(National Motor Museum)*

as a cycle manufacturer. George M. Hendee was the founder, but in 1900 he became associated with Oscar Hedstrom, and this led to the first Indian motorised bicycles and in 1905 to the first Indian V-twin. In the early part of the century Indian machines were perhaps the most popular foreign make of machine on the British market, this reputation being enhanced by the factory's spectacular victory in 1911 when Indian machines took the first three places in the Senior TT to become the first foreign factory to win the Isle of Man event. The Hendee Company maintained a progressive outlook and introduced a spring frame in 1913 and then the world's first electric starter a year later. Their domestic output was considerable. After the First World War they introduced the 596 cc Scout, which led to other models which found favour with American motorcycle-mounted police.

In racing and sport, Indian machines were prominent. Ed Walker claimed the world outright speed record at 104·12 mph (167·56 km/h) in 1920. Much earlier Jake de Rosier and some ten years later, Bert Le Vack (winning the Brooklands 500-mile race in 1921) gained racing distinction for Indian machines. Unfortunately, little progress in the design of Indian machines was evident after about 1930 and although they were to struggle along for some years, and purchase the once-famous Ace company in an effort to survive, they had seen their best days.

HARLEY-DAVIDSON have acquired an outstanding reputation in almost all branches of motorcycling. The first Harley-Davidsons appeared in 1903 and six years later the first V-twins, setting the pattern for their reputation which exists to the present time for the manufacture of big V-twin machines. Many innovations, including the twist grip, were pioneered by Harley-Davidson in the early years, and in 1914, following the successes of many private riders in national races, Harley-Davidson set up their first competitions department. Floyd Clymer set a new world one-hour dirt-track record in 1916 on a technically advanced 1000 cc V-twin which had four valves to each cylinder head and a three-speed gearbox.

Harley-Davidson solo and motorcycle combinations were used extensively by the American army in the First World War, the firm producing 20 000 machines in two years. In the early 1920s Britain's Freddie Dixon raced Harley-Davidson successfully at Brooklands, in 1923 bringing the factory the world speed record at 106·5 mph (197·2 km/h). About this time pedal cycle production was abandoned and in 1926 a 350 cc side-valve single-cylinder Harley-Davidson machine was added to the range of large capacity V-twins and, as an overhead track-racing version, scored significant success in short-track American racing.

The 750 cc side-valve V-twin was introduced in 1929 and witnessed little real development, though the firm survived the depression and was boosted by the American forces use of their machines during the Second World War. As America took increasingly to the motor car in post-war years, Harley-Davidson struggled, but kept going through their resistance to imported models and by securing a revision to the racing rules of the AMA which gave them the advantage and kept Harley-Davidson machines strongly in the results. Their amalgamation with the Italian Aermacchi company, Aeronautica Macchi, was established in 1960, and although the name was changed to Aermacchi-Harley-Davidson, the Italian lower-capacity bikes were sold under the American name in the United States.

Harley-Davidson continued to be known for their lumbering big twins which, however, were appealing less and less to the motorcycle buying public, so in order to stay in business the firm moved out of the original Harley and Davidson families' hands and became a public corporation in 1965, four years later being taken over by the American Machine and Foundry Group (AMF). Production was rationalised and although the basic policy of the company didn't seem to alter dramatically, a new generation of two-stroke machines led to Harley-Davidson's first road-racing world championship in 1974. These machines, designed by Walter Villa and his brother and ridden successfully by Walter, originated from their base

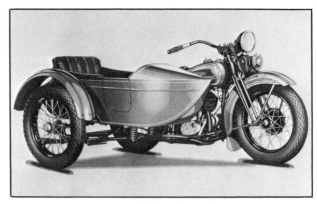

This Harley-Davidson, from America's most famous and enduring motorcycle manufacturer, is fitted with a 1932 model sidecar

in Italy, and Walter was to secure the 250 cc world championship again in 1975 and 1976, the latter year adding the 350 cc title. Harley-Davidson continue, however, to be known for their extraordinarily bulky motorcycles for which there appears to be a steady demand in the United States.

Although France was active in the early days of motorcycle development, and **PEUGEOT** and **MOTOBECANE** continue to make motorcycles, Italy and Germany are the countries which became known more than others for their motorcycle industries. The best known and most significant Italian manufacturers have been (alphabetically), Benelli, Ducati, Garelli, Gilera, (Moto) Guzzi, Mondial, Morini and MV Agusta.

The **BENELLI** company, founded in 1911 by five brothers, began as a motorcycle and parts manufacturer and the factory began to show interest in racing in the mid-1920s, achieving some success just prior to the outbreak of the war when British rider Ted Mellors won the Lightweight TT on the Isle of Man on the only Benelli machine in the race. With racing ambitions, Benelli developed what was generally accepted as a superb water-cooled, four-cylinder 250, but the war intervened and the post-war ban on supercharged machines made it obsolete. The Benelli works was destroyed in the war, but was built up substantially afterwards to employ some 700 people. In 1972 it became part of the De Tomaso group, which also, later that year, encompassed Moto Guzzi.

After the war Benelli returned to racing with a version of their pre-war double overhead-camshaft single and in 1950, through Dario Ambrosini, they caused a major upset by unseating the previously all-conquering Guzzi factory to win the 250 cc world championship. The Italian rider's death while racing the following year caused Benelli to lose interest in racing until 1959 when they

161

returned with new machines to show promise with Dickie Dale and Geoff Duke riding. Later still, Renzo Pasolini rode Benelli machines with distinction before the Japanese were to dominate racing.

Benelli have manufactured road-going machines of all kinds and their 750 cc Sei was the only six-cylinder motorcycle in the world when introduced in 1974.

DUCATI began motorcycle manufacture in 1950 with mopeds and ultra-lightweight machines and made significant progress following the appointment of Fabio Taglioni as chief designer in 1954. A single-cylinder machine of Taglioni design won its debut race in the 125 cc Swedish Grand Prix of 1956 and was the first racing machine to incorporate the technical characteristic of desmodromic valves – positively operated valves being used to close the valves as well as open them. Though the idea was not new, and it had been used in racing cars, Ducati was the first factory to use the principle successfully in motorcycles. The factory later made larger-capacity, more powerful machines with a view to claiming sales in the United States, and in the 1970s Ducati became known for their big V-twins which did so well in endurance racing.

GARELLI was established in 1913 and produced successful 350 cc 2-stroke singles in the early 1920s. In 1967 Garelli merged with Agrati, and the factory at Sesto San Giovanni now concentrates on the manufacture of 2-stroke engines. Garelli is now best known for a successful and wide range of mopeds and mini bikes, though it also manufactures components for the motorcycle and bicycle industries.

One of the oldest motorcycle manufacturers in Italy is **GILERA**, founded by Count Giuseppe

Gilera in 1909. Nothing much was heard of them until 1937 when Piero Taruffi achieved a world speed record of 170·37 mph (274·18 km/h) and a new distance One Hour record at 121·23 mph (195·10 km/h) on a fully enclosed, water-cooled, four-cylinder machine developed from the Italian Rondine. After the war, with supercharging banned, Gilera engineer Pietro Remor redesigned the pre-war record breaker and the new version appeared with an air-cooled engine developing bhp at 10 000. Its power was more than a match for the winning single-cylinder Nortons, and once its handling was improved, the new Gilera took command and captured the 500 cc world title in 1950. Apart from 1951, Gileras were to take the title every year until the factory retired from racing at the end of 1957. Italian riders Umberto Masetti, Gilberto Milani and Libero Liberati, and Britons Geoffrey Duke and John Surtees were the riders.

The importance of Gilera was also that their design became the standard for all modern high-performance motorcycles with a transverse four-cylinder engine. Achievements of Gilera include the first 100 mph lap of the Assen Circuit in the Dutch TT (Umberto Masseti in 1952) and of the Isle of Man Mountain Circuit in the TTs (Bob McIntyre in 1957). At Monza that year, McIntyre raised the One Hour record to 141·37 mph (261·82 km/h) on the 350 cc version, not to be exceeded until Mike Hailwood's Daytona triumph in 1964.

After Gilera's withdrawal from racing MV Agusta continued to be successful with broadly the same basic design, as did Honda even later, confirming Gilera's theories for high-performance machines of fairly large capacity.

Domestically, Gilera was never exceptionally strong internationally and in 1969 financial problems were resolved only through the selling of the company's assets and famous name to the makers of Vespa scooters, Piaggio. In the 1970s the range consisted of touring and sporting lightweights and mopeds.

Two other famous Italian companies retired from racing at the time of Gilera's withdrawal, Mondial and Guzzi. **MONDIAL** are remembered for the work of their brilliant designer Alfonso Drusiani who produced superbly built double overhead-camshaft 125 cc racers for competition in a lightweight class which, until then, had not been taken too seriously. But these excellent Mondials brought enormous prestige to the class and were perhaps faster than many of the then current 250 cc and 350 cc racers. For three years they were superior to their rivals. Drusiani later left the factory but after his return new 125 cc and

Bob McIntyre on a Gilera at Ballaugh Bridge in the 1957 Senior TT *(B.R. Nicholls)*

250 cc machines were produced, but the factory's withdrawal from racing sadly ended further development.

GUZZI are remembered for their astonishing versatility in design and for their technical brilliance. The full name of the factory was Moto Guzzi and their advanced approach to machine development, exemplified in the special wind tunnel they built at their headquarters at Mandello to test and develop streamlining for their machines, was reflected in their prolific success in racing and record breaking. At their peak they held more than 120 international records.

Guzzi entered racing in the early 1920s and retired in 1957. In road racing they gained 8 world championships and 11 TT victories. After winning numerous continental Grands Prix Guzzi's victory in both the Lightweight and Senior TTs of 1935 was the first 'foreign' Senior victory for 24 years. The 500 cc Guzzi was virtually a 'doubled-up' version of the successful 250 cc model, itself unusual because of its wide angle 120° V-twin engine, with a horizontal front 'pot' and a magneto set between the cylinders. It was also the first TT winner to incorporate rear springing. The British rider Stanley Woods steered it to victory. From the early days Guzzi consistently favoured a unique horizontal single-cylinder engine of basic design and four years after Woods' TT victories in 1935 came their epic defeat of the all-conquering DKWs in the 250 cc German Grand Prix. They dominated 250 cc racing from 1947 to 1953 when they upgraded their machines and, with a 350 cc version of basically the same design, won the 350 cc world title at their first attempt. They had already won the 250 cc world championship in 1949, the inaugural year of the modern championships, through the Italian rider Bruno Ruffo.

In addition to their famous 'singles', Guzzi produced V-twins, across-the-frame-3s, in-line-4s. . .and a V-8 machine! This extraordinary model, of 500 cc, was introduced in 1954 and developed 65 bhp at 1200 rpm. A later version came in 1957 and had a speed of around 174 mph (280 km/h), but the full potential of this machine, because of Guzzi's racing withdrawal that year, was never fully exploited.

The company was founded in 1921 by Carlo Guzzi and Giorgio Parodi and over the years introduced numerous innovations including a sprung frame in 1936 and a rotary disc-valve after the First World War. Guzzi himself did much of the early design work, but most of the factory's fame came from the brilliant design work of, first, Giulio Cesare Carcano and then Lino Tonti. In the motorcycling recession of the 1960s Guzzi made an attempt to break into the American market, but in 1967 they were taken over by the Societa Esercizio Industrie Moto Mecanniche (SEIMM) and reorganised under Alejandro de Tomaso. By the late 1970s Moto Guzzi were producing some 85 000 vehicles a year – mopeds, motorcycles and three-wheeler transport vehicles – of which about half went for export. Many police and armed forces have bought Guzzi machines.

Two smaller Italian factories are Moto Morini and Morbidelli. **MORINI** was founded in 1937 to manufacture motor cars and tricycles, but in 1946 they began to specialise in motorcycles and, in particular, two-stroke mopeds and four-stroke lightweights for road and enduro riding. They also introduced a 350 cc model and the Corsaro Special, a 5-speed 150 cc single with a top speed of 87 mph (140 km/h). Morini have been spasmodically interested in racing. Their first 125 cc two-stroke race-special won the Italian championship in 1948. Talented rider Tarquinio Provini took them nearest to world championship honours with a second place in the 250 cc class in 1963.

MORBIDELLI, conversely, have made remarkable impact in racing in more recent times. Unknown until the early 1970s, when they began competing in 125 cc and 250 cc Grands Prix, they were soon in the news. The Italian rider Paolo Pileri brought them their first world championship in the 125 cc class in 1975, the factory retaining it in 1976 through fellow Italian Pierpaolo Bianchi. In 1977 Bianchi made it three in a row and Italy's Mario Lega also brought them their first 250 cc world title.

BIANCHI was an Italian factory which achieved a certain amount of racing success in the 1920s and '30s, and ran the MV-four close in the Italian Grand Prix of 1960, but after the demise of the racing Guzzis and Gileras in 1957, **MV AGUSTA** was to establish an Italian legend in motorcycling. Although MV, founded by the enigmatic Count Domenico Agusta, never went in for volume production of road models, the bikes they did produce for domestic use were to extremely high specifications and priced accordingly. In racing, however, they became the most successful factory of all time, amassing 38 individual world championships, 37 manufacturers titles and a staggering 270 world championship wins. Les Graham, John Surtees, Gary Hocking, Mike Hailwood, Phil Read and Giacomo Agostini all rode successfully for MV and the factory secured the 500 cc crown every year from 1958 to 1974 inclusive, though for much of this time serious works opposition was limited. In 1958 and 1959 they won all four solo classes of the world championships.

An Italian factory less well known outside Italy than the 'established' names is **LAVERDA**, which began making motorcycles in 1949, though the family-owned Laverda industrial group began as early as 1873 when Pietro Laverda started the manufacture of agricultural machinery. Laverda have always paid much attention to performance and after the introduction of their large twin-cylinder machines in 1968, became very successful in long-distance road racing. In earlier days Laverda produced lightweight machines up to 175 cc and gained many victories in production races. About half of Laverda's current production is exported.

HUSQVARNA is the only motorcycle of note to be made in Sweden, being most prominent in motocross. The factory began making motorcycles in 1903 and in the early 1930s were active in road racing. Before the outbreak of war, however, their road-racing performances were in decline, but in 1960 a modified version of their single-cylinder overhead-valve 500 cc roadster, first seen in 1936, took Bill Nilsson to Husqvarna's first world 500 cc motocross championship in 1960.

Spain has an impressive pedigree of motorcycle manufacture, through Montesa, Bultaco, Ossa and Derbi. **MONTESA** was the country's first major manufacturer, the business originating in 1941 in Barcelona. After a period of difficulty in the 1950s they introduced more modern production techniques, leading to the production of a wide range of motocross and trials machinery which did well in international competition.

BULTACO are better known for their success, largely through the Spanish rider Angel Nieto, in Grand Prix road racing. The company was set up in 1958 by former Montesa designer Signor Francesco Bulto who quickly sought recognition through racing success. Bultaco's reputation was first established in international motocross and trials. In the latter their brilliance brought them the World Trials Championship every year since its introduction in 1975 up to and including 1979, and they also contested Grand Prix road-racing events in the lower capacity classes. From a production peak of 40 000 in 1976, however, there followed a serious decline to only 12 000 in 1979 and in 1980, with the company reported to be about £7 million in debt, the future of Bultaco appeared seriously in doubt.

Harry Everts (Bultaco) winning in Germany after a dazzling duel with Jaroslav Falta (CZ) in 1978 *(J. Burnicle)*

Spain's small **OSSA** Company began life making projector equipment but switched to motorcycle manufacture in 1946. The firm has been closely identified with off-road models, being very succesful during the 1970s in the United States market. Ossa have achieved recognition in trials, winning many international competitions. The British rider Mick Andrews was the first trials rider to use Ossa machinery and, following their suggestion that he concentrate his efforts on this sport (to the exclusion of his interest in motocross), he brought them top-level success.

Ossa are also vividly remembered for their remarkable impact in 250 cc racing in 1969 through the Spanish rider Antiago Herrero. Designed by Eduardo Giro, the Ossa's performance startled the Japanese twins and Italian machines. With just one rider and one machine, Ossa almost accomplished the 'miracle' – only Herrero's fall in the last race of the year in Yugoslavia robbing him and Ossa of the title after winning three rounds. The factory in the late 1970s, however, were kept going with aid from the Spanish Government.

DERBI is also a small Spanish company, a family concern, being founded by Señor Rabosa after the Second World War. They began to concentrate on the manufacture of small capacity machines, for which they are now world famous, in the mid-1960s, outstanding road racing success through the achievements of Spain's own Angel Nieto giving them a tremendous boost. On a racer specially designed by Francisco Tombias, Nieto won the 50 cc world championship for the first time in 1969, winning again in 1970 and 1972. A copy of this successful model was made available to the general public and sold well. Derbi also developed a successful 125 cc racer, Nieto taking the world title in both 1971 and 1972.

In Eastern Europe, Czechoslovakia is the country mostly identified with motorcycles, through its two major factories, JAWA and CZ, run as a nationalised industry. The **JAWA** company developed from armaments production when its founder, Frantisek Janecek, began to build German motorcycles under licence in 1929. In the years before the Second World War, British Villiers engines were used by Jawa, leading to the development of their own technically advanced two-stroke machines. Post-war years saw the concentration on rugged off-road models, with Jawa bikes becoming dominant in 250 cc world motocross and the International Six-Days Trial.

CZ also made a name in motocross; and in speedway. By converting a 175 cc trials model into a motocross special the factory, after a couple of years' further development, finished second in the Czech National Championships. This gave them confidence to move into Europe and on improved machinery, Vlastimil Valek and Karel Pilar did well in the early 1960s. The big break came after Valek had ridden to second place in the world motocross championship in 1963, the famous Belgian ace Joel Robert then switching to CZ in place of the British Greeves machine. He took the world title on a CZ machine in 1964. Extremely reliable, CZ machines have since won a number of world motocross championships. The factory at Strakonice produces about 30 000 bikes a year and makes engines for Jawa models, which are manufactured at Sazavou.

Countries perhaps less well known for motorcycle production are Portugal (Casal), USSR (Cossack), Holland (Batavas and Van Veen) and Austria (KTM and Puch). Of these makes **PUCH** is noted for large-scale production of mopeds and sports motorcycles, and **KTM**, in production since the last war, has achieved success in trials and motocross. **VAN VEEN** is the Dutch concessionaire for West German Kreidler models, but in 1972 founder Henk Van Veen introduced his own impressive OCR 1000 cc superbike, a top-quality high-speed, limited production luxury machine, as a personal venture.

A review of motorcycling factories could not be complete without reference to the strength of Germany. **ZUNDAPP**, while perhaps enjoying less general recognition than firms like BMW, Kreidler, MZ and DKW, nevertheless developed from the manufacture of their first motorcycles in 1921 to become one of Germany's most important and largest manufacturers. Zundapp were active in the 1930s in other forms of motorised transport, but came back strongly into motorcycle manufacture in the years following the Second World War, showing particular interest in endurance trials and cross-country events and gaining a number of world records. Their factory is in Munich.

Two German factories which share some common ground are **DKW** and **MZ**, for after the Second World War, when Germany was divided, the old DKW works at Zschopau, south west of Dresden, was reorganised under Russian control as MZ (Motorradwerk Zschopau). DKW had even earlier experienced uneasy times since their formation in Saxony in 1920 by Jorgen Skafte Rasmussen, a Dane. After a 122 cc auxiliary engine designed by Hugo Ruppe became enormously successful in the early years, and the factory in the late 1920s gained recognition with a loop scavenge system for their two-stroke engine, DKW became part of the Auto-Union car group in 1932. After supplying the German army with two-stroke motorcycles during the war, DKW found their premises in the Russian zone of Germany after hostilities, and under Russian control motorcycle production continued under the new name, MZ. The well known engineer Walter Kaaden and rider Ernst Degner were closely associated with MZ and pioneered technical developments and racing success. Kaaden produced 125 cc and 250 cc racing machines with novel disc valve two-stroke motors which were soon to upset the superiority of four-stroke machines in the smaller capacity classes. Degner took MZ to the verge of world championship honours, and would most likely have taken the title had he not chosen to seek refuge in the West. The firm also gained a reputation for highly successful motocross models. MZ is the brand name of the IFA-Kombinat Zweirader Group, East Germany's nationalised vehicle industry.

DKW production, meantime, was continued from Ingolstadt, in West Germany, where the company had been re-formed, but in 1966 the Auto-Union Group was absorbed into Volkswagen and DKW was acquired by Zweirad Union, then making a range of motorcyles and mopeds. The firm became the first to use a Wankel engine in a production motorcycle in 1974 with the introduction of the W2000, known in certain markets as a Hercules model, but elsewhere as a DKW. The 1966 merger brought the interests of DKW, Express, Victoria and Hercules motorcycles under one umbrella to create the largest manufacturer of two-wheel production in Germany.

MAICO is another German name deeply respected for splendid off-road machines with an international reputation. They made a particularly strong impact in the United States and have been successful in both 250 cc and 500 cc motocross world championships. The firm was started by the brothers Otto and Wilhelm Maisch in 1934 with a 100 cc road bike. Touring scooters and a 400 cc twin were put into production in the early 1950s. They scored heavily with the M250, used extensively by the German Federal army.

A much younger company in Germany is **KREIDLER**, now famous for lightweight motorcycle manufacture, but which was founded only in 1950. The factory's reputation has been formed solidly on racing, their first 50 cc world championship machine being introduced in 1962 and in this category Kreidler's very first Grand Prix win came in Spain through Hans-Georg Anscheidt. Later, through the initiative of Dutch importer Henk Van Veen, the Kreidler name gained further successes and in the 1970s was strongly represented in 50 cc racing, gaining world titles in 1971, 1973, 1974, 1975, and 1979.

Unlike Kreidler, the German **NSU** concern has a long history, dating back to 1873. They began making motorised pedal cycles in 1900 in the factory at Neckarsulm, from which the initials NSU are derived. After a reasonably quiet existence, NSU thrust themselves into racing in the early 1950s, when their works machines and riders dominated the 125 cc and 250 cc world championships in 1953 and 1954. NSU had involved themselves earlier in sport, their machines competing in the TT Races regularly from 1907 to 1914; and again in the 1930s they gave consistent support to racing. Developed supercharged 350 cc and 500 cc twin-cylinder machines were raced before the war and afterwards, in 1950, there was a four-cylinder machine with atmospheric induction, but this was unsuccessful. By this time, however, their greatest effort was being directed into the smaller classes. NSU are also famous for their record-breaking success, Wilhelm Herz capturing the world outright speed record in 1951, and twice more in 1956. Gustav Baumm also shattered the 50 cc world speed record at 121·9 mph (196·2 km/h).

The best known German factory of all is undoubtedly **BMW**. The Bayerische Motorenwerkse at Munich was founded during the First World War to make engines for the German Air Force, beginning motorcycle production in 1923. That year, at the Paris Motor Show, the BMW 500 cc R32 model was unveiled and its basic concept of a transversely mounted horizontally opposed engine with shaft drive – it was designed by Dr. Ing Max Friz – was to set the pattern of BMW tradition down the ages. BMW entered racing in the early 1920s, but had little success in international competition. Careful development brought a measure of success, however, and with supercharged versions of the 500 cc flat twin machine, with telescopic front forks and rear springing, BMW gained prominence. But although Jock West won the Ulster Grand Prix for BMW in 1937 and 1938, and in 1939 Georg Meier caused a sensation by becoming the first foreign rider on a foreign (BMW) machine to win the Senior TT, it was to be in the sidecar class that BMW achieved such phenomenal success. The outstanding low-speed torque and incredible reliability of the BMW made it ideal in sidecar racing and after the war they concentrated their efforts in this class, being less active in the solo classes. BMW took the sidecar world championship every year from 1954 to 1974 inclusive.

BMW have been responsible for a number of technical advances in motorcycle design, being the first factory to use hydraulically damped telescopic forks, in 1935, and twin leading shoe drum brakes in the 1950s. In the middle 1960s, when motorcycle sales slumped generally in the United States and Europe, the BMW company almost discontinued motorcycle production, but a new range of superbikes in the 1970s enabled them to recover their fortunes. They have built up a firm reputation for the sheer quality of their machines, in both construction and finish.

BMW are also remembered, of course, for their world speed records in the 1930s and the claiming of the outright world speed record on two wheels through Ernst Henne at almost 174 mph (280 km/h), a record which stood for 14 years.

The German DKW factory distinguished its Hercules W 2000 model with an air-cooled Wankel engine *(M. Decet)*

Chapter 17

The Race for World Titles

After the Second World War motorcycling struggled to find its feet again and road racing looked to the Isle of Man and to the continental Grands Prix to rekindle interrupted glories. Events like the German, Belgian, Italian and Ulster Grands Prix, along with the Dutch TT, were first held in the 1920s, but in the beginning they were boringly long and punishing affairs with little spectator interest. Races were run over normal roads, specially closed for the occasion, and seemed to go on for ever – some events taking three and four hours to complete. The 500 cc class was the one that mattered most and although there were 350 cc and 250 cc machines, the entry for the latter classes was generally so low that all machines ran together, with each capacity starting out at set intervals.

In the 1930s races were becoming recognisable with their modern counterparts, being shorter, better organised and with separate classes. But although each country had its own Grand Prix and riders formed themselves into what became

Above: Alec Bennett, on a Norton, making a pit stop during the 1924 French Grand Prix *(National Motor Museum)*

Below: Time to celebrate. Jon Ekerold, Anton Mang and Michel Frutschi finish one, two and three in the 350 cc German Grand Prix at Hockenheim in 1979 *(All Sport/Don Morley)*

Nortons outside the Shelley Works *(National Motor Museum)*

known as the 'continental circus' – travelling from one country to another in a season-long schedule of races, there was no formal championship series. Each race was individual with its own prestige and its own heroes.

These were the days when the British Norton factory dominated racing. Competition-proved on the rugged Isle of Man Mountain Course, British riders and British machinery were supreme. Norton were virtually invincible in both the 350 cc and 500 cc classes and that remarkable Scottish rider Jimmy Guthrie was top-of-the-bill, once winning nine continental Grands Prix in succession. It was a painful disaster for the sport when Guthrie was killed when leading the German Grand Prix at Sachsenring in 1937. By this time Germany was set to challenge the all-conquering superiority of the British industry and, sponsored heavily by a fanatically nationalistic government, their factories were pushing Britain hard on the race tracks in the last few years leading up to the outbreak of war. Norton's single-cylinder models, despite their handling and road-holding qualities, were finding the supercharged flat-twin 500 cc of BMW an insistent opponent, while the finely-engineered DKW two-strokes were beginning to make an impact in the 250 cc and 350 cc classes.

There had been talk of a championships series before the war and in 1938 the Fédération Internationale des Clubs Motor Cyclistes (FICM), the international governing body of motorcycle sport, organised a European championship based on eight races, including the TT, Dutch TT, and Grands Prix in Belgium, France, Germany and Switzerland. It was not totally representative, but the 500 cc title went to BMW through Germany's Georg Meier, the British rider Ted Mellors on the British Velocette took the 350 cc title, and the honours in the 250 cc class went to Germany through Ewald Kluge on the DKW – Kluge also earning himself the title of Champion of Europe by scoring more points than any other rider in all three classes.

The following year, as Italy, through Gilera and a passionate drive to follow Germany's example by gaining sporting achievement, entered the fray, Norton withdrew from racing to concentrate their energies on making as many of their side-valve 490 cc 16 H models as possible for military use. The four-cylinder 500 cc supercharged Gilera ridden by Dorino Serafini was more than a match for the BMW, taking the 500 cc title, while Mellors and Velocette retained their 350 cc crown and Kluge and DKW were once more supreme in the 250 cc class. The championship, originally scheduled for nine rounds, was curtailed to seven because of the outbreak of war and motorcycle sport went into hibernation for six years.

So by the time racing was resumed in 1946, the seeds of a championship series had been set. It was curious, therefore, that in 1947, when racing could get back to some semblance of normality, the FICM decided to abandon the series idea and instead ran each event as an individual race. A similar arrangement took place in 1948, but for 1949 the FICM, having now become the FIM (Fédération Internationale Motocycliste), decided to reintroduce the idea of a series of races, adding prestige to their decision by calling them the World Championships. It was the start of the modern series and the beginning of a new era for international road racing.

The intervening years since the armistice had witnessed little real change from pre-war days. General scarcities, the use of low-grade 'pump' petrol, the outlawing of supercharging and the immediate postwar ban on Germany in international competition (a fate escaped by Italy), put a brake on progress, though British Nortons and Velocettes fared better than others from the new set of rules – their pre-war racers, hit by the fuel regulations, being quickly adapted to new octane levels. The supercharged Gileras, however, were now illegal – the 'blown' ban also killing off the

post-war promise of a 500 cc twin Velocette which had been completed in 1939 and known as the 'Roarer'. Norton, Velocette, Moto Guzzi, new unsupercharged air-cooled Gileras – these were the machines dominant in these immediate post-war races with Britain overall taking the honours. In 1948 the racing 350 cc 7R AJS became available to private owners and new four-cylinder Gileras were seen for the first time at the Dutch TT, but the only one raced was overtaken by Artie Bell on a Norton with a fastest lap of 87·75 mph (141·28 km/h). With the AJS 'Porcupine' showing its paces, along with the Nortons, Gileras, Moto Guzzis and Velocettes, the year witnessed some stimulating racing.

The first series of world championships in 1949 was a shadow of the extensive series of present times, but it was a start, there being just six events in the 500 cc class, five for the 350s, four for the 250 cc class and a mere three for the 125 cc machines and the sidecars. Come the 1950s and we would see the memorable years of Italian and German domination; then the 1960s and the scintillating years of Honda and the other Japanese factories. But in 1949, Britain still had a stake in top-level racing and although Italy's performance bore witness of their future strength, Britain took the honours in the more prestigious heavier machine classes. Nello Pagani won Italy an easy 125 cc world title and caused some palpitating moments for British 500 cc riders by winning in this class in Holland and Italy, but the talented and dedicated Les Graham took the AJS 'Porcupine' to a couple of wins and a second place to gain the title by a single point. Riding the 350 cc Velocette, Freddie Frith was untouchable in the class, winning all five rounds. The Italian Guzzi

British rider Les Graham won the first 500 cc world championship in 1949 though in the Senior TT he pushed his AJS home to finish tenth *(Motor Cycle Weekly)*

Above: Britain took the world sidecar champion-ship in 1977, for the first time since 1953, through George O'Dell, seen here at the Dutch TT with passenger Cliff Holland *(All Sport/Don Morley)*

Left: The Austrian Grand Prix at Salzburgring and the 350 cc class is fast away *(All Sport/Don Morley)*

Right: Virginio Ferrari, one of Italy's rising stars, riding his Suzuki with style and attack in 1977 *(All Sport/Don Morley)*

and Benelli factories dominated 250 cc racing with Bruno Ruffo winning the title for Guzzi. Eric Oliver won the first of his four sidecar world titles in five years with three outright wins.

In 1949 Britain had maintained her position in the 500 cc class because of the greater reliability of the AJS machines and the superior riding of Les Graham, Bill Doran and Ted Frend, though the Gileras were decidedly faster, and the once invincible Norton factory, still fielding the old racers, was left behind. For 1950 Norton entered the fray with new single-cylinder racers – the noted 'Featherbed' – and although they fell just one point short at the end of the season through the effective riding of Geoffrey Duke, the new Nortons were good enough to win back the coveted 500 cc crown for Britain in 1951, Duke winning four of the eight rounds. Duke became the first rider to win a world championship 'double' for his five wins in the 350 cc class were enough to give Norton their second title that year. Mondial continued to dominate the 125 cc class, as they had done in 1950, and the Italian Guzzi and Benelli factories stayed ahead in 250 cc racing, Benelli's world championship of 1950 being relinquished to Guzzi in 1951.

Geoffrey Duke caused a sensation by riding in trimly-fitting one-piece leathers, instead of the customary two-piece baggy outfits which until then had been standard wear for racing men, and by his extremely fast, neat style. He moved through corners with great pace, heeling the Norton over at what, for those times, were alarmingly acute angles.

The riding of Duke, the technical brilliance of Norton manager Joe Craig and the new McCandless 'featherbed' frame had prolonged Norton's life at the top, but the writing was on the wall at Monza at the end of 1951 when Gilera occupied the first three positions in the 500 cc race.

It was clear that the more advanced machines of Italy were much faster and as the British racing effort faded, and the much heralded new multi-cylinder machine failed to materialise, one further move only was needed to put Italy firmly on top in racing. Britain still had the best riders and once the Italian factories realised how successful their machines would be in the hands of British riders, the best days of UK racing, led by the Norton factory, were at an end. The Italians offered lucrative contracts and acknowledged the true status of top riders. Once it was evident that the greatest days for British motorcycling were past, ambitious British racers saw plainly that their only hope of gaining a world title was in 'going foreign'.

World champion Les Graham went first – to MV Agusta at the end of 1950. Geoff Duke then

became the big prize and although intensely patriotic and remaining with Norton for 1952, he became a Gilera works rider for 1953. His last season for Norton was eventful. He secured the 350 cc world title with four straight wins in the first half of the season, but in the 500 cc class the Norton was well outpaced by the multi-cylinder Gileras, although Duke was well in the lead in the Senior TT on the Isle of Man when the Norton's clutch failed and put him out of the race. He found a tempting big-money offer to ride in a non-championship event at Schotten in Germany irresistible, but he crashed and was fortunate to escape with only a broken arm. The injury kept him out of racing for the remainder of the season.

The Italians, however, weren't to have things all their own way in 1953, for by now the Germans had been readmitted to the FIM and in the 125 cc class NSU and Werner Haas took up the challenge. The West German factory hadn't contemplated championship racing seriously before, but their superbly engineered single-cylinder overhead-camshaft 125 cc racer and 250 cc twin made an immediate impact. In the 125 cc class Haas brushed aside an MV Agusta challenge and in the 250 cc class was superior to the Guzzi machines ridden by Anderson and the Italian Lorenzetti. It seemed strange to see British riders like Cecil Sandford, Les Graham and Fergus Anderson now riding continental machinery. After the departure of Geoffrey Duke to Gilera, Norton had regrouped their racing team with the Rhodesian rider Ray Amm as team leader. A win in the opening round on the Isle of Man gave some hope of a British revival in the 500 cc class, but Duke on the Gilera won in Holland and again in France, Switzerland and Monza to take the title back to Italy. Such was Gilera's command of the season's racing that their riders also occupied second and third places. In the 350 cc class the British rider Fergus Anderson made sure of the title for Guzzi. Only in the sidecar class did Britain retain a world title – the incomparable Eric Oliver driving to what was to be Britain's last victory in this class for more than 20 years.

This was a golden age of motorcycling with many brilliant riders, intense machine development, and Grand Prix racing gaining pace and professionalism. Among British racers with reputations on the Continent, in addition to Geoff Duke of course, were Fergus Anderson, who was to win his first world title on a 350 cc Guzzi in 1954, Dickie Dale, riding MV Agusta machinery, Jack Brett on Norton and Bob McIntyre on AJS. Among noted continental riders of the day were Werner Haas, Tarquinio Provini and a rapidly emerging Carlo Ubbiali.

In machine development Moto Guzzi broke new ground with an experimental 500 cc water-cooled, four-cylinder racer with the cylinders in line with, and not set across, the frame as in the MV Agusta and Gilera: and streamlining became the big issue of the day in almost all factories, the Italian example being followed by the Germans and the British. Most factories added streamlining to orthodox bikes, but Norton went further and produced a racer designed with streamlining as an integral part. Intended as a Grand Prix machine, it was never raced in a world championship event because rider Ray Amm's practice times were not sufficiently impressive. Later it succeeded in sprinting, shattering a number of world records at the Montlhery track near Paris.

The world championship series was by now gaining momentum and in 1954 the number of rounds in the 125 cc class and Sidecar class was increased to six – double the number of 1949; there were seven 250 cc races and nine rounds in the 350 cc and 500 cc classes. NSU again dominated lightweight racing, with Austria's Ruppert Hollaus taking the 125 cc title and Germany's Werner Haas the 250 cc crown. British rider prestige was well maintained by Anderson's success in the 350 cc series, and by Geoffrey Duke on the Gilera, who was again untouchable in a 500 cc class reduced to eight effective rounds. The Ulster Grand Prix did not count towards the championship because bad weather reduced the distance to 117·28 miles (188·82 km), below the minimum 124 miles (200 km) distance imposed by the FIM for a 500 cc championship race.

While 1954 was itself a spectacular year with racing activity intense, it was also to witness the end of an era. But more of that later. In the meantime, Norton had produced for 1954 one of their best race machines of all time, having developed their 500 cc classic bike to the point where, with an over-square engine measuring 90 mm bore and 78·4 mm stroke, it revved to 8000 rpm and produced 55 bhp. With Gilera, MV Agusta, Moto Guzzi and AJS also in the hunt for honours, the season rejoiced at the sight and sound of five works teams in competition displaying an impressive number of factory bikes at most races.

It was in 1954 that streamlining, in the race for extra mph, was developed to an exceptional degree. NSU, who started out with a modest dolphin fairing which left the front wheel exposed, finished the season with the full 'dustbin' version of a type originally used by Moto Guzzi. Norton streamlining extended over the front wheel, but although it was no surprise that so much attention should be given to streamlining (for it could add as much as 10 mph to a machine's top speed), the riders didn't

Geoff Duke swings into the saddle of the Gilera four. He won three 500 cc world titles in three years on the famous Italian machine (*Associated Press*)

like it, nor the spectators. Riders found streamlined bikes more difficult to handle at speed, particularly in windy conditions, and for spectators it obscured most of the machine. In four years' time it would be banned altogether, on safety grounds.

The year also brought a great deal of concentration on gearboxes, with Gilera, Moto Guzzi and MV Agusta fitting five-speeders to many of their racing specials and the 125 cc MV and the NSUs being equipped with six-speed units.

But in 1954 the critical problem was that factories were finding the pursuit of championship honours just too costly. Racing machinery was

The impressive style of Bob McIntyre as he takes Quarter Bridge in the 1961 TT (*B.R. Nicholls*)

moving further away from the character of bread-and-butter roadsters, making it hard for manufacturers to justify the cost of racing against over-the-counter sales; and the additional problem facing British manufacturers was that, if they weren't to be left behind, an enormous investment programme was vital to develop multi-cylinder machines comparable with the Italians and Germans. There was hardly a crust of comfort for the British factories in the sales of road-going bikes, which in Europe were tending to level off after the comparative boom of the early post-war years. At the end of the year Norton and AJS withdrew from racing, as did NSU, the latter's remarkable racers being silenced and stilled when they were well ahead of the competition in their class. Only three years later racing suffered another appalling blow with

the departure from the race scene of Gilera, Moto Guzzi and Mondial.

Meantime, Grand Prix racing claimed plenty of attention. Early in 1955 Ray Amm, having switched from Norton to MV Agusta, was killed in his first race for the Italian factory at Imola on a new 350 cc four-cylinder machine, and at the Dutch TT there was the first riders' boycott when a number of private riders (those without factory contracts) did only one lap of the 500 cc race, at slow speed, and then returned to the pits because they considered their 'start money' too low. Thirteen riders were subsequently suspended for six months by the FIM, including Reg Armstrong and Geoffrey Duke, because of their sympathetic action in support of the private riders, and a number of Italian riders were suspended for four months. It

Above: Britain's golden boy of racing, Barry Sheene, enjoying his success after winning the 1977 German Grand Prix *(All Sport/Don Morley)*

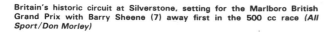

Britain's historic circuit at Silverstone, setting for the Marlboro British Grand Prix with Barry Sheene (7) away first in the 500 cc race *(All Sport/Don Morley)*

was to be Geoff Duke's last really effective season for although he went on to win the 500 cc crown that year (his third in succession and his fourth title in five years), his suspension became effective in 1956 and kept him out of racing until July, letting John Surtees through to take his first world title. A serious accident at Imola at the start of 1957 hindered his come-back and he retired at the end of 1959 without regaining the championship.

Norton and AJS, though not fielding full works teams, had taken some of their catalogued racers and prepared them specially for selected riders, but the season ended without success for the British factories. In the 125 cc class Carlo Ubbiali romped home on the fleeting MV with five wins out of six starts and the West German veteran Herman-Peter Muller, with works support, took

the 250 cc title on one of the new single-cylinder NSU Sportsmax models. Britain's Bill Lomas, who convincingly took the 350 cc crown for Guzzi, would have taken the 250 cc title as well, but in Holland his win over Luigi Taveri was downgraded to second place because he allegedly took on petrol without stopping his engine.

By 1956 MV Agusta were emerging as the powerful force in lightweight racing and Ubbiali secured both 125 cc and 250 cc titles for the factory. Lomas was again supreme in the 350 cc class on the Guzzi in his final season of racing and, as already noted, Surtees took advantage of Duke's absence through suspension to gain his first world title to give MV Agusta three of the four solo world championships. Surtees himself had his share of misfortune, a heavy crash in the

German Grand Prix ending his chances in the 350 cc category, which it seemed he might win, though with three straight wins he had already made sure of the 500 cc crown.

Much of MV's success could be attributed to Surtees' advice in the workshop as well as his prowess on the race machines, but the following year MV Agusta's confidence was shattered by Mondial who, through Provini in the 125 cc class and Sandford in the 250 cc category, took two world titles in a final blaze of glory. In the 350 cc class the Australian Keith Campbell caused a sensation on the equally sensational eight-cylinder 500 cc Moto Guzzi with a new lap record at the Belgian Grand Prix, the combination also being good enough to take the class championship back to Italy once again. In the 500 cc class Italy's own Libero Liberati became champion on the Gilera.

It was also an outstanding year for the great Scottish rider, Bob McIntyre. On the Isle of Man, in the Golden Jubilee TTs, his brilliant riding shattered the 100 mph (161 km/h) lap barrier for the first time ever. It was a memorable ride for McIntyre took the first lap at 99·99 mph (160·98 km/h) from a standing start to shatter Geoff Duke's existing record. His second lap was clocked at 101·03 mph (162·66 km/h) and on lap 3 he averaged 100·54 mph (161·87 km/h). An epic fourth lap was even better, at 101·12 mph (162·80 km/h) and on lap 6 he reached 100·35 mph (161·56 km/h). The dedicated Scot raced on to become the hero of the Island races, collecting both Senior and Junior TT titles.

McIntyre is considered by many to have been the best rider never to win a world championship. Born in Glasgow in 1928, his first road race was at Kirkcaldy on a borrowed 350 cc BSA Gold Star, after success in club level scrambling. He appeared on the Isle of Man for the first time in 1952 in the Senior Manx Grand Prix. Two years later he was a works rider with AJS and later joined forces with the celebrated Scottish tuner Joe Potts, riding Nortons and AJSs successfully. He joined Gilera for 1957, finishing second in the 500 cc class and third on the 350 cc Gilera. Then came his famous world one-hour record at Monza, some consolation for the ill-luck which robbed him of the 500 cc title that year. A win in the final round at Monza would have been enough to give him the championship, but he was ill and could not race. McIntyre died racing a five-speed experimental Norton at Britain's Oulton Park circuit in 1962.

In 1957 all solo world championship titles had been secured by Gilera, Guzzi and Mondial and with racing done for the year all three sensationally announced their racing withdrawal, without, it was claimed, even their works riders having any prior knowledge. For a time it seemed that MV Agusta might also join the departing factories, but with their main opposition removed they decided to stay and collect the honours. This they did with remarkable regularity, for three years – 1958, 1959 and 1960 – winning all solo classes. In an astonishing, if monotonous, record of success unequalled in the history of the modern championships, MV Agusta in those three sensational years won 64 Grand Prix races out of 76 and in 1960 won all except two races.

Britain, Germany and then Italy had been the driving force of world championship racing during its first decade and at the start of the 1960s the position of MV Agusta seemed impregnable. A challenge to their Grand Prix leadership was to come from a totally unexpected quarter and began quietly enough on the Isle of Man in 1959. In Japan the motorcycle industry had seen spectacular growth in the early post-war years and Honda, then virtually unknown in Europe, was the most enterprising and ambitious factory. To gain brand awareness and prove their products, Honda sent riders and machines to contest the 125 cc TT. It was the beginning of a startling revolution in world championship racing and MV Agusta's days of racing success, in all except the 500 cc category, were numbered.

At the time the Japanese were noted for their ability as painstaking copyists and those first Hondas on the Isle of Man looked very much like scaled-down versions of the successful 250 cc NSUs of a few years before. Though beautifully made they were orthodox machines and made no impression against the MV, Ducati and MZ entries. Within a year Honda proved that they were also quick to learn, for in 1960 they returned to Europe with a completely new 125 cc twin and a 250 cc four which showed a good deal of originality. Their own riders were replaced by Rhodesian Jim Redman and Australians Tom Phillis and Bob Brown and although this new oriental challenge was again repelled by the works MVs, the dismissive attitude of many observers to Honda's initial arrival on the Isle of Man was rapidly changing.

Any doubts about Honda's intentions were shatteringly dispelled in 1961. Fate played into their hands for as sales of motorcycles in Italy sagged disastrously, MV were forced to cut back on their racing programme. They pulled out of the lightweight classes, leaving Honda with a clear field. Even had MV been able to stand their ground it is doubtful if they would have been a match for Honda. The Japanese factory flooded the classics with works machines, signed the Swiss rider Luigi Taveri to replace Bob Brown (who sadly had been killed in the German Grand Prix

One-two-three on the Isle of Man in 1960 and all MV Agusta riders. Ubbiali *(centre)* winner, Hocking *(left)* second, and Taveri *(right)* third, in the Lightweight 125 cc race *(Motor Cycle Weekly)*

at Solitude in 1960), gave new contracts to Phillis and Redman and provided bikes for an up-and-coming Mike Hailwood and the resolute Bob McIntyre. Phillis won the 125 cc title and in the 250 cc class Honda swept aside all opposition to finish the season with their riders occupying the top five places, Hailwood claiming the title. Gary Hocking kept MV Agusta in the picture by gaining the 350 cc and 500 cc titles.

The four-cylinder Hondas which made such an impact in the 250 cc series were inspired by the classic Gilera and MV design with the in-line engine set across the frame, but they introduced four valves per cylinder, itself not new since the British Rudge factory had experimented with this layout in pre-war days. But the use of smaller valves and multi-cylinders gave the Hondas about

43 bhp at around 13 000 rpm. Honda's 125 cc crown was also gained with fortune on their side because Ernst Degner on the MZ was equal on points with Phillis until he chose to forfeit any further chance of gaining the title by seeking asylum in the West.

In 1961 the Japanese reinforced their effort in Grand Prix racing. Suzuki, who had followed Honda to the Isle of Man in 1969 with 125 cc racers, added a 250 cc challenge in 1961 and Yamaha, led by Fumio Ito, of former BMW fame, arrived in Europe with 125 cc and 250 cc two-strokes. They made little immediate impact, being slower than the current MZ machinery, but after Degner had taken his skills to Suzuki the picture changed.

For 1962 the 50 cc class was given world status

The most successful Grand Prix road racer of all time – Giacomo Agostini, 15 times world champion *(All Sport/Don Morley)*

for the first time and Degner took Suzuki to their first world championship. Honda increased their challenge with 50 cc and 350 cc machines and although in the tiddler class they were no match for Suzuki and the West German Kreidler of Hans-Georg Anscheidt, they gained an impressive double victory through Jim Redman, who brought home the 250 cc and 350 cc titles.

The season is remembered for the inter-factory battle between the MV Agustas of Hailwood and Hocking and the Honda of Jim Redman in the 350 cc category. Honda had enlarged their successful 250 cc four-cylinder design and with a 49 × 45 bore and stroke engine, the new 350 had a power output of 50 bhp at 12 500 rpm. Tragically its debut on the Isle of Man was marred by the death of Tom Phillis, who crashed while chasing the MVs, which were scaled down versions of the Italian factory's race-winning 500s. In the 250 cc class Redman's main challenge came from the Honda of Bob McIntyre, and Honda's 125 cc world championship was won by Luigi Taveri, whose international career had started in 1954 on privately-owned 350 cc and 500 cc Nortons. After being spotted by MV Agusta, works rides followed with Ducati, MZ and Kreidler. His big break came in 1961, when he signed for Honda.

By now the tide had turned totally in favour of the Japanese. Their record was staggering. In 1959 Japanese machines were virtually unheard of in Grand Prix racing. In 1962 they had taken four of the five solo world championships, an astonishing performance. Domination continued in 1963 with Suzuki narrowly retaining their 125 cc title after a season-long battle with Kreidler, and thrashing Honda resoundingly to take the 125 cc championship. The New Zealander Hugh Anderson was the championship rider in both classes. For Honda it was a hard season and Redman only retained the 250 cc title by winning the final race of the season, at Suzuka in Japan, Tarquinio Provini on a single-cylinder four-stroke Morini almost causing the season's greatest upset. Redman took the 350 cc title with ease from Hailwood on the MV Agusta.

MV Agusta, meantime, continued to dominate the 500 cc class and in 1963 took the title yet again – their sixth championship in as many years. The run had started with John Surtees (1958, 1959 and 1960), then Gary Hocking in 1961, and finally Mike Hailwood in 1962 and 1963. The monotony of it all had led former racing champion Geoffrey Duke to come forward with a novel idea and after a good deal of discussion he persuaded

Superbike sensation Australian Gregg Hansford, with mechanic Neville Doyle, competing in the FIM Formula 750 world championship *(All Sport/Don Morley)*

One of the most dedicated of world champions, John Surtees, racing in the Belgian Grand Prix of 1957 *(Motor Cycle Weekly)*

the Gilera factory to take the dust covers off their 1957-winning racers in an attempt to knock MV Agusta off their championship pedestal. With the former champion managing the team under the 'Scuderia Duke' banner, riders Derek Minter and John Hartle were signed to 'take on' the formidable Hailwood MV Agusta combination. But after impressive practice rides in Italy and good performances in British international meetings, the Gilera challenge faded. Minor irritations between Minter and Hartle and then Minter and Duke took the edge off the challenge, and the enterprise was left without hope when Minter crashed in a domestic meeting at Britain's Brands Hatch circuit, breaking his back. Some observers believe that, but for the crash, Minter might well have won the 500 cc world title that year on the Gilera, but by the time he rejoined the team it was too late and he wasn't really fit enough. Phil Read had meantime been drafted in to uphold the challenge with Hartle, but in the end it was Hailwood and, once again, MV Agusta, who headed the 500 cc table at the end of the year.

The 1960's were a particularly exciting and glamorous time for world championship racing. From 1964 the competition between the Japanese factories became intense and vast sums of money were invested in the quest for international racing honours. Never before had so much money gone into the development of exotic racing machinery, and the top riders became superstars, jet-setting to and from Japan to test machines and sign lucrative contracts. With Honda opening up vast new global markets for motorcycles and changing completely the very character of two-wheel motorised travel, Yamaha and Suzuki were keen to claim some of the action and for three years the three Japanese giants were locked in an exceptional power-struggle on the race track, fighting for recognition which they hoped would pay off in showroom sales throughout the world.

It was a four-stroke/two-stroke confrontation. Honda, for policy reasons, continued to race four-stroke machines, but by 1964 they were coming under increasing pressure from the Suzuki and Yamaha two-strokes, now highly developed and exceptionally competitive. As one factory tried to out-race the others, costs of racing rose astronomically. Honda poured money into a new, phenomenal 50 cc machine after Hugh Anderson on the mini-Suzuki had won three Grands Prix out of the first four. They cast off the single-cylinder model in favour of a 50 cc twin with tiny cylinders (33×29.2mm) which gave 13 bhp and could travel at more than 100 mph (161 km/h). Ulster's Ralph Bryans took the new Honda to three wins in succession, but although he again won in the last round in Japan, Anderson's Suzuki had done enough in the early part of the season to clinch the title by eight points.

For the 125 cc and 250 cc classes, Honda stayed in the race by wheeling out a new 125 cc four-cylinder machine with an eight-speed gearbox and a top speed in excess of 120 mph (193 km/h), and a remarkable six-cylinder 250 cc, seen for the first time towards the end of 1964, in an attempt to stem the success of Yamaha's twin-cylinder RD56 machines. The new Honda gave out 53 bhp at 16 500 rpm and had an eight-speed gearbox. Top speed approached 150 mph (242 km/h). Taveri did well to regain the 125 cc title for Honda, but Yamaha held their ground to take the 250 cc title through Phil Read. Redman and Honda were supreme in 350 cc racing and Hailwood once more roared home an easy champion on the MV Agusta in the 500 cc class.

In all except the 500 cc category, the Japanese now monopolised classic road racing, though British and Commonwealth riders were still the best

Jim Redman on his way to victory in the 250 cc TT of 1964 *(B.R. Nicholls)*

in the world. The Japanese were producing incredible machines and in 1965 Suzuki hit back with a redesigned water-cooled, disc-valve twin on which Hugh Anderson gave them back the 125 cc title. Honda again dominated the 50 cc and 350 cc categories and Yamaha was untouchable in the 250 cc class. Redman's 350 cc wins were particularly good performances, for MV Agusta had moved back into the fray with a brand new three-cylinder racer which handled better and was lighter than the rival Hondas, and a new rider called Giacomo Agostini, who won three rounds to give him second place behind Redman with only six points between them at the end of the season. In fact, had not the new MV broken down in the final Grand Prix in Japan, Honda would have surrendered their 350 cc title for the first time in four years.

So enormous was Honda's ambition that for 1966 they decided to contest all five solo classes. They retained their 50 cc, 125 cc and 250 cc machines, introduced an enlarged version of the six-cylinder 250 for 350 cc competition, and added a 500 cc machine to challenge MV Agusta. With a fat contract they tempted Mike Hailwood from the Italian factory, for whom he had won the 500 cc crown for the past four years, but Honda underestimated the staying power and reliability of the MV, and perhaps the emerging talent of Agostini, and the Italian factory kept the title. Even though the new Honda was inferior to the

MV, Hailwood's talent might still have brought them the title, but team captain Jim Redman went after the 500 cc title himself. When Hailwood was able to take up the challenge after Redman's effort ended with a crash in Belgium which put him out of action for the remainder of the season, he came near to pulling off the title. He impressively won the 350 cc and 250 cc titles for Honda, Taveri gave them a third in the 125 cc class and Suzuki, through Anscheidt, won the 50 cc crown.

After three momentous years of rich and stimulating racing with prodigious sums of money being pumped into an almost reckless bid for world championship honours, it was clear that, even for the Japanese factories, the race was getting out of control, financially. The body-blow, all the more savage because of their massive contribution to racing, was struck in 1967 when Honda announced their withdrawal. It was complete in the 50 cc and 125 cc classes, but they agreed to give limited factory backing to Hailwood and Ralph Bryans on existing works machines in the three bigger machine classes. Suzuki, too, were feeling the financial strain and eased back their challenge, though Yamaha stepped up their effort as development work neared completion on new 250 cc and 125 cc machines.

Off to a good start are Heinz Rosner (MZ), 19, Phil Read (Yamaha) 1, Kevin Cass (Bultaco) 44 and Ginger Molloy (Bultaco) 17, in the 250 cc Ulster Grand Prix of 1966, won by the New Zealander Ginger Molloy *(Motor Cycle Weekly)*. *Inset:* Bill Ivy, racing the 250 cc Yamaha four in Belgium *(Mick Woollett)*

Motorcycle enthusiasm in the United States, the world's biggest market for bikes (All Sport/Don Morley)

Bill Ivy had now joined Phil Read in the Yamaha team and Hailwood confronted them on a six-cylinder 250 cc Honda. It was nail-biting tension as Read won in Spain, Hailwood on the Isle of Man and in Holland, Read again in East Germany and Czechoslovakia. The season of Grand Prix racing had by now been extended and in 1967 there were no fewer than 13 rounds. At the end of it all Hailwood and Read tied with 50 points each, but Hailwood took the title with five wins to Read's four. Hailwood secured a second world championship for Honda in the 350 cc class, just beating Agostini and MV Agusta, and there was another season-long battle in the prestigious 500 cc class with Hailwood once more trying to take the title on the Honda. After a momentous duel on the Isle of Man, won by Hailwood after Agostini's machine broke down, the MV Agusta rider fought back strongly and at the end of the season Hailwood and Agostini were tied on 46 points. Moreover, both had the same number of wins, so second places were taken into account, Agostini retaining the title with three second places to Hailwood's two. Ivy secured the 125 cc crown for Yamaha and Anscheidt the 50 cc title for Suzuki.

Suzuki left the racing arena at the end of 1967 and Honda cut back even further, forbidding Bryans and Hailwood to compete in world championship races, fearing results might damage their reputation if the bikes were proved uncompetitive. Yamaha decided to continue and 1968 is remembered for the bitter feud which developed within the Yamaha team between Phil Read and Bill Ivy. Dominating 125 cc and 250 cc racing, Yamaha decided that Read should take the former title and Ivy, now regarded by the factory as their number 1 rider, should take the latter. Tension and rivalry between the riders grew as the season developed and once Read had secured the 125 cc crown by mid-season, he defied team orders and fought Ivy successfully for the 250 cc championship. Both riders finished with the same number of points and both had five wins and two second places! Read was declared champion once the times of each rider in the races they had both completed were calculated. The FIM stepped in when the feud was at its height to warn Yamaha that riders should be left alone to win races if they could and any attempt to direct the course of a race was against the best interest of racing and could end in suspension for the factory.

It had been a sensational season – and if anyone doubted that, then BMW's failure to win the world sidecar championship removed all doubt. Every year since 1954 a BMW-powered sidecar unit had taken the title, but in 1968 a four-cylinder engine with a double over-head camshaft and fuel injection developed by former champion Helmut Fath took the West German ace to a resounding victory ahead of the BMW outfits of Auerbacher and Schauzu. Fath had been seriously injured while racing in 1960 and had spent his recuperation creating the unit, which he named the URS, taken from the first three letters of the town near his home, Ursenbach.

Sidecar racing had been popular since the early days when racing pioneers like Bert Le Vack took frail-looking, unsteady combinations round Brooklands. The first sidecar TT was held in 1923 and attracted 14 entries from Norton, Douglas, Scott and Sunbeam. Freddie Dixon gained early recognition with his unique outfit which could be 'banked' on corners. There was no Sidecar TT in 1926 because of lack of support and the event wasn't included again until 1954. Britain's Eric Oliver was the first world sidecar champion in 1949 and in 1950 and 1951 continued to dominate, toughest opposition coming from Gilera. He looked sure to repeat his success in 1952, but he broke a leg in a minor meeting in France, leaving the way clear for Britain's Cyril Smith to take the title. That year Eric Oliver's keenest rival, the Italian Ercole Frigerio, was killed while racing and Oliver went on to collect his fourth title, winning the 1953 championship with four victories from the five-round series.

Oliver fought hard to take the title again in 1955, a titanic struggle developing between his famous Norton-Watsonian combination and the BMW of Wilhelm Noll. Oliver looked equal to the challenge, but after winning the first three rounds, a broken arm sustained in a non-championship race lost Oliver his chance and although Oliver and Noll finished all square on wins, BMW took the title on better placings. BMW were then to dominate sidecar racing for close on 20 years.

Sidecar outfits were at first nothing more scientific than a motorcycle with a crude sidecar attached by swivel joints. They weren't easy to steer and there was always the tendency for the sidecar wheel to lift on corners taken at speed. Oliver and the Swiss rider Hans Haldemann contributed towards the 'kneeler' method of sidecar racing, with the driver operating from a kneeling position, his knees in specially made gutters or troughs. The 'kneeler' became a considerable force in sidecar racing and no longer was it necessary for the passenger to hang out over the large wheel of the sidecar. A streamlined version built by the famous British sidecar manufacturer Watsonian caused a sensation when Oliver brought it out for practice at the Belgian Grand Prix in 1954.

Above: Sidecar racing for world titles in Holland in 1970. Auerbacher and Hahn (BMW) no. 4, won the race, but Enders and Kallaugh took the world championship that year *(Mick Woollett)*

Right: In action on the Isle of Man in 1968, Helmut Fath and Wolfgang Kallaugh with the URS outfit. The URS broke the 14-year BMW domination of the world championship in the sidecar class that year *(Mick Woollett)*

Spectacularly exciting, colourful and often dramatic, sidecar racing lacks the status of solo events because it has little commercial value for manufacturers, but it attracts a lot of interest among race-going crowds. Periodic moves to run sidecars-only meetings have not been successful and diversions into separate categories have resulted in a quick return to one event with all outfits racing together.

The Swiss rider Florian Camathias helped the cause of sidecar racing with his extremely low-to-the-ground design which became the basis of the modern, flatter outfits to follow and one of sidecar's major controversies occurred in 1966 when the tall, bespectacled and highly-respected Swiss driver, Fritz Scheidegger, was disqualified after winning the Sidecar TT on the Isle of Man for alleged infringement of fuel regulations. After personal appeals and support from the Swiss Federation he was finally reinstated as winner, but he died the following year while racing at Britain's Mallory Park.

In 1969 the world championships suffered severe withdrawal symptoms as the Japanese factories lost interest in Grand Prix road racing. At the end of the year only one oriental factory figured in the results, the British rider Dave Simmonds on a Kawasaki winning the 125 cc class. Although the factory, new to European racing, lent Simmonds the bike, they gave him no other support. Closer contests were evident in the 50 cc and 250 cc classes. There was success for Spain in the former, Angel Nieto on a Derbi taking the title by a single point from the Dutchman Aalt Toersen on a Kreidler, while the 250 cc class lived up to its cliff-hanger reputation, and was decided in the final round. The Australian

Bikes . . . bikes . . . and more bikes. An impressive view of the bike park at a Grand Prix (All Sport/Steve Powell)

Kel Carruthers took the title on a four-cylinder works Benelli from Kent Andersson on a Yamaha and Spain's Santiago Herrero on a remarkably fast single-cylinder two-stroke Ossa machine. After leaving racing in disgust after the squabbles with Phil Read and Yamaha, Bill Ivy had been tempted back when the Czech Jawa factory offered him works rides and he looked a serious threat to Agostini in the 350 cc class in 1969. After riding brilliantly to win the Dutch TT, when he proved himself superior to Agostini on the MV Agusta, Ivy was tragically killed while practising for the East German Grand Prix and Agostini had no trouble thereafter in taking both the 350 cc and 500 cc championships.

In the scintillating mid-1960s the Japanese factories had turned to the production of exotic multi-cylinder machines to stay in the race. The sheer costs were in the end self-defeating from a racing standpoint leading to their eventual withdrawal and, while they were racing, the discouragement of smaller manufacturers with far less resources. In an attempt to avoid a similar situation in the future and to encourage the smaller factories back into the sport, the FIM restricted 50 cc machines to single-cylinder engines and six-speed gearboxes and later, limited 125 cc and 250 cc machines to twin-cylinders and six-speed gearboxes. The scheme worked, with Derbi, Kreidler (through their Dutch agent Van Veen) and the tiny Dutch Jamathi company all giving support to the 50 cc class through factory teams in 1969. The new rules in 1970 gave Yamaha the advantage in the 250 cc class and unfortunately eliminated the challenging Benelli. The year ended with Nieto champion on the Derbi in 50 cc racing, Dieter Braun (Suzuki) in the 125 cc class, Rodney Gould (Yamaha) 250 cc, and Agostini yet again supreme in 350 cc and 500 cc racing.

It was towards the end of the 1960's that Yamaha produced their new and very competitive TD2 250 cc and TR2 350 cc race-developed machines for the American market. Prototypes were seen at Daytona, but now they made a batch of these racers for Europe and riders were, for the first time in years, able to buy a machine which gave them some chance of finishing in the results. Thus began the Yamaha phenomenon of production line racers based on track-tested specials and soon both classes were to be dominated in depth by Yamaha-mounted riders.

The early 1970s also saw the start of the two-stroke challenge in the 500 cc championship, the only category where four-stroke machinery still dominated, through MV Agusta. The changeover was dramatic. In 1969 four-stroke machines occupied the top 12 places in the 500 cc championship

Nürburgring in 1972 and the excitement is intense as the 250 cc riders get away *(Mick Woollett)*

table. In 1970 the two-stroke Kawasaki ridden by New Zealand's Ginger Molloy finished second to Agostini and in 1971 Agostini was pursued by two-strokes which, at the end of the season, took the next six places in the championship table. MV Agusta were forced to increase their racing budget to stay in front. It was in 1971 that Phil Read, who had ignored world championship racing since his bitter battles with Ivy in 1968 – preferring to race only in Britain, returned to the international scene and took the 250 cc world championship on a Yamaha-based machine he and Helmut Fath had developed.

Finland's Jarno Saarinen was the new racing sensation as the world championships gained momentum once more in 1972. Yamaha brought out a new water-cooled model based on the earlier air-cooled version and in the hands of Saarinen it was so competitive that Agostini and the MV Agusta were beaten in the 350 cc Grands Prix in Germany and France, the first time in five years that the Italian combination had been beaten. MV Agusta were forced to introduce a new machine later in the season to retain the 350 cc crown.

Saarinen made no mistake riding a Yamaha in the 250 cc class while Angel Nieto was the outstanding lightweight racer, collecting 50 cc and 125 cc titles.

The year 1972 was historic, for not a single world championship had been won by a British rider. In 24 years of world championship racing that hadn't happened before.

The following year the Derbi factory didn't race, leaving the way clear for the Dutch rider Jan De Vries to take the 50 cc title in his last season before retirement. Kent Andersson secured the 125 cc crown and in the 250 cc class, following the fatal crash at Monza which took the lives of Saarinen and Pasolini, Dieter Braun won the championship. To strengthen his MV team, Count Agusta had signed Phil Read to partner Agostini and although the Italian secured the 350 cc title for the sixth consecutive time, the 500 cc class was sensationally won by the British rider, ending Agostini's absolute dominance. He had won the 500 cc title every year since 1966.

After the amalgamation of Aermacchi and Harley-Davidson in 1960, the new racers produced by talented Walter Villa and his brother enabled Walter to win the 250 cc class in 1974, breaking

Renzo Pasolini races the 350 cc Benelli round the TT course in 1968, but the race was won by Giacomo Agostini on the MV Agusta *(Mick Woollett)*

Left: A celebration 'wheelie' from Yamaha rider Kenny Roberts, America's first motorcycling road race world champion *(All Sport/Don Morley)*

the stranglehold which Yamaha had exerted since the end of the 1960s, and the big news of 1975 was that Yamaha, who had signed Giacomo Agostini following his row with MV Agusta over team mate Phil Read's position, took the 500 cc world championship, dislodging MV Agusta after 17 years. Johnny Cecotto, from Venezuela, rocketed into the headlines to win a world championship (350 cc) in his first year of championship racing and the Italian rider Paolo Pileri was to give an indication of future trends by winning the 125 cc title. Italian riders were to become very strong contenders in the world championships during the 1970s.

Over the years the method of scoring points in world championship races has been amended and is now looked at each year by the FIM. When the modern series started in 1949 points were given to the first five finishers in each race – 10 for the winner, then 8, 7, 6 and 5, plus one point for the fastest lap if this was raced by a finisher. In 1950 the reward for the fastest lap was abandoned and the first six finishers gained points – 8 for the winner and then from 6 points in descending order to 1 for a sixth place. This method was retained until 1969 when points were awarded down to tenth position. The winner gained 15 points, and the other nine finishers were awarded 12, 10, 8, 6, 5, 4, 3, 2 and 1 for the tenth place. Not all scores counted towards a world championship. Under the road-racing rules of the FIM only up to half the number of Grands Prix were counted, plus one (ignoring fractions). In a Grand Prix series of 12 rounds, for instance, a rider's seven best performances only would count towards his final world championship table placing.

In 1976 the FIM was to introduce a new scoring system, taking a rider's best three scores from the first five rounds and adding his best three scores from the remaining five rounds of the championship to calculate his overall points tally. The object of this was to reduce the number of

For some years a formidable combination in lightweight races. Angel Nieto riding the Derbi in the Belgian Grand Prix of 1971 *(Mick Woollett)*

Above: On his way to yet another Grand Prix victory. Agostini on the 500 cc MV Agusta in the 1970 Dutch TT *(Mick Woollett)*. *Below:* The 500 cc version of the three-cylinder 350 cc and 500 cc MV Agustas which, ridden by Giacomo Agostini, dominated Grand Prix racing from 1968 to 1972 *(All Sport)*

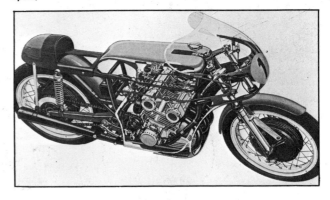

Left: Dutchman Jan De Vries riding the Kreidler at Monza in 1970. He secured his first world title the following year *(Mick Woollett)*

Centre: Walter Villa (Harley-Davidson) and Johnny Cecotto (Yamaha) in the 350 cc in the German Grand Prix *(Mick Woollett)*

Below: Down the hill at the start of the Belgian Grand Prix *(Mick Woollett)*

events a rider could ignore once he had achieved his championship target. All rounds now count.

The rules and regulations of Grand Prix racing are based on cylinder capacity of machines and on safety considerations. There are restrictions on the numbers of cylinders and gears, there is a minimum dry weight for machines, minimum rim widths and tyre sections for each machine class. Noise levels are controlled, as is the consistency of the fuel used; and the length of exhaust pipes is strictly restricted, again on safety grounds. Minimum classic race distances are laid down, though these distances may be reduced by 10 per cent provided the duration of the race does not fall below 45 minutes (30 minutes in the 50cc class).

In addition to the riders' individual world championships there is a manufacturers' counterpart which, though important, doesn't carry the public appeal of the rider tables. It reflects the changing pattern over the years of factory participation and success in Grand Prix racing.

In the 25 years of the world championships from 1949 to 1973, the number of rounds increased and circuits gained and lost favour. There were 12 races each in 1973 in the 500 cc, 250 cc and 125 cc classes, 11 in the 350 cc class and 7 in the 50 cc class, compared with the 1949 tally of six 500 cc races, five 350 cc events, four rounds in the 250 cc series and only three races for 125 cc machines. There was no 50 cc competition.

Some of the early venues, like the Dutch Grand Prix circuit at Assen and Belgium's Spa Francorchamps, continue to be popular today, though they have changed over the years. There is a carnival atmosphere about the Dutch TT and this famous motorcycle race is regarded as the country's most important sporting occasion with crowds of 100 000 attending. The Francorchamps Spa in Belgium, has a picturesque setting and is the world's fastest Grand Prix circuit. Until the political situation forced its withdrawal, the Ulster Grand Prix held on the 7½-mile road race circuit at Dundrod, was a regular and popular world championship round, as of course was the Isle of Man Mountain Circuit until 1976. Switzerland was also included until the country banned racing and while the Italian Grand Prix has always been included in the world championship calendar, it has taken place at a number of circuits, Monza, an early choice, later being considered too dangerous.

Spain and France were granted world championship status in 1951 with rounds at the famous Barcelona circuit and at Albi, and the Solitude track in Germany was included for the first time in 1952. The Nürburgring was later tried. In the 1960s the FIM began allocating rounds to more

Johnny Cecotto crests the hill, but Barry Sheene is ahead in the 1978 500 cc German Grand Prix *(Motor Cycle Weekly)*

Britain in 1977 gained the world sidecar championship for the first time since 1953 through George O'Dell with passenger Cliff Holland *(Mick Woollett)*

America's top two of the late 1970s in action. Kenny Roberts (Yamaha) leads Pat Hennen (Suzuki) at Venezuela in 1978 *(Mick Woollett)*

distant countries, bringing in Argentina and, in recognition of the immense contribution being made to world championship racing by the Japanese factories, the Suzuka circuit just outside

Tokyo. During this period Sweden and Finland were included and for a time Germany had two Grands Prix, the West German at Hockenheim and Nürburgring alternately, and the East German at Sachsenring. Massive crowds of around 200 000 would travel from all parts of Eastern Germany to watch the East German event, and the special magic and festival nature of the occasion was heightened, literally, by the enthusiasts who designed, built and erected tall poles, some 30 feet (9 metres) high and supported by rubber guy lines, to gain vantage points. After 1972 the East German authorities did not apply to be included in the championships and the series from then on took in just one round in Germany, in the Western sector.

Of the newer circuits, Saltzburgring in Austria became important in 1971 when it was included in the world championship programme for the first time. It was specially constructed for racing and although it has a picturesque setting, it suffered a riders' sit-down strike by 125 cc competitors and a boycott of the 500 cc race in 1977 because of the riders' lack of confidence in the track-side organisation's ability to deal with emergencies. The Opatija circuit in Yugoslavia has also seen turbulent times.

World championship racing in the 1970s ushered in the era of Barry Sheene, Americans riding in Britain, a more positive claim than ever before by riders to have a greater say in the running of racing, and the emergence of continental riders, particularly the Italians. In 1976 the French Grand Prix reverted to the circuit at Le Mans because Clermont-Ferrand, a natural choice since 1970, was considered unable to control the crowds; they had spilled over onto the circuit in 1974. Suzuki were challenging strongly in the 500 cc class and Barry Sheene won the opening round, going on to take the 500 cc world title. Tepi Lansivuori from Finland was second and American Pat Hennen finished third. Hennen became the first American to win a road-racing Grand Prix, winning in Finland in August. Walter Villa succeeded in taking Harley-Davidson to 350 cc and 250 cc world championships, the Italian Pierpaola Bianchi, riding a Morbidelli, won the 125 cc class and evergreen Angel Nieto won the 50 cc crown on a Bultaco.

In 1977 the Venezuelan circuit at San Carlos, though it had hosted 750 cc racing, was included in the Grand Prix calendar for the first time, Sheene collecting maximum points in the 500 cc class. An exceptional dice developed between Sheene and Pat Hennen on works Suzukis and brand new factory Yamahas ridden by Johnny Cecotto and American Steve Baker. Although

Sheene retained his 500 cc crown in 1977, Italian riders did well, Mario Lega and Pierpaola Bianchi, both Morbidelli mounted, winning the 250 cc and 125 cc classes. Nieto repeated his performance in the 50 cc class on the Bultaco, and a new champion emerged to take the 350 cc crown, the Korean-born Japanese rider, Takezumi Katayama. Japan dominated motorcycling, yet their riders had never fully succeeded in international racing. Katayama had been a Yamaha works rider in Japan, winning national titles in 1972 and 1973. When he first contested the world championships in 1974 he finished fourth. A hard and uncompromising rider, Katayama helped with the development work on the new three-cylinder Yamaha and raced it, and his own Yamaha twin, to success in Germany, France, Yugoslavia, Sweden and Finland to take the title.

In the sidecar class there was a remarkable turnabout. Although British drivers like Pip Harris, Colin Seeley and Chris Vincent had gained some recognition in world championship events (Harris third in 1960, Seeley third in 1964 and 1966, and Vincent fourth in 1972), sidecar racing had never been regarded as being other than German or Swiss drivers' territory. But in 1977, for the first time since Eric Oliver's success in 1953, a British driver won the world sidecar championship. George O'Dell, with a Seymaz outfit bought from Swiss ace Rolf Biland, was the man to work the miracle, beating the famous opposition of sidecar specialists Biland, Werner Schwarzel, Rolf Steinhausen and the rest to take the title. O'Dell proved the value of consistent performance, for throughout the season he didn't win a single world championship race! Yet he won the title.

For the first time since the modern championships began in 1949 there was no place for the Isle of Man events in 1977, the historic races becoming a victim to the increasingly vigorous lobby from many top riders to outlaw natural road circuits, and some others, on the grounds of safety. Racing, of course, continued on the Isle of Man, but Britain's world championship event was switched to Silverstone, where South African Kork Ballington was the hero, winning 350 cc and 250 cc events on Yamaha machinery.

The remainder of the 1970s was dominated by the impact of Kenny Roberts, the amazing public recognition and acclaim of Barry Sheene, the success in Grand Prix racing, at long last, of the Kawasaki factory, and the continued influence of Italian riders in the championship series. Roberts left America to conquer Europe and he did this with such conviction that he won the 500 cc world championship on Yamaha machinery in 1978 and

The East German Grand Prix at Sachsenring in 1967 . . . and those oh so enthusiastic crowds *(Mick Woollett)*

1979, the first American to win a road-racing world title. Kawasaki eventually proved themselves unassailable in 'middleweight' racing, Kork Ballington gaining the 250 cc and 350 cc world titles in 1978 and 1979, a remarkably consistent performance, and his Kawasaki team mate, Australian Gregg Hansford, gaining a second and third place both years. Spain's Ricardo Tormo, Italy's Virginio Ferrari, Eugenio Lazzarini and Franco Uncini, and Holland's Wil Hartog, were among a new generation of riders claiming the headlines in the late 1970s: and although he was beaten to the world championship by Kenny Roberts in 1978 and 1979, Barry Sheene seemed to lose none of his mass popularity.

Further major incidents in 1979 were the return to Grand Prix racing of Honda, the riders' strike in Belgium, and the failure of the new dual championship for sidecars. Honda had been out of Grand Prix racing for well over a decade and with a new generation of race goers (and domestic motorcyclists!) they felt the need to rekindle the spirit of their past glories. Their debut with new

NR 500 cc racers at Britain's Silverstone circuit, however, was a dismal failure, the machines being pathetically slow and clearly not ready for top competition.

Top riders refused to race in the Belgian Grand Prix because they considered the Spa-Francorchamps circuit unsafe, and the idea of splitting the sidecar championship into B2A and B2B categories, to cater for the more modern and unconventional outfits, proved a dismal experiment. There was little excitement or enthusiasm in the unconventional category, and it was no real surprise when the FIM abandoned the idea at the end of the season.

The major sensation as world championship racing nudged towards the 1980s was the open challenge to authority put forward by the unofficial world series, brain-child of Kenny Roberts and colleague Barry Coleman, with solid support coming from Barry Sheene and other top Grand Prix racers, and the first real possibility of a union for riders.

Chapter 18

Superbike Sensations

From the early days of motorcycling there have been superbikes in all except the name. That came in the 1960s when motorcycle manufacture became a science and modern marketing demanded neat packages and convenient name-tags. And anyway, it's an apt description for the superbly styled, comprehensively equipped, top-of-the-range 'wonder bikes' available today from Honda, Kawasaki, BMW and the rest.

Luxurious and powerful motorcycles are not a new idea. In the beginning they were crude and brutish. At Brooklands the quality was better and the speed more under control. Between the wars the Brough Superior was the 'Rolls Royce of Motorcycles' because of its exceptional and exclusive quality. Later still the Vincent-HRD Black Shadow had the power to reach 125 mph (201 km/h), even in 1948.

But until the 1960s exceptional machines of this kind sold only in small numbers to committed enthusiasts. Their modern equivalents go to a much larger and wider market, growth having come from an accelerating interest in high-powered, high-performance machines. And, of course, the vast American market.

Bike enthusiasm in the United States has always been based on the big, V-twin Harley-Davidsons and Indians. Lightweight models carried no impact. So when the Japanese identified the potential of the North Amercian market they quickly saw the future in terms of more powerful models.

It's true to say that the European industry, Britain included, got the message earlier. Dependent more and more on an expanding American market for its survival, it was forced to comply with buying needs. Hence the development of the big-engined Triumphs, BSAs and Nortons. The Triumph 650 cc Bonneville was introduced as

Tepi Lansivuori leads during the Imola 200-miler in 1974 *(Mick Woollett)*

early as 1959. In the 1970s the Triumph Trident and the BSA Rocket were three-cylinder, high-speed cruising models offering plenty of style and comfort.

But the real breakthrough came in 1975 when Honda introduced their CB750. It was the first of a new generation of superbikes and, with a four-cylinder, race-bred overhead camshaft engine, and 'superior' specifications which included a five-speed gearbox and electric starting, it was an immediate and massive success. Britain responded by making the Norton Commando into an 850, but the effort was puny compared with the onslaught of Kawasaki, Suzuki and Yamaha, who were to join Honda in the race to produce faster, bigger and more sophisticated superbikes.

While Britain appeared daunted by the Japanese drive and initiative, the Italians reasoned that in the making of superbikes they had a chance to compete with their Japanese rivals. Mass production, where the Japanese were untouchable, was less important and while they couldn't hope to compete with the Japanese in technological innovation and motorcycle research, they had a long pedigree of technical excellence which could be applied to superbike production.

The superbike is now a familiar and admired part of the motorcycle scene. To qualify as a superbike, a machine must have at least a 650 cc engine, exceptional performance, and it must look what it is – a 'king of the road' – with high standards of luxury, comfort and mechanical refinement. Superbikes are aimed at the ultimate bike lover and can cost more than a car. They seem to get bigger, faster and more expensive as manufacturers cater for a specialised market which, until the new conception of the modern superbike, simply didn't exist.

Laverda are Italy's superbike specialists and have based their reputation on a series of 1000 cc three-cylinder double overhead camshaft machines. More traditional in approach are Germany's BMW superbikes, relying heavily on the outstanding quality of construction and finish. Carrying evidence of typically American styling, Harley-Davidson superbikes are noted for their trouble-free, go-all-day power, while the Dutch Van Veen, was powered by a transverse twin rotor rotary engine, being heavy, speedy and expensive; but nonetheless an exceptional superbike. Italy has been particularly active in superbike production with Ducati, Moto Guzzi, Benelli and MV Agusta all bringing out interesting models. Add the flourishing output of the Japanese 'big four' and you have some idea of the way the superbike market has developed and expanded in a relatively short time.

With the success of road-going superbikes came, not unexpectedly, the *racing* of superbikes. This brought a boost to the long-distance endurance events (*see* Chapter 13) and heralded the introduction of Formula 750 cc racing. American influence again played its part and, following the re-admission of the AMA to the FIM in 1970, strong efforts were made by Britain's A-CU to arrange a series of races in Britain and America. Based on road engines and with strong manufacturer support, Formula 750 cc racing was seen in Europe as a means of significantly extending the scope of racing, and in 1971 a Formula 750 cc TT was introduced into the Isle of Man race programme, Alan Jeffries being first home on a Triumph at an average of 102.85 mph (165.59 km/h).

In 1973 the FIM acknowledged Formula 750 racing as an international class and in a series which included rounds in Italy, the United States, Britain, France, Finland and West Germany, Britain's Barry Sheene on a Yamaha was the winner. Australians John Dodds and Jack Findlay, both on Yamahas, took the title in 1974 and 1975, followed by Spain's Victor Palomo in 1976. This was an exciting series of races building up to sensational drama when the points were totted up at the end of the season.

Focal point of a row which developed between Palomo and American Gary Nixon was the second round of the championship in Venezuela, early in the season. In the first leg of the race American Steve Baker ran his Yamaha into the pits for a minor adjustment to the carburettor. He re-joined the race quickly, but thereafter the timekeepers seemed doubtful about which lap he was on. Gary Nixon harboured no such doubts. He was convinced that he (Nixon) was a lap ahead and when Baker stormed up from behind, offered no opposition, allowing Baker to move ahead. When the results were declared the timekeepers sided with Nixon, placing him second behind Johnny Cecotto with Steve Baker down in fifth position. Baker protested, claiming he, and not Nixon, had finished in second place. The second leg started with the dispute still unsettled and Cecotto moved into first slot once again. Baker was running second. The intense South American heat got the better of the local hero and Cecotto pulled into the pits suffering from exhaustion and sunstroke, leaving Baker to become a clear winner with Nixon in second place.

At the end of the race the timekeepers rejected Steve Baker's earlier protest and upheld Nixon's claim to that first leg victory. Baker lodged a second protest and the officials sat down to work it all out again. Four hours later, with the riders back in the hotel, they declared Baker to be the winner. Now it was Nixon's turn to protest and

Kawasaki, with a reputation built on a performance image, showed their 750 cc racer at Daytona in 1974 (Mick Woollett)

The 1980 version of the CB900, the big four-cylinder in Honda's range (Honda UK Ltd)

the wrangle was to go on until the authorities declared that a final decision could only be made at the FIM Congress in Belgium in October.

How crucial to the championship their decision was to be could not be anticipated at the time, but at the end of the season there was the incredible situation of both Victor Palomo and Gary Nixon claiming the championship title. Assuming that Steve Baker had run second in the race in scorching-hot Venezuela, then Palomo had beaten Nixon to the title by 61 points to 59. But if the FIM found in favour of Nixon, then the title would undoubtedly be his, by just one point.

But finally at the October meeting, and not without some difficulty, for the Bureau Centrale of the FIM referred the case to their road-race committee meeting later in the week, Baker was given the verdict and Palomo won the title.

In 1977 Formula 750 racing was granted world status and almost immediately doubts about the wisdom of the move began to be heard. Rounds at Daytona in the United States and Imola in Italy were dramatic and glamorous, attracting huge publicity, but other rounds fell short of what might have been expected. The racing calendar, even without another world championship, was crowded and the new Formula 750 cc championship merely added to the problem and for the average fan, the complications and confusions. There already seemed to be quite enough world champions.

Winner of the first FIM Formula 750 world championship was the little American Steve Baker. He had started racing in 1968 and was initially sponsored by Yamaha in Canada, because he lived near to the Canadian border. In Canada he was the number 1 road racer in 1974 and 1975 and in the latter year made his first racing trips to Europe. Baker won in America, Spain, Britain, Austria and Belgium and with creditable second places in Holland and in the second American round at Laguna Seca in California, he romped home with a 131 total, against the 55 of runner up Christian Sarron of France. In 1978 Johnny Cecotto won the championship and in 1979, France's Patrick Pons. It was the end of Formula 750 as a major series, for the FIM had already decided that the races would lose their world status for 1980.

Formula 750 racing hadn't fulfilled its early promise. Perhaps the heavyweight bikes didn't have that essential flourish and dash that made the 500 cc Grand Prix series a greater joy to follow. Certainly, the endless parade of Yamaha machines hadn't helped to add variety and sparkle to what, after all, was supposed to be a race between riders and machines – a variety of makes if possible.

In Britain, superbike racing really took off in 1971 with the beginning of the Superbike Championship, sponsored by the weekly newspaper *Motor Cycle News*, and the first Anglo-American Match Race Series. Both events have done much to raise the status of superbike racing in Britain and despite the fate of the international series, continue to be eagerly anticipated and enjoyed by large numbers of enthusiasts.

Chapter 19

The Modern Scene

Motorcycling today is a kaleidoscope which reflects the variety and ramifications of modern life. It touches the world at many points. What possible common ground could there be between the colourful Grand Prix road-racing professional and the ordinary man-in-the-street who lives next door. Motorcycling could be the link. To one it has given the opportunity of becoming a highly-paid international superstar; the other an easier, more convenient, cheaper way of getting to and from his work.

Motorcycling means different things to different people. To some it's a way of life. For others it's a fascinating hobby. It can be a sport, a weekend recreation, an obsession, a means of simply getting from A to B.

One motorcyclist who rides a bike for more exotic reasons is the stunt man. The most famous is the American phenomenon, Evel Knievel. He's the most spectacular motorcycle showman of all with his flying leaps over rows of cars and buses. In a blaze of publicity which spread like a prairie fire almost round the world, Knievel prepared himself in the autumn of 1974 for his most daring (and some would say foolhardy) stunt of all: a miracle-leap over the near-mile wide, 600 ft drop of Snake River Canyon in Idaho, USA, on his remarkable machine, Sky Cycle Z2. The fact that the extraordinary attempt failed didn't appear to affect the public image of a man who claims to have broken almost every bone in his body and is a self-confessed jailbird. Born in 1949, Evel Knievel is a former traditional motorcycle racer whose conversion to flamboyant and spectacular stunt-riding made him a multi-millionaire and something of a living legend in the United States.

Britain's best known stunt rider is Eddie Kidd. He made his name, like Knievel, in leaping over buses. He is also the man the film makers call for when they need someone to stand in for an actor in a motorcycle stunt sequence. He has also graduated into specialised feature filming. Londoner Dave Taylor is a stunt rider of less flamboyant style. 'Wheelies' – riding with the front wheel hoisted high in the air – are Dave's speciality. Amazingly, he can ride like this for long distances and at high speed, round corners and up and down hills. Dave travels to many countries to give displays which are warmly acclaimed.

Motorcycle display teams are another popular public attraction. The feats a number of skilful and precision-trained riders can accomplish on motorcycles are extraordinary and most routines include the daring leap through a burning hoop and the traditional finale with all members of the team climbing onto one machine for an astonishing display of balance, courage and coordination.

A motorcycle phenomenon of more recent origins is the chopper. Originally a product of the United States, the chopper is immediately recognisable for its gross distortion from the norm – extra-long front forks, tiny front wheels, high-rise swept-back handlebars, tilted seat, forward located footrests and armchair riding position. In the late 1950s and 1960s 'chops' became a cult. They are monuments to their owners' devotion, with glistening chrome, highly-polished paintwork, exotic and often highly-expensive extras and accessories. What first started perhaps with the tuning of the engine and developed into a shift in the riding position to gain more comfort, could end with the ultimate 'customising' of the bike with so many additions that it is difficult to find the motorcycle under all the trimming.

Evel Knievel's unsuccessful attempt to propel his Sky Cycle across the Snake River Canyon. In the air, but the 'rogue' chute is already out (*Motor Cycle Weekly*)

Chopper scene at Daytona *(Mick Woollett)*

The American dream! There's a bike somewhere underneath all that 'illumination' *(Mick Woollett)*

At best these 'showbikes' are incredible, ingenious and in their own special way, handsome. At worst they are the ultimate degradation of motorcycling and in appallingly bad taste. Always they incorporate powerful machines. Pride of ownership is one factor all showbike owners have in common. The best and most exciting examples of the showbike can take years of painstaking effort to build and are admirable examples of the cult. Nowadays there are special shows for such bikes where proud owners come together in competition for cups and other prizes.

Another comparatively recent vogue is to make ordinary road bikes look more like racers. A substantial business has developed in recent years in these 'cafe racers', which are often extremely fast and look very much like the real thing. 'Cafe racing' originated in Kent before the days of motorways and speed limits when groups of enthusiasts used to congregate at cafes in the Brands Hatch area to discuss their bikes and 'race' each other from one cafe to the next. The idea was much more recently taken up and popularised in America and is now a significant part of the modern bike scene. You can now buy 'cafe racers' from the manufacturers and from smaller firms and individuals who specialise in the motorcycle customising business.

Less exhibitionist are the large number of police forces throughout the world who use powerful, fast-travelling superbikes in the cause of law and order. The comprehensively and specialist-equipped power bikes move fluently, even through heavy traffic, and when occasion demands, have the speed necessary for motorway apprehension.

Motorcycles are also often used on organised mercy missions. A good example of this voluntary service is the Freewheelers, based on the Lister Hospital at Stevenage, England. This team of riders make life-saving nightly journeys with emergency blood, breast milk and X-ray plates. They have to reach a high standard of riding proficiency, know something about blood groups and two-way radio receivers, and they maintain their own machines and finance their outgoings through voluntary contributions.

Far removed from the thrills of stunt riding, the fairy-tale world of the chopper and show machines, and the functional police patrol bikes, is the calm, innocuous power of the long-distance touring model. Many riders gain immense pleasure from loading up their panniers and taking off on cross-country journeys. They enjoy the freedom of the road, the open spaces and the sheer joy of riding in relatively docile comfort. It is a relaxing form of recreation. Some riders develop the idea by undertaking long expeditions which are as much of a personal challenge as a pleasure. Distance, not speed, is generally the measure of this particular performance and fun is found in travelling from one side of America to the other and back, through Africa, South America, or even through Scandinavia to the frozen north.

A more light-hearted form of recreational motorcycling is the local rally. This type of event has a social, club-like atmosphere, with pillion passengers often acting as navigators. A local rally is competition riding in a mild form and consists of travelling over public roads from start to finishing point at an average speed which has been established beforehand. Checks have to be made at a series of control points on the way. Points are gained or lost for timekeeping, number of control points visited, and for proficiency in any special tests which might be organised. A variation on this form of competition riding, but still good fun, is the local treasure hunt where riders have to interpret clues based on road signs, pub names, churches and so on – the solution to one clue providing the link to the next.

The ubiquitous nature of motorcycling makes it appealing to enthusiasts of varying interests. The need to buy a commuter model to save petrol, time or harassment in today's traffic-clogged city streets, can lead to an interest in motorcycle touring; or to a passion for trials or drag racing. Motocross club events are where many of today's top road racers learned the skills of their trade. Some bike enthusiasts don't even own a machine or ride regularly; but they follow intently the exploits of Barry Sheene, Kenny Roberts, or their favourite riders at the local circuit.

Those who do venture into competition will find numerous officials available to ensure that meetings run smoothly and safety precautions are upheld. Stewards of the meeting are responsible for the supervision of a competition and for making sure that the programme is carried out in accordance with the regulations. The Clerk of the Course is responsible to the stewards and to the promoter for the good management and conduct of the competition, and controls the riders. He also collects reports from the timekeepers and other officials and prepares and publishes the provisional results of the meeting. The Secretary of the meeting sees that all necessary documents and badges are supplied and deals with official correspondence. Judges supervise the start and finish of races. Timekeepers record and report times required by the conditions of the competition. Scrutineers are there for safety reasons and to make sure machines are fit for competition. The measurers' responsibility is to check the specifications of suspect machines.

In Britain two exciting projects captured the imagination of motorcycle enthusiasts in the early 1980s. First came reliable reports of a Japanese interest (possibly through Suzuki) in some kind of liaison with the Triumph workers co-operative at Meriden. Then came the unveiling of a new 1000 cc high performance superbike by Lord Hesketh. The race-enthusiastic peer was said to have spent more than £500 000 ($1 000 000) designing and developing the machine – the first major new British motorcycle to be introduced in 11 years.

Motorcycling can be a hobby. It is also big business providing employment for hundreds of thousands of people throughout the world. Motorcycle racing has developed from a crude spectacle into a highly-sophisticated entertainment. There have been enormous advances in the last fifteen years. What might happen in the next fifteen years can only add to the overall magic of motorcycling.

Hospital mercy riders during a charity run

Chapter 20

Take your Choice

Puch Maxi Range

The Puch Maxi has a 49 cc single-cylinder, air-cooled, two-stroke engine with light-alloy cylinder head and barrel. A flywheel generator provides current for ignition and direct lighting.

Gear primary drive transmits power through a centrifugally-operated clutch to a single-speed transmission and a chain final drive. On the two-speed versions gear change is automatic by means of another centrifugal clutch.

Lubrication of the engine is by a 2 per cent of 50 to 1 petrol and oil mixture; separate oil is used for lubrication of the transmission.

The carburettor has an automatic choke which releases when the throttle is opened fully.

The Maxi Quickly, SW and Two-Speed models retain pedalling gear but the remainder of the range by the early 1980s had fixed footrests and kick start pedals.

The Maxi frame is a pressed steel fabrication with integral fuel tank. All models have a telescopic front fork and, except for the Quickly and Zippy, pivoted fork rear suspension. Drum brakes in light-alloy hubs are used on front and rear wheels on all models. Except for the Maxi Super DK, all models have a luggage carrier as standard.

A later addition to the Puch's line up of powered two-wheelers was the Magnum X fun bike. Aimed at the younger members of the family it was intended for off-road use. With good styling, knobbly tyres, telescopic front fork, pivoted rear fork suspension and the Puch 49 cc engine with single-speed transmission and automatic clutch like its moped stable mates, it looks a very smart mini motocross machine.

The comprehensive Puch moped range plus purpose-built accessories combines to create a variety of specifications. The X50 Alpine was introduced in 1979 as the latest addition to a colourful and rugged moped range.

Honda Step-Through Models

Honda has been synonymous with lightweight commuter machines since the motorcycling revolution they created some 30 years ago, and the popularity of the step-through range of Hondas is legendary. More of these machines have been sold around the world than any other single design from the beginning of motorcycling.

The C50 is the basic utility bike, with a 49 cc engine. The C70 is the 72 cc version with an air-cooled, ohc, four-stroke, single-cylinder engine, and the C90 is a popular top-of-the range step-through offering improved engine performance.

Engine Unit

Type:	Air-cooled, single-cylinder, ohc four-stroke
Bore and Stroke:	50 x 45.6mm
Displacement:	89cc
Compression ratio:	8.2:1
Carburettor:	Piston valve type
Lubrication system:	Wet sump
Oil capacity:	0.9 litre
Starting system:	Kickstarter
Maximum horsepower:	7.2ps/8000rpm (DIN)
Maximum torque:	0.69kg-m/6000rpm

Frame

Type:	Backbone design
Front suspension:	Bottom link
Rear suspension:	Swing arm
Front tyre:	2.50 x 17-4PR
Rear tyre:	2.50 x 17-4PR
Front brake:	Expanding shoes
Rear brake:	Expanding shoes

Electrical System

Ignition:	Battery and ignition coil
Alternator:	0.042kW/5000rpm
Battery capacity:	6V-5.5AH
Headlight low/high:	25/25 watt
Tail/Stoplight:	5/21 watt
Indicator light:	18 watt

Transmission

Type:	3-speed constant mesh
Clutch:	Automatic centrifugal type
Primary Reduction:	3.722
Gear ratios: 1st	2.538
2nd	1.555
3rd	1.000
Final reduction:	2.857

Dimensions

Overall length:	71.7in
Overall width:	25.2in
Overall height:	38.6in
Wheelbase:	46.5in
Seat height:	30.7in
Ground clearance:	5.1in
Fuel capacity:	5.5 litre
Dry weight:	84kg
Curb weight:	88kg
Colours available:	Red, blue

Puch 50 cc Super Executive

Suzuki GSX1100

onda C50L

Honda XL125 Trail Bike

Yamaha XS250 Twin

BMW R100RT

Kawasaki Z1300

Moto Guzzi V1000 automatic

Yamaha XS1100

Honda CX500A

Honda XL125 Trail Bike

Honda now produce a variety of on/off road machines in their trail, motocross, and enduro range. The XL125 is a successful trail machine featuring a six-speed constant-mesh transmission, long travel front forks and 'lay down' rear suspension capable of handling both on and off road-riding demands.

Engine Unit

Type:	Air-cooled, single-cylinder, ohc four-stroke
Bore and Stroke:	56.5 x 49.5mm
Displacement:	124cc
Compression ratio:	9.4:1
Carburettor:	Piston valve type
Lubrication system:	Wet sump
Oil capacity:	1.1 litre
Starting system:	Kickstarter
Maximum horsepower:	13ps/9500rpm (DIN)
Maximum torque:	1.05kg-m/8000rpm

Frame

Type:	Diamond cradle design
Front suspension:	Telescopic (travel)
Rear suspension:	Swing arm (travel)
Front tyre:	2.75 x 21-4PR block pattern
Rear tyre:	4.10 x 18-4PR block pattern
Front brake:	Expanding shoes
Rear brake:	Expanding shoes
Trail length:	4.8in
Caster angle:	62° 10'

Electrical System

Ignition:	Capacitive discharge ingnition
Alternator:	0.09kW/5000rpm
Battery capacity:	6V-4AH
Headlight low/high:	35/35 watt
Tail/Stoplight:	5/21 watt
Indicator light:	21 watt

Transmission

Type:	6-speed constant mesh
Clutch:	Wet multi-plate type
Primary Reduction:	3.333
Gear ratios: 1st	3.083
2nd	1.941
3rd	1.400
4th	1.130
5th	0.923
6th	0.785
Final reduction:	3.357
Drive sprocket:	14T
Driven sprocket:	47T

Dimensions

Overall length:	85.43in
Overall width:	33.07in
Overall height:	44.49in
Wheelbase:	51.57in
Seat height:	32.28in
Ground clearance:	10.43in
Fuel capacity:	1.54 gallons
Dry weight:	233.5lb
Curb weight:	249lb
Colours available:	Red, white, blue

Suzuki GSX 1100

This new flagship of the Suzuki range was launched to take the famous Japanese factory dramatically into the 1980s. It had its international debut in Britain in early 1980 and was the most powerful motorcycle ever produced by Suzuki and probably the fastest production motorcycle in the world. It had a claimed top speed of 160 mph (250 km/h). Though extremely powerful, Suzuki worked hard at giving it lightness (for a heavy machine) and good handling characteristics.

Engine Unit

Type:	Air-cooled, four cylinder, 16 valve, dohc four-stroke
Bore and Stroke:	72.0 x 66.0mm
Displacement:	1075cc
Compression ratio:	9.5:1
Lubrication system:	Wet sump
Starting system:	Transistorised

Frame

Front suspension:	Telescopic, pneumatic fork
Rear suspension:	Swing arm, oil dampened
Front tyre:	3.50V x 19-4PR
Rear tyre:	4.50V x 17-4PR
Front brake:	Twin perforated disc
Rear brake:	Disc

Transmission

Clutch:	Wet multi-plate
Gearbox:	5-speed
Ignition:	Electrical

Dimensions

Overall length:	2220mm
Overall width:	870mm
Overall height:	1175mm
Wheelbase:	1515mm
Fuel capacity:	24 litre
Dry weight:	256kg
Colours available:	Red, silver, blue

Yamaha XS250 Twin

A handsome machine which meets the demands of the 'commuter' and also the owner who rides for fun is the Yamaha XS250, its engine easy and smooth throughout the rev-range. Described by Yamaha as incorporating a race-bred chassis and sporting styling for a get-up-and-go image without detracting from its utilitarian virtues.

Engine Unit

Type:	Four-stroke, twin, ohc
Bore and Stroke:	55.0 x 52.4mm
Displacement:	248cc
Compression ratio:	9.3:1
Carburettor:	Mikuni, BS32 (X2)
Lubrication system:	Pressure-fed set sump
Oil capacity:	2.6 litre
Starting system:	Electric and kickstarter
Maximum horsepower:	27.0kW(19.8hp)/9500 rpm
Maximum torque:	20.5Nm(2.1kg-m)/8500 rpm

Frame

Front tyre:	300S-18-4PR
Rear tyre:	3,75S-18-4PR
Front brake:	Hyd. disc ϕ267mm
Rear brake:	Drum

Electrical System

Ignition:	Battery CB/Coil
Battery capacity:	12V, 12AH
Charging system:	A.C. Generator

Transmission

Clutch:	Multi-plate, wet
Gearbox:	6-speed
Primary:	Gear
Final:	Chain

Dimensions

Overall length:	2080mm
Overall width:	745mm
Overall height:	1065mm
Wheelbase:	1380mm
Seat height:	780mm
Fuel capacity:	17.0 litre

BMW R100RT Flat Twin

One of the most impressive looking touring motorcycles, it is said to provide absolutely fatigue-free and comfortable riding conditions, even over long distances.

Engine Unit

Type:	Air-cooled, two-cylinder, four-stroke, twin-flat. Light alloy construction for good heat dissipation
Bore and Stroke:	94 x 70.6mm
Displacement:	980cc (59.8 cu in)
Compression ratio:	9.5:1
Maximum horsepower:	51kW (70 bhp) 7250rpm
Maximum torque:	77.0Nm (55.7ft/lb 5500rpm

Frame

Front tyre:	3.25H x 19
Rear tyre:	4.00H x 18
Front brake:	Drilled, floating-calliper twin brake, dia 260mm
Rear brake:	Drilled, floating-calliper single-disc brake, dia 260mm

Electrical System

Alternator:	280 watt three-phase
Battery capacity:	12 volt, 28 Amps/hr

Transmission

Clutch:	Single-disc dry with diaphragm spring, dia 200mm
Gearbox:	5-speed with jaw clutch and hook shift
Gear ratios: 1st	4.40
2nd	2.86
3rd	2.07
4th	1.67
5th	1.50

Dimensions

Overall length:	2210mm
Overall width:	746mm
Wheelbase:	1465mm
Seat height:	820mm
Ground clearance:	165mm
Fuel capacity:	24 litre inc. 3 litre reserve
Handlebar width:	690mm
Maximum height unladen:	1465mm
Empty weight:	214kg
Ready for the road inc. fuel:	234kg
Maximum permissible weight:	398kg

Kawasaki Z1300 Water-Cooled Six

Some say it's the ultimate superbike … and it would be a brave man to argue. Smooth and the most powerful sports-touring machine that Kawasaki has ever produced, the Z1300 is a water-cooled, 1286 cc double overhead-camshaft, six-cylinder machine which, despite its impressive size and power output, is surprisingly docile and manoeuvrable. First introduced at the Cologne Show in West Germany in 1978 after five years of consideration and development.

Engine Unit

Type:	Four-stroke, six-cylinder, water-cooled, dohc
Bore and Stroke:	62 x 71mm
Displacement:	1286cc
Compression ratio:	9.9:1
Lubrication system:	Forced lubrication (wet sump)
Starting system:	Electric
Maximum horsepower:	120hp/8000rpm
Maximum torque:	11.8kg-m/6500rpm

Frame

Type:	Tubular, double cradle
Front suspension:	Telescopic fork
Rear suspension:	Swing arm
Front tyre:	110/90 V-18 4PR
Rear tyre:	130/90 V-17 6PR
Front brake:	Dual disc, effective disc diameter 260mm
Rear brake:	Disc, effective disc diameter 250mm

Electrical System

Ignition:	Full transistor

Transmission

Type:	5-speed constant mesh, return shift
Clutch:	Wet, multi-disc
Shift pattern:	I-N-2-3-4-5

Dimensions

Overall length:	2335mm*/2295mm
Overall width:	840mm*/905mm
Overall height:	1155mm*/1280mm
Wheelbase:	1580mm
Ground clearance:	137mm
Fuel capacity:	27 litre
Dry weight:	297kg

*General model specifications

Yamaha XS 1100 Shaft Drive Four

Yamaha's top-of-the-line superbike has a pedigree of powerful performance and endurance riding. In the United States a brand new XS1100 was taken from its shipping crate and immediately, on a drag-racing strip, recorded standing quarter-mile times in the low 11-second bracket. This was followed without any appreciable delay by a non-stop 5000 km ride from Los Angeles to New York, completed in less than 60 hours.

Engine Unit

Type:	Four-stroke, four-cylinder, dohc
Bore and Stroke:	71.5 x 68.6mm
Displacement:	1101cc
Compression ratio:	9.2:1
Lubrication system:	Pressure-fed wet sump
Oil capacity:	4.2 litre
Starting system:	Electric and kickstarter
Maximum horsepower:	69.9kW (95hp)/8000 rpm
Maximum torque:	90.2Nm (9.2kg-m)/6500 rpm

Frame

Front tyre:	3.50V-19-4PR
Rear tyre:	4.50V-17-4PR
Front brake:	Hydraulic discs ϕ298mm (x2)
Rear brake:	Hydraulic disc ϕ298mm

Electrical System

Ignition:	Transistor
Battery capacity:	12V, 20AH
Charging system:	A.C. Generator

Transmission

Clutch:	Multi-plate, wet
Gearbox:	5-gear
Primary:	HY-VO Chain + Gear
Final:	Shaft

Dimensions

Overall length:	2260mm
Overall width:	755mm
Overall height:	1145mm
Wheelbase:	1545mm
Seat height:	810mm
Ground clearance:	150mm
Fuel capacity:	24 litre
Dry weight:	256kg

Moto Guzzi V1000 Automatic

Significant features of this powerful model are the automatic transmission and the integral brake system. All Moto Guzzi V-twins are unique in having this integral braking system, with its emphasis on safety. One of the twin front disc brakes and the rear disc brakes are operated by the foot pedal with about 70 per cent of the power going to the front wheel and approximately 30 per cent to the rear wheel. There is also a pressure release valve which eliminates the risk of skidding, thus providing the motorcyclist with the same kind of powerful and balanced brakes as offered to the motor car driver.

Engine Unit

Type:	Twin cylinder, four-stroke
Bore and Stroke:	88 x 78mm
Displacement:	949cc
Compression ratio:	9.2:1
Starting system:	Electric
Maximum torque:	8.6kg a5200g/m

Frame

Type:	Duplex cradle, disassemblable
Suspension:	Telescopic with hydraulic dampers
Front tyre:	4.10H – 18
Rear tyre:	4.10H – 18
Front brake:	Hydraulic disc. Left foot operated, right brake operated from handlebar
Rear brake:	Hydraulic disc, foot operated

Electrical System

Ignition:	Battery with twin contact breaker

Transmission

Type:	Two-speed (low and high) foot controlled from the left of vehicle
Clutch:	Multiplate, dry

Dimensions

Fuel capacity:	24 litre
Dry weight:	240kg

Honda CX500 Transverse V-Twin

For sports riding and touring, this Honda special combines a lightweight approach and good handling characteristics with comfort and the kind of maintenance-free operation demanded by the touring rider.

Engine Unit

Type:	Water-cooled, twin cylinder ohv four-stroke
Bore and Stroke:	78 x 52mm
Displacement:	496cc
Compression ratio:	10.0:1
Carburettor:	CV type (35mm bore) x 2
Lubrication system:	Wet sump
Oil capacity:	3.0 litre
Starting system:	Electric
Maximum horsepower:	50ps/9000rpm (DIN)
Maximum torque:	4.4kg-m/7000rpm

Frame

Type:	Diamond
Front suspension:	Telescopic (travel 139.5mm)
Rear suspension:	Swing arm (travel 85mm)
Front tyre:	3.25S x 19
Rear tyre:	3.75S x 18
Front brake:	Twin discs
Rear brake:	Expanding shoes
Trail length:	3.9in
Caster angle:	68°30'

Electrical System

Ignition:	Capacitive discharge ignition
Alternator:	0.17kW/5000rpm
Battery capacity:	12V-14H
Headlight low/high:	55/60 watt Halogen
Tail/Stoplight:	5/21 watt x 2
Indicator light:	21 watt

Transmission

Type:	5-speed constant mesh
Clutch:	Wet multi-plate
Primary reduction:	2.242
Gear ratios: 1st	2.733
2nd	1.850
3rd	1.416
4th	1.148
5th	0.931
Final reduction:	3.091
Drive sprocket:	11T
Driven sprocket:	34T

Dimensions

Overall length:	86.8in
Overall width:	29.1in
Overall height:	44.3in
Wheelbase:	57.3in
Seat height:	31.9in
Ground clearance:	5.9in
Fuel capacity:	3.74 gallons
Dry weight:	441lb
Curb weight:	459lb
Colours available:	Red, blue, black

Chapter 21

Statistics

ROAD RACING

World Championships

1949

125cc
1 Nello Pagani, Italy (Mondial)
2 R.Magi, Italy (Morini)
3 Umberto Masetti, Italy (Morini)

250cc
1 Bruno Ruffo, Italy (Guzzi)
2 Dario Ambrosini, Italy (Benelli)
3 R.Mead, GB (Mead Norton)

350cc
1 Freddie Frith, GB (Velocette)
2 Reg Armstrong, Ireland (AJS)
3 Albert Foster, GB (Velocette)

500cc
1 Les Graham, GB (AJS)
2 Nello Pagani, Italy (Gilera)
3 A.Artesiani, Italy (Gilera)

Sidecar
1 Eric Oliver, GB (Norton)
2 Ercole Frigerio, Italy (Gilera)
3 F.Vanderschrick, Belgium (Norton)

1950

125cc
1 Bruno Ruffo, Italy (Mondial)
2 G.Leoni, Italy (Mondial)
3 Carlo Ubbiali, Italy (Mondial)

250cc
1 Dario Ambrosini, Italy (Benelli)
2 Maurice Cann, GB (Guzzi)
3 Fergus Anderson, GB (Guzzi)

350cc
1 Bob Foster, GB (Velocette)
2 Geoffrey Duke, GB (Norton)
3 Les Graham, GB (AJS)

500cc
1 Umberto Masetti, Italy (Gilera)
2 Geoffrey Duke, GB (Norton)
3 Les Graham, GB (AJS)

Sidecar
1 Eric Oliver, GB (Norton)
2 Ercole Frigerio, Italy (Gilera)
3 Hans Haldemann, Switzerland (Norton)

1951

125cc
1 Carlo Ubbiali, Italy (Mondial)
2 G.Leoni, Italy (Mondial)
3 Bill McCandless, Ireland (Mondial)

250cc
1 Bruno Ruffo, Italy (Guzzi)
2 Tommy Wood, GB (Guzzi)
3 Dario Ambrosini, Italy (Benelli)

350cc
1 Geoffrey Duke, GB (Norton)
2 Johnny Lockett, GB (Norton)
3 Bill Doran, GB (AJS)

500cc
1 Geoffrey Duke, GB (Norton)
2 Alfredo Milani, Italy (Gilera)
3 Umberto Masetti, Italy (Gilera)

Sidecar
1 Eric Oliver, GB (Norton)
2 Ercole Frigerio, Italy (Gilera)
3 Albino Milani, Italy (Gilera)

1952

125cc
1 Cecil Sandford, GB (MV)
2 Carlo Ubbiali, Italy (Mondial)
3 E. Mendogni, Italy (Morini)

250cc
1 Enrico Lorenzetti, Italy (Guzzi)
2 Fergus Anderson, GB (Guzzi)
3 Leslie Graham, GB (Velocette)

350cc
1 Geoffrey Duke, GB (Norton)
2 Reg Armstrong, Ireland (Norton)
3 Ray Amm, Rhodesia (Norton)

500cc
1 Umberto Masetti, Italy (Gilera)
2 Leslie Graham, GB (MV)
3 Reg Armstrong, Ireland (Norton)

Sidecar
1 Cyril Smith, GB (Norton)
2 Albino Milani, Italy (Gilera)
3 Jacques Drion, France (Norton)

1953

125cc
1 Werner Haas, W. Germany (NSU)
2 Cecil Sandford, GB (MV)
3 Carlo Ubbiali, Italy (MV)

250cc
1 Werner Haas, W. Germany (NSU)
2 Reg Armstrong, Ireland (NSU)
3 Fergus Anderson, GB (Guzzi)

350cc
1 Fergus Anderson, GB (Guzzi)
2 Enrico Lorenzetti, Italy (Guzzi)
3 Ray Amm, Rhodesia (Norton)

500cc
1 Geoffrey Duke, GB (Gilera)
2 Reg Armstrong, Ireland (Gilera)
3 Alfredo Milani, Italy (Gilera)

Sidecar
1 Eric Oliver, GB (Norton)
2 Cyril Smith, GB (Norton)
3 Hans Haldemann, Switzerland (Norton)

1954

125cc
1 Ruppert Hollaus, Austria (NSU)
2 Carlo Ubbiali, Italy (MV)
3 Herman Müller, W. Germany (NSU)

250cc
1 Werner Haas, W. Germany (NSU)
2 Ruppert Hollaus, Austria, (NSU)
3 Herman Müller, W. Germany (NSU)

350cc
1 Fergus Anderson, GB (Guzzi)
2 Ray Amm, Rhodesia (Norton)
3 Rod Coleman, New Zealand (AJS)

500cc
1 Geoffrey Duke, GB (Gilera)
2 Ray Amm, Rhodesia (Norton)
3 Ken Kavanagh, Australia (Norton)

Sidecar
1 Wilhelm Noll, W. Germany (BMW)
2 Eric Oliver, GB (Norton)
3 Cyril Smith, GB (Norton)

1955

125cc
1 Carlo Ubbiali, Italy (MV)
2 Luigi Taveri, Switzerland (MV)
3 Remo Venturi, Italy (MV)

250cc
1 Herman Müller, W. Germany (NSU)
2 Cecil Sandford, GB (Guzzi)
3 Bill Lomas, GB (MV)

350cc
1 Bill Lomas, GB (Guzzi)
2 Dickie Dale, GB (Guzzi)
3 A. Hobl, W. Germany (DKW)

500cc
1 Geoffrey Duke, GB (Gilera)
2 Reg Armstrong, Ireland (Gilera)
3 Umberto Masetti, Italy (MV)

Sidecar
1 Willy Faust, W. Germany (BMW)
2 Wilhelm Noll, W. Germany (BMW)
3 Walter Schneider, W. Germany (BMW)

1956

125cc
1 Carlo Ubbiali, Italy (MV)
2 R. Ferri, Italy (Gilera)
3 Luigi Taveri, Switzerland (MV)

250cc
1 Carlo Ubbiali, Italy (MV)
2 Luigi Taveri, Switzerland (MV)
3 Enrico Lorenzetti, Italy (Guzzi)

350cc
1 Bill Lomas, GB (Guzzi)
2 A. Hobl, W. Germany (DKW)
3 Dickie Dale, GB (Guzzi)

500cc
1 John Surtees, GB (MV)
2 Walter Zeller, W. Germany (BMW)
3 John Hartle, GB (Norton)

Sidecar
1 Wilhelm Noll, W. Germany (BMW)
2 Fritz Hillebrand, W. Germany (BMW)
3 Pip Harris, GB (Norton)

1957

125cc
1 Tarquinio Provini, Italy (Mondial)
2 Luigi Taveri, Switzerland (MV)
3 Carlo Ubbiali, Italy (MV)

250cc
1 Cecil Sandford, GB (Mondial)
2 Tarquinio Provini, Italy (Mondial)
3 Sammy Miller, Ireland (Mondial)

350cc
1 Keith Campbell, Australia (Guzzi)
2 Bob McIntyre, Scotland (Gilera)
3 Libero Liberati, Italy (Gilera)

500cc
1 Libero Liberati, Italy (Gilera)
2 Bob McIntyre, Scotland (Gilera)
3 John Surtees, GB (MV)

Sidecar
1 Fritz Hillebrand, W. Germany (BMW)
2 Walter Schneider, W. Germany (BMW)
3 Florian Camathias, Switzerland (BMW)

1958

125cc
1 Carlo Ubbiali, Italy (MV)
2 A. Gandossi, Italy (Ducati)
3 Luigi Taveri, Switzerland (Ducati)

250cc
1 Tarquinio Provini, Italy (MV)
2 H. Fugner, E. Germany (MZ)
3 Carlo Ubbiali, Italy (MV)

350cc
1 John Surtees, GB (MV)
2 John Hartle, GB (MV)
3 Geoffrey Duke, GB (Norton)

500cc
1 John Surtees, GB (MV)
2 John Hartle, GB (MV)
3 Dickie Dale, GB (BMW)

Sidecar
1 Walter Schneider, W. Germany (BMW)
2 Florian Camathias, Switzerland (BMW)
3 Helmut Fath, W. Germany (BMW)

1959

125cc
1 Carlo Ubbiali, Italy (MV)
2 Tarquinio Provini, Italy (MV)
3 Mike Hailwood, GB (Ducati)

250cc
1 Carlo Ubbiali, Italy (MV)
2 Tarquinio Provini, Italy (MV)
3 Gary Hocking, Rhodesia (MZ)

350cc
1 John Surtees, GB (MV)
2 John Hartle, GB (MV)
3 Bob Brown, Australia (Norton)

500cc
1 John Surtees, GB (MV)
2 Remo Venturi, Italy (MV)
3 Bob Brown, Australia (Norton)

Sidecar
1 Walter Schneider, W. Germany (BMW)
2 Florian Camathias, Switzerland (BMW)
3 Fritz Scheidegger, Switzerland (BMW)

1960

125cc
1 Carlo Ubbiali, Italy (MV)
2 Gary Hocking, Rhodesia (MV)
3 Ernst Degner, E. Germany (MZ)

250cc
1 Carlo Ubbiali, Italy (MV)
2 Gary Hocking, Rhodesia (MV)
3 Luigi Taveri, Switzerland (MV)

350cc
1 John Surtees, GB (MV)
2 Gary Hocking, Rhodesia (MV)
3 John Hartle, GB (MV/Norton)

500cc
1 John Surtees, GB (MV)
2 Remo Venturi, Italy (MV)
3 John Hartle, GB (Norton/MV)

Sidecar
1 Helmut Fath, W. Germany (BMW)
2 Fritz Scheidegger, Switzerland (BMW)
3 Pip Harris, GB (BMW)

1961

125cc
1 Tom Phillis, Australia (Honda)
2 Ernst Degner, E. Germany (MZ)
3 Luigi Taveri, Switzerland (Honda)

250cc
1 Mike Hailwood, GB (Honda)
2 Tom Phillis, Australia (Honda)
3 Jim Redman, Rhodesia (Honda)

350cc
1 Gary Hocking, Rhodesia (MV)
2 Frantisek Stastny, Czechoslovakia (Jawa)
3 G.Havel, Czechoslovakia (Jawa)

500cc
1 Gary Hocking, Rhodesia (MV)
2 Mike Hailwood, GB (Norton/MV)
3 Frank Perris, GB (Norton)

Sidecar
1 Max Deubel, W. Germany (BMW)
2 Fritz Scheidegger, Switzerland (BMW)
3 E.Strub, Switzerland (BMW)

1962

50cc
1 Ernst Degner, W. Germany (Suzuki)
2 Hans-Georg Anscheidt, W. Germany (Kreidler)
3 Luigi Taveri, Switzerland (Honda)

125cc
1 Luigi Taveri, Switzerland (Honda)
2 Jim Redman, Rhodesia (Honda)
3 Tommy Robb, Ireland (Honda)

250cc
1 Jim Redman, Rhodesia (Honda)
2 Bob McIntyre, Scotland (Honda)
3 A.Wheeler, GB (Guzzi)

350cc
1 Jim Redman, Rhodesia (Honda)
2 Mike Hailwood, GB (MV)
3 Tommy Robb, Ireland (Honda)

500cc
1 Mike Hailwood, GB (MV)
2 Alan Shepherd, GB (Matchless)
3 Phil Read, GB (Norton)

Sidecar
1 Max Deubel, W. Germany (BMW)
2 Florian Camathias, Switzerland (BMW)
3 Fritz Scheidegger, Switzerland (BMW)

1963

50cc
1 Hugh Anderson, New Zealand (Suzuki)
2 Hans-Georg Anscheidt, W. Germany (Kreidler)
3 Ernst Degner, W. Germany (Suzuki)

125cc
1 Hugh Anderson, New Zealand (Suzuki)
2 Luigi Taveri, Switzerland (Honda)
3 Jim Redman, Rhodesia (Honda)

250cc
1 Jim Redman, Rhodesia (Honda)
2 Tarquinio Provini, Italy (Morini)
3 Fumio Ito, Japan (Yamaha)

350cc
1 Jim Redman, Rhodesia (Honda)
2 Mike Hailwood, GB (MV)
3 Luigi Taveri, Switzerland (Honda)

500cc
1 Mike Hailwood, GB (MV)
2 Alan Shepherd, GB (Matchless)
3 John Hartle, GB (Gilera)

Sidecar
1 Max Deubel, W. Germany (BMW)
2 Florian Camathias, Switzerland (BMW)
3 Fritz Scheidegger, Switzerland (BMW)

1964

50cc
1 Hugh Anderson, New Zealand (Suzuki)
2 Ralph Bryans, Ireland (Honda)
3 Hans-Georg Anscheidt, W. Germany (Kreidler)

125cc
1 Luigi Taveri, Switzerland (Honda)
2 Jim Redman, Rhodesia (Honda)
3 Hugh Anderson, New Zealand (Suzuki)

250cc
1 Phil Read, GB (Yamaha)
2 Jim Redman, Rhodesia (Honda)
3 Alan Shepherd, GB (MZ)

350cc
1 Jim Redman, Rhodesia (Honda)
2 Bruce Beale, Rhodesia (Honda)
3 Mike Duff, Canada (AJS)

500cc
1 Mike Hailwood, GB (MV)
2 Jack Ahearn, Australia (Norton)
3 Phil Read, GB (Matchless)

Sidecar
1 Max Deubel, W. Germany (BMW)
2 Fritz Scheidegger, Switzerland (BMW)
3 Colin Seeley, GB (BMW)

1965

50cc
1 Ralph Bryans, Ireland (Honda)
2 Luigi Taveri, Switzerland (Honda)
3 Hugh Anderson, New Zealand (Suzuki)

125cc
1 Hugh Anderson, New Zealand (Suzuki)
2 Frank Perris, GB (Suzuki)
3 Denis Woodman, GB (MZ)

250cc
1 Phil Read, GB (Yamaha)
2 Mike Duff, Canada (Yamaha)
3 Jim Redman, Rhodesia (Honda)

350cc
1 Jim Redman, Rhodesia (Honda)
2 Giacomo Agostini, Italy (MV)
3 Mike Hailwood, GB (MV)

500cc
1 Mike Hailwood, GB (MV)
2 Giacomo Agostini, Italy (MV)
3 Paddy Driver, S. Africa (Matchless)

Sidecar
1 Fritz Scheidegger, Switzerland (BMW)
2 Max Deubel, W. Germany (BMW)
3 Georg Auerbacher, W. Germany (BMW)

1966

50cc
1 Hans-Georg Anscheidt, W. Germany (Suzuki)
2 Ralph Bryans, Ireland (Honda)
3 Luigi Taveri, Switzerland (Honda)

125cc
1 Luigi Taveri, Switzerland (Honda)
2 Bill Ivy, GB (Yamaha)
3 Ralph Bryans, Ireland (Honda)

250cc
1 Mike Hailwood, GB (Honda)
2 Phil Read, GB (Yamaha)
3 Jim Redman, Rhodesia (Honda)

350cc
1 Mike Hailwood, GB (Honda)
2 Giacomo Agostini, Italy (MV)
3 Renzo Pasolini, Italy (Aermacchi)

500cc
1 Giacomo Agostini, Italy (MV)
2 Mike Hailwood, GB (Honda)
3 Jack Findlay, Australia (Matchless)

Sidecar
1 Fritz Scheidegger, Switzerland (BMW)
2 Max Deubel, W. Germany (BMW)
3 Colin Seeley, GB (BMW)

1967

50cc
1 Hans-Georg Anscheidt, W. Germany (Suzuki)
2 Yoshi Katayama, Japan (Suzuki)
3 Stuart Graham, GB (Suzuki)

125cc
1 Bill Ivy, GB (Yamaha)
2 Phil Read, GB (Yamaha)
3 Stuart Graham, GB (Suzuki)

250cc
1 Mike Hailwood, GB (Honda)
2 Phil Read, GB (Yamaha)
3 Bill Ivy, GB (Yamaha)

350cc
1 Mike Hailwood, GB (Honda)
2 Giacomo Agostini, Italy (MV)
3 Ralph Bryans, Ireland (Honda)

500cc
1 Giacomo Agostini, Italy (MV)
2 Mike Hailwood, GB (Honda)
3 John Hartle, GB (Matchless)

Sidecar
1 Klaus Enders, W. Germany (BMW)
2 Georg Auerbacher, W. Germany (BMW)
3 Siegfried Schauzu, W. Germany (BMW)

1968

50cc
1 Hans-Georg Anscheidt, W. Germany (Suzuki)
2 P. Lodewijkx, Holland (Jamathi)
3 B. Smith, Australia (Derbi)

125cc
1 Phil Read, GB (Yamaha)
2 Bill Ivy, GB (Yamaha)
3 Ginger Molloy, New Zealand (Bultaco)

250cc
1 Phil Read, GB (Yamaha)
2 Bill Ivy, GB (Yamaha)
3 Heinz Rosner, E. Germany (MZ)

350cc
1 Giacomo Agostini, Italy (MV)
2 Renzo Pasolini, Italy (Benelli)
3 Kel Carruthers, Australia (Aermacchi)

500cc
1 Giacomo Agostini, Italy (MV)
2 Jack Findlay, Australia (Matchless)
3 Gyula Marsovszky, Switzerland (Matchless)

Sidecar
1 Helmut Fath, W. Germany (URS)
2 Georg Auerbacher, W. Germany (BMW)
3 Siegfried Schauzu, W. Germany (BMW)

1969

50cc
1 Angel Nieto, Spain (Derbi)
2 Aalt Toersen, Holland (Kreidler)
3 B. Smith, Australia (Derbi)

125cc
1 Dave Simmonds, GB (Kawasaki)
2 Dieter Braun, W. Germany (Suzuki)
3 C. van Dongen, Holland (Suzuki)

250cc
1 Kel Carruthers, Australia (Benelli)
2 Kent Andersson, Sweden (Yamaha)
3 Santiago Herrero, Spain (Ossa)

350cc
1 Giacomo Agostini, Italy (MV)
2 Silvio Grassetti, Italy (Yamaha/Jawa)
3 G. Visenzi, Italy (Yamaha)

500cc
1 Giacomo Agostini, Italy (MV)
2 Gyula Marsovszky, Switzerland (Linto)
3 G. Nash, GB (Norton)

Sidecar
1 Klaus Enders, W. Germany (BMW)
2 Helmut Fath, W. Germany (URS)
3 Georg Auerbacher, W. Germany (BMW)

1970

50cc
1 Angel Nieto, Spain (Derbi)
2 Aalt Toersen, Holland (Jamathi)
3 Rudolph Kunz, W. Germany (Kreidler)

125cc
1 Dieter Braun, W. Germany (Suzuki)
2 Angel Nieto, Spain (Derbi)
3 Borje Jansson, Sweden (Maico)

250cc
1 Rodney Gould, GB (Yamaha)
2 Kel Carruthers, Australia (Yamaha)
3 Kent Andersson, Sweden (Yamaha)

350cc
1 Giacomo Agostini, Italy (MV)
2 Kel Carruthers, Australia (Benelli/Yamaha)
3 Renzo Pasolini, Italy (Benelli)

500cc
1 Giacomo Agostini, Italy (MV)
2 Ginger Molloy, New Zealand (Kawasaki)
3 Angelo Bergamonti, Italy (Aermacchi/MV)

Sidecar
1 Klaus Enders, W. Germany (BMW)
2 Georg Auerbacher, W. Germany (BMW)
3 Siegfried Schauzu, W. Germany (BMW)

1971

50cc
1 Jan de Vries, Holland (Kreidler)
2 Angel Nieto, Spain (Derbi)
3 J. Schurgers, Holland (Kreidler)

125cc
1 Angel Nieto, Spain (Derbi)
2 Barry Sheene, GB (Suzuki)
3 Borje Jansson, Sweden (Maico)

250cc
1 Phil Read, GB (Yamaha)
2 Rodney Gould, GB (Yamaha)
3 Jarno Saarinen, Finland (Yamaha)

350cc
1 Giacomo Agostini, Italy (MV)
2 Jarno Saarinen, Finland (Yamaha)
3 K-I. Carlsson, Sweden (Yamaha)

500cc
1 Giacomo Agostini, Italy (MV)
2 K. Turner, New Zealand (Suzuki)
3 R. Bron, Holland (Suzuki)

Sidecar
1 Horst Owesle, W. Germany (Munch)
2 A. Butscher, W. Germany (BMW)
3 Siegfried Schauzu, W. Germany (BMW)

1972

50cc
1 Angel Nieto, Spain (Derbi)
2 Jan de Vries, Holland (Kreidler)
3 Theo Timmer, Holland (Jamathi)

125cc
1 Angel Nieto, Spain (Derbi)
2 Kent Andersson, Sweden (Yamaha)
3 Charles Mortimer, GB (Yamaha)

250cc
1 Jarno Saarinen, Finland (Yamaha)
2 Renzo Pasolini, Italy (Aermacchi)
3 Rodney Gould, GB (Yamaha)

350cc
1 Giacomo Agostini, Italy (MV)
2 Jarno Saarinen, Finland (Yamaha)
3 Renzo Pasolini, Italy (Aermacchi)

500cc
1 Giacomo Agostini, Italy (MV)
2 Alberto Pagani, Italy (MV)
3 Bruno Kneubuhler, Czechoslovakia (Yamaha)

Sidecar
1 Klaus Enders, W. Germany (BMW)
2 Heinz Luthringshauser, W. Germany (BMW)
3 Siegfried Schauzu, W. Germany (BMW)

1973

50cc
1 Jan de Vries, Holland (Van Veen Kreidler)
2 Bruno Kneubuhler, Czechoslovakia (Van Veen Kreidler)
3 Theo Timmer, Holland (Jamathi)

125cc
1 Kent Andersson, Sweden (Yamaha)
2 Charles Mortimer, GB (Yamaha)
3 J. Schurgers, Holland (Bridgestone)

250cc
1 Dieter Braun, W. Germany (Yamaha)
2 Tepi Lansivuori, Finland (Yamaha)
3 John Dodds, Australia (Yamaha)

350cc
1 Giacomo Agostini, Italy (MV)
2 Tepi Lansivuori, Finland (Yamaha)
3 Phil Read, GB (MV)

500cc
1 Phil Read, GB (MV)
2 K. Newcombe, New Zealand (Konig)
3 Giacomo Agostini, Italy (MV)

Sidecar
1 Klaus Enders, W. Germany (BMW)
2 Werner Schwarzel, W. Germany (Konig)
3 Siegfried Schauzu, W. Germany (BMW)

1974

50cc
1 Henk van Kessell, Holland (Van Veen Kreidler)
2 Herbert Rittberger, W. Germany (Kreidler)
3 Julien van Zeebroeck, Belgium (Kreidler)

125cc
1 Kent Andersson, Sweden (Yamaha)
2 Bruno Kneubuhler, Czechoslovakia (Yamaha)
3) Otello Buscherini, Italy (Malanca)
3) Angel Nieto, Spain (Derbi)

250cc
1 Walter Villa, Italy (Harley-Davidson)
2 Dieter Braun, W. Germany (Yamaha)
3 Patrick Pons, France (Yamaha)

350cc
1 Giacomo Agostini, Italy (Yamaha)
2 Dieter Braun, W. Germany (Yamaha)
3 Patrick Pons, France (Yamaha)

500cc
1 Phil Read, GB (MV)
2 Gianfranco Bonera, Italy (MV)
3 Tepi Lansivuori, Finland (Yamaha)

Sidecar
1 Klaus Enders, W. Germany (Busch BMW)
2 Werner Schwarzel, W. Germany (Konig)
3 Siegfried Schauzu, W. Germany (BMW)

1975

50cc
1 Angel Nieto, Spain (Kreidler)
2 Eugenio Lazzarine, Italy (Piovaticci)
3 Julien van Zeebroeck, Belgium (Kreidler)

125cc
1 Paolo Pileri, Italy (Morbidelli)
2 Pierpaolo Bianchi, Italy (Morbidelli)
3 Kent Andersson, Sweden (Yamaha)

250cc
1 Walter Villa, Italy (Harley-Davidson)
2 Michel Rougerie, France (Harley-Davidson)
3 Dieter Braun, W. Germany (Yamaha)

350cc
1 Johnny Cecotto, Venezuela (Yamaha)
2 Giacomo Agostini, Italy (Yamaha)
3 Penti Korhonen, Finland (Yamaha)

500cc
1 Giacomo Agostini, Italy (Yamaha)
2 Phil Read, GB (MV)
3 Hideo Kanaya, Japan (Yamaha)

Sidecar
1 Rolf Steinhausen, W. Germany (Konig)
2 Werner Schwarzel, W. Germany (Konig)
3 Rolf Biland, Switzerland (Yamaha)

1976

50cc
1 Angel Nieto, Spain (Bultaco)
2 Herbert Rittberger, W. Germany (Kreidler)
3 Ulrich Graf, Switzerland (Kreidler)

125cc
1 Pierpaolo Bianchi, Italy (Morbidelli)
2 Angel Nieto, Spain (Bultaco)
3 Paolo Pileri, Italy (Morbidelli)

250cc
1 Walter Villa, Italy (Harley-Davidson)
2 Takazumi Katayama, Japan (Yamaha)
3 Gianfranco Bonera, Italy (Harley-Davidson)

350cc
1 Walter Villa, Italy (Harley-Davidson)
2 Johnny Cecotto, Venezuela (Yamaha)
3 Charles Mortimer, GB (Yamaha)

500cc
1 Barry Sheene, GB (Suzuki)
2 Tepi Lansivuori, Finland (Suzuki)
3 Pat Hennen, USA (Suzuki)

Sidecar
1 Rolf Steinhausen, W. Germany (Busch Konig)
2 Werner Schwarzel, W. Germany (König)
3 Herman Schmid, Switzerland (Yamaha)

1977

50cc
1 Angel Nieto, Spain (Bultaco)
2 Eugenio Lazzarini, Italy (Kreidler)
3 Ricardo Tormo, Spain (Bultaco)

125cc
1 Pierpaolo Bianchi, Italy (Morbidelli)
2 Eugenio Lazzarini, Italy (Morbidelli)
3 Angel Nieto, Spain (Bultaco)

250cc
1 Mario Lega, Italy (Morbidelli)
2 Franco Uncini, Italy (Harley-Davidson)
3 Walter Villa, Italy (Harley-Davidson)

350cc
1 Takazumi Katayama, Japan (Yamaha)
2 Tom Herron, GB (Yamaha)
3 Jon Ekerold, South Africa (Yamaha)

500cc
1 Barry Sheene, GB (Suzuki)
2 Steve Baker, USA (Yamaha)
3 Pat Hennen, USA (Suzuki)

Sidecar
1 George O'Dell, GB (Seymaz-Yamaha & Windle-Yamaha)
2 Rolf Biland, Switzerland (Schmid-Yamaha)
3 Werner Schwarzel, W.Germany (Aro)

Formula 750
1 Steve Baker, USA (Yamaha)
2 Christian Sarron, France (Yamaha)
3 Giacomo Agostini, Italy (Yamaha)

1978

50cc
1 Ricardo Tormo, Spain (Bultaco)
2 Eugenio Lazzarini, Italy (Kreidler)
3 Patrick Plisson, France (ABF)

125cc
1 Eugenio Lazzarini, Italy (MBA)
2 Angel Nieto, Spain (Bultaco/Minarelli)
3 Pierpaolo Bianchi, Italy (Minarelli)

250cc
1 Kork Ballington, S. Africa (Kawasaki)
2 Gregg Hansford, Australia (Kawasaki)
3 Patrick Fernandez, France (Yamaha)

350cc
1 Kork Ballington, S. Africa (Kawasaki)
2 Takazumi Katayama, Japan (Yamaha)
3 Gregg Hansford, Australia (Kawasaki)

500cc
1 Kenny Roberts, USA (Yamaha)
2 Barry Sheene, GB (Suzuki)
3 Johnny Cecotto, Venezuela (Yamaha)

Sidecar
1 Rolf Biland, Switzerland (Beo-Yamaha & TTM Yamaha)
2 Alain Michel, France (Seymaz-Yamaha)
3 Bruno Holzer, Switzerland (LCR-Yamaha)

Formula 750
1 Johnny Cecotto, Venezuela (Yamaha)
2 Kenny Roberts, USA (Yamaha)
3 Christian Sarron, France (Yamaha)

1979

50cc
1 Eugenio Lazzarini, Italy (Kreidler)
2 Rolf Blatter, Switzerland (Kreidler)
3 Patrick Plisson, France (ABF)

125cc
1 Angel Nieto, Spain (Morbidelli)
2 Maurizio Massimiani, Italy (Morbidelli)
3 Hans Müller, Switzerland (MBA)

250cc
1 Kork Ballington, S. Africa (Kawasaki)
2 Gregg Hansford, Australia (Kawasaki)
3 Graziano Rossi, Italy (Morbidelli)

350cc
1 Kork Ballington, S. Africa (Kawasaki)
2 Patrick Fernandez, France (Yamaha)
3 Gregg Hansford, Australia (Kawasaki)

500cc
1 Kenny Roberts, USA (Yamaha)
2 Virginio Ferrari, Italy (Suzuki)
3 Barry Sheene, GB (Suzuki)

Sidecar B2A
1 Rolf Biland, Switzerland (Yamaha)
2) Rolf Steinhausen, W. Germany (Yamaha)
2) Dick Greasley, GB (Yamaha)

Sidecar B2B
1 Bruno Holzer, Switzerland (LCR)
2 Rolf Biland, Switzerland (LCR)
3 Masato Kumano, Japan (Yamaha)

Formula 750
1 Patrick Pons, France (Yamaha)
2 Michel Frutschi, Switzerland (Yamaha)
3 Johnny Cecotto, Venezuela (Yamaha)

World Championships – Manufacturer's Category

	50cc	125cc	250cc	350cc	500cc	Sidecar
1949		Mondial	Moto Guzzi	Velocette	AJS	Norton
1950		Mondial	Benelli	Velocette	Norton	Norton
1951		Mondial	Moto Guzzi	Norton	Norton	Norton
1952		MV Agusta	Moto Guzzi	Norton	Gilera	Norton
1953		MV Agusta	NSU	Moto Guzzi	Gilera	Norton
1954 No award during this year						
1955		MV Agusta	MV Agusta	Moto Guzzi	Gilera	BMW
1956		MV Agusta	MV Agusta	Moto Guzzi	MV Agusta	BMW
1957		Mondial	Mondial	Gilera	Gilera	BMW
1958		MV Agusta	MV Agusta	MV Agusta	MV Agusta	BMW
1959		MV Agusta	MV Agusta	MV Agusta	MV Agusta	BMW
1960		MV Agusta	MV Agusta	MV Agusta	MV Agusta	BMW
1961		Honda	Honda	MV Agusta	MV Agusta	BMW
1962	Suzuki	Honda	Honda	Honda	MV Agusta	BMW
1963	Suzuki	Suzuki	Honda	Honda	MV Agusta	BMW
1964	Suzuki	Honda	Yamaha	Honda	MV Agusta	BMW
1965	Honda	Suzuki	Yamaha	Honda	MV Agusta	BMW
1966	Honda	Honda	Honda	Honda	Honda	BMW
1967	Suzuki	Yamaha	Honda	Honda	MV Agusta	BMW
1968	Suzuki	Yamaha	Yamaha	MV Agusta	MV Agusta	BMW
1969	Derbi	Kawasaki	Benelli	MV Agusta	MV Agusta	RMW
1970	Derbi	Suzuki	Yamaha	MV Agusta	MV Agusta	BMW
1971	Kreidler	Derbi	Yamaha	MV Agusta	MV Agusta	BMW
1972	Kreidler	Derbi	Yamaha	MV Agusta	MV Agusta	BMW
1973	Kreidler	Yamaha	Yamaha	Yahama	MV Agusta	BMW
1974	Kreidler	Yamaha	Yamaha	Yamaha	Yamaha	Konig
1975	Kreidler	Morbidelli	Harley-Davidson	Yamaha	Yamaha	Konig
1976	Bultaco	Morbidelli	No award	Yamaha	No award	No award
1977	Bultaco	Morbidelli	Yamaha	Yamaha	Suzuki	Yamaha
1978	Bultaco	No award	Kawasaki	Kawasaki	Suzuki	Yamaha
1979	Kreidler	Minarelli	Kawasaki	Kawasaki	Suzuki	Yamaha

MOTOCROSS

World Championships

125cc

1975   1 Gaston Rahier, Belgium (Suzuki)
      2 Gilbert De Roover, Belgium (Zundapp)
      3 Antoin Baborowsky, Czechoslovakia (CZ)
1976   1 Gaston Rahier, Belgium (Suzuki)
      2 Jiri Churavy, Czechoslovakia (CZ)
      3 Marty Smith, USA (Honda)
1977   1 Gaston Rahier, Belgium (Suzuki)
      2 Gerard Rond, Netherlands (Yamaha)
      3 André Massant, Belgium (Yamaha)
1978   1 Akira Watanabe, Japan (Suzuki)
      2 Gaston Rahier, Belgium (Suzuki)
      3 Gerard Rond, Denmark (Yamaha)
1979   1 Harry Everts, Belgium (Suzuki)
      2 Akira Watanabe, Japan (Suzuki)
      3 Gaston Rahier, Belgium (Yamaha)

250cc

1962   1 Torsten Hallman, Sweden (Husqvarna)
      2 Jeff Smith, GB (BSA)
      3 Arthur Lampkin, GB (BSA)
1963   1 Torsten Hallman, Sweden (Husqvarna)
      2 Vlastimil Valek, Czechoslovakia (CZ)
      3 Igor Grigoriev, USSR (CZ)
1964   1 Joel Robert, Belgium (CZ)
      2 Torsten Hallman, Sweden (Husqvarna)
      3 Victor Arbekov, USSR (CZ)
1965   1 Victor Arbekov, USSR (CZ)
      2 Joel Robert, Belgium (CZ)
      3 Dave Bickers, GB (Greeves)
1966   1 Torsten Hallman, Sweden (Husqvarna)
      2 Joel Robert, Belgium (CZ)
      3 Petr Dobry, Czechoslovakia (CZ)
1967   1 Torsten Hallman, Sweden (Husqvarna)
      2 Joel Robert, Belgium (CZ)
      3 Olle Petersson, Sweden (Husqvarna)
1968   1 Joel Robert, Belgium (CZ)
      2 Torsten Hallman, Sweden (Husqvarna)
      3 Silvain Geboers, Belgium (CZ)
1969   1 Joel Robert, Belgium (CZ)
      2 Silvain Geboers, Belgium (CZ)
      3 Olle Petersson, Sweden (Suzuki)
1970   1 Joel Robert, Belgium (Suzuki)
      2 Silvain Geboers, Belgium (Suzuki)
      3 Roger De Coster, Belgium (CZ)
1971   1 Joel Robert, Belgium (Suzuki)
      2 Hakan Andersson, Sweden (Husqvarna)
      3 Silvain Geboers, Belgium (Suzuki)
1972   1 Joel Robert, Belgium (Suzuki)
      2 Hakan Andersson, Sweden (Yamaha)
      3 Silvain Geboers, Belgium (Suzuki)
1973   1 Hakan Andersson, Sweden (Yamaha)
      2 Adolf Weil, Germany (Maico)
      3 Heikki Mikkola, Finland (Husqvarna)
1974   1 Gennady Moisseev, USSR (KTM)
      2 Jaroslav Falta, Czechoslovakia (CZ)
      3 Harry Everts, Belgium (Puch)
1975   1 Harry Everts, Belgium (Puch)
      2 Hakan Andersson, Sweden (Yamaha)
      3 Willy Bauer, Germany (Suzuki)
1976   1 Heikki Mikkola, Finland (Husqvarna)
      2 Gennady Moisseev, USSR (KTM)
      3 Vladimir Kavinov, USSR (KTM)

1977   1 Gennady Moisseev, USSR (KTM)
      2 Vladimir Kavinov, USSR (KTM)
      3 André Malherbe, Belgium (KTM)
1978   1 Gennady Moisseev, USSR (KTM)
      2 Torleif Hansen, Sweden (Kawasaki)
      3 Hans Maisch, Germany (Maico)
1979   1 Hakan Carlqvist, Sweden (Husqvarna)
      2 Neil Hudson, GB (Maico)
      3 Vladimir Kavinov, USSR (KTM)

500cc

1957   1 Bill Nilsson, Sweden (AJS)
      2 René Baeten, Belgium (FN)
      3 Sten Lundin, Sweden (BSA)
1958   1 René Baeten, Belgium (FN)
      2 Bill Nilsson, Sweden (Crescent)
      3 Sten Lundin, Sweden (Monark)
1959   1 Sten Lundin, Sweden (Monark)
      2 Bill Nilsson, Sweden (Crescent)
      3 Dave Curtis, GB (Matchless)
1960   1 Bill Nilsson, Sweden (Husqvarna)
      2 Sten Lundin, Sweden (Monark)
      3 Don Rickman, GB (Metisse)
1961   1 Sten Lundin, Sweden (Lito)
      2 Bill Nilsson, Sweden (Husqvarna)
      3 Gunnar Johansson, Sweden (Lito)
1962   1 Rolf Tibblin, Sweden (Husqvarna)
      2 Gunnar Johansson, Sweden (Lito)
      3 Sten Lundin, Sweden (Lito)
1963   1 Rolf Tibblin, Sweden (Husqvarna)
      2 Sten Lundin, Sweden (Lito)
      3 Jeff Smith, GB (BSA)
1964   1 Jeff Smith, GB (BSA)
      2 Rolf Tibblin, Sweden (Husqvarna)
      3 Sten Lundin, Sweden (Lito)
1965   1 Jeff Smith, GB (BSA)
      2 Paul Friedrichs, E. Germany (CZ)
      3 Rolf Tibblin, Sweden (Husqvarna)
1966   1 Paul Friedrichs, E. Germany (CZ)
      2 Rolf Tibblin, Sweden (CZ)
      3 Jeff Smith, GB (BSA)
1967   1 Paul Friedrichs, E. Germany (CZ)
      2 Jeff Smith, GB (BSA)
      3 Dave Bickers, GB (CZ)
1968   1 Paul Friedrichs, E. Germany (CZ)
      2 John Banks, GB (BSA)
      3 Ake Jonsson, Sweden (Husqvarna)
1969   1 Bengt Aberg, Sweden (Husqvarna)
      2 John Banks, GB (BSA)
      3 Paul Friedrichs, E. Germany (CZ)
1970   1 Bengt Aberg, Sweden (Husqvarna)
      2 Arne King, Sweden (Husqvarna)
      3 Ake Jonsson, Sweden (Husqvarna)
1971   1 Roger De Costa, Belgium (Suzuki)
      2 Ake Jonsson, Sweden (Maico)
      3 Adolf Weil, Germany (Maico)
1972   1 Roger De Coster, Belgium (Suzuki)
      2 Paul Friedrichs, E. Germany (CZ)
      3 Heikki Mikkola, Finland (Husqvarna)
1973   1 Roger De Coster, Belgium (Suzuki)
      2 Willy Bauer, Germany (Maico)
      3 Jaak Van Velthoven, Belgium (Yamaha)
1974   1 Heikki Mikkola, Finland (Husqvarna)
      2 Roger De Coster, Belgium (Suzuki)
      3 Adolf Weil, Germany (Maico)
1975   1 Roger De Coster, Belgium (Suzuki)
      2 Heikki Mikkola, Finland (Husqvarna)
      3 Gerrit Wolsink, Netherlands (Suzuki)

1976 1 Roger De Coster, Belgium (Suzuki)
      2 Gerrit Wolsink, Netherlands (Suzuki)
      3 Adolf Weil, Germany (Maico)
1977 1 Heikki Mikkola, Finland (Yamaha)
      2 Roger De Coster, Belgium (Suzuki)
      3 Gerrit Wolsink, Netherlands (Suzuki)

1978 1 Heikki Mikkola, Finland (Yamaha)
      2 Brad Lackey, USA (Honda)
      3 Roger De Coster, Belgium (Suzuki)
1979 1 Graham Noyce, GB (Honda)
      2 Gerrit Wolsink, Netherlands (Suzuki)
      3 André Malherbe, Belgium (Honda)

Moto-Cross des Nations

1947 Great Britain (Nicholson, Rist, Ray)
1948 Belgium (Jansen, Cox, Milhoux)
1949 Great Britain (Lines, Manns, Scovell)
1950 Great Britain (Draper, Hall, Lines)
1951 Belgium, (Leloup, Jansen, Meunier)
1952 Great Britain (Stonebridge, Ward, Nex)
1953 Great Britain (Archer, Draper, Ward)
1954 Great Britain (Ward, Stonebridge, Curtis)
1955 Sweden (Nilsson, Lundin, Gustafsson)
1956 Great Britain (Smith, Ward, Draper)
1957 Great Britain (Smith, Curtis, Martin)
1958 Sweden (Nilsson, Gustafsson, Lundell)
1959 Great Britain (D. J. Rickman, Smith, Draper)
1960 Great Britain (D. J. Rickman, Curtis, Smith)
1961 Sweden (Nilsson, Tibblin, Lundell)
1962 Sweden (Tibblin, Johansson, Nilsson)
1963 Great Britain (D. J. Rickman, D. E. Rickman, Smith)
1964 Great Britain (Smith, D. J. Rickman, D. E. Rickman)
1965 Great Britain (D. J. Rickman, Smith, Eastwood)
1966 Great Britain (Bickers, D. J. Rickman, Lampkin)
1967 Great Britain (Smith, Bickers, Eastwood)
1968 USSR (Shinkarenko, Petushkov, Pogrebniak)
1969 Belgium (De Coster, Geboers, Robert)
1970 Sweden (Aberg, Hammergren, Johansson)
1971 Sweden (Aberg, Hammergren, Johansson)
1972 Belgium (De Coster, Robert, van de Vorst)
1973 Belgium (De Coster, van Velthoven, Geboers)
1974 Sweden (Aberg, Andersson, Kring)
1975 Czechoslovakia (Barborovsky, Novacek, Velky)
1976 Belgium (De Coster, Rahier, Everts, van Velthoven)
1977 Belgium (De Coster, Malherbe, Mingels, van Velthoven)
1978 USSR (Moisseev, Kavinov, Khudiakov, Korneev)
1979 Belgium (De Coster, Everts, Malherbe, van de Broeck)

Trophee des Nations

1961 Great Britain (Bickers, Smith, Lampkin)
1962 Great Britain (Bickers, Smith, Lampkin
1963 Sweden (Hallman, Forsberg, Loof)
1964 Sweden (Hallman, Jonsson, Peterson)
1965 No result, meeting null and void
1966 Sweden (Hallman, Petterson, Tornblom)
1967 Sweden (Hallman, Pettersen, Eneqvist)
1968 Sweden (Aberg, Hammargran, Bonn)
1969 Belgium (De Coster, Geboers, Robert)
1970 Belgium (De Coster, Geboers, Robert)
1971 Belgium (De Coster, Geboers, van Velthoven)
1972 Belgium (De Coster, Robert, van Velthoven)
1973 Belgium (De Coster, Geboers, van Velthoven)
1974 Belgium (De Coster, Everts, van Velthoven)
1975 Belgium (De Coster, Everts, van Velthoven)
1976 Belgium (De Coster, Rahier, Everts, van Velthoven)
1977 Belgium (De Coster, Everts, van Velthoven, Malherbe)
1978 Belgium (De Coster, Rahier, Everts, van Velthoven)
1979 USSR (Moisseev, Kavinov, Korneev, Khudiakov)

SPEEDWAY

Individual World Championships
1936	Lionel Van Praag
1937	Jack Milne
1938	Bluey Wilkinson
1949	Tommy Price
1950	Fred Williams
1951	Jack Young
1952	Jack Young
1953	Fred Williams
1954	Ronnie Moore
1955	Peter Craven
1956	Ove Fundin
1957	Barry Briggs
1958	Barry Briggs
1959	Ronnie Moore
1960	Ove Fundin
1961	Ove Fundin
1962	Peter Craven
1963	Ove Fundin
1964	Barry Briggs
1965	Bjorn Knutsson
1966	Barry Briggs
1967	Ove Fundin
1968	Ivan Mauger
1969	Ivan Mauger
1970	Ivan Mauger
1971	Ole Olsen
1972	Ivan Mauger
1973	Jerzy Szczakiel
1974	Anders Michanek
1975	Ole Olsen
1976	Peter Collins
1977	Ivan Mauger
1978	Ole Olsen
1979	Ivan Mauger

Team World Championships
1960	Sweden
1961	Poland
1962	Sweden
1963	Sweden
1964	Sweden
1965	Poland
1966	Poland
1967	Sweden
1968	Great Britain
1969	Poland
1970	Sweden
1971	Great Britain
1972	Great Britain
1973	Great Britain
1974	England
1975	England
1976	Australia
1977	England
1978	Denmark
1979	New Zealand

TRIALS
1975	H Martin Lampkin, GB (Bultaco)
1976	Yrjo Vesterinen, Finland (Bultaco)
1977	Yrjo Vesterinen, Finland (Bultaco)
1978	Yrjo Vesterinen, Finland (Bultaco)
1979	Bernie Schreiber, USA (Bultaco)

International Six-Days Trial
1947	Trophy:	Czechoslovakia
	Vase:	Czechoslovakia
1948	Trophy:	GB
	Vase:	GB
1949	Trophy:	GB
	Vase:	Czechoslovakia
1950	Trophy:	GB
	Vase:	GB
1951	Trophy:	GB
	Vase:	Holland
1952	Trophy:	Czechoslovakia
	Vase:	Czechoslovakia
1953	Trophy:	GB
	Vase:	Czechoslovakia
1954	Trophy:	Czechoslovakia
	Vase:	Holland
1955	Trophy:	Germany
	Vase:	Czechoslovakia
1956	Trophy:	Czechoslovakia
	Vase:	Holland
1957	Trophy:	Germany
	Vase:	Czechoslovakia
1958	Trophy:	Czechoslovakia
	Vase:	Czechoslovakia
1959	Trophy:	Czechoslovakia
	Vase:	Czechoslovakia
1960	Trophy:	Austria
	Vase:	Italy
1961	Trophy:	W. Germany
	Vase:	Czechoslovakia
1962	Trophy:	Czechoslovakia
	Vase:	W. Germany
1963	Trophy:	E. Germany
	Vase:	Italy
1964	Trophy:	E. Germany
	Vase:	E. Germany
1965	Trophy:	E. Germany
	Vase:	E. Germany
1966	Trophy:	E. Germany
	Vase:	W. Germany
1967	Trophy:	E. Germany
	Vase:	Czechoslovakia
1968	Trophy:	W. Germany
	Vase:	Italy
1969	Trophy:	E. Germany
	Vase:	W. Germany
1970	Trophy:	Czechoslovakia
	Vase:	Czechoslovakia
1971	Trophy:	Czechoslovakia
	Vase:	Czechoslovakia
1972	Trophy:	Czechoslovakia
	Vase:	Czechoslovakia
1973	Trophy:	Czechoslovakia
	Vase:	USA
1974	Trophy:	Czechoslovakia
	Vase:	Czechoslovakia
1975	Trophy:	W. Germany
	Vase:	Italy
1976	Trophy:	W. Germany
	Vase:	Czechoslovakia
1977	Trophy:	Czechoslovakia
	Vase:	Czechoslovakia
1978	Trophy:	Czechoslovakia
	Vase:	Italy
1979	Trophy:	Italy
	Vase:	Czechoslovakia

Index

INDEX

INDEX